THIS is the ninth large edition of this great work.

This book is the story of a man's fight for the right to think. Through its pages there flow the surge and flux of a battle greater than any battle of bullet and sword. It is a battle for Tolerance, the struggle of the unsubdued and unsubduable spirit of man for his own thoughts, his own beliefs and his own expression of those beliefs.

There is murder in its pages that drags men from quiet beds and hangs them to a rafter because they have chosen to think apart from the mob; there is lust and rapine here that make of sane men a great many-fanged beast-mob that blindly burns and slays; there is love that prompts them to die clutching a nebulous dream; there is arson and sabotage, intrigue and cruelty, ugliness and beauty.

Strange figures move through these pages; brave men and cravens; martyrs and madmen; all of them once lived and had their being; all were intrigued in that glorious warfare to speak as their consciences dictated or to suppress the speech of conscience by intimidation and the sword; all are recreated here in an unforgettable manner.

Erasmus and Kant, Spinoza and Montaigne, Martin Luther and Socrates, Copernicus and Pascal, Abélard and Galileo are some of the men who come to a thrilling rebirth in these pages.

TOLERANCE

Why should we not all live in peace and harmony? We look up at the same stars, we are fellow-passengers on the same planet and dwell beneath the same sky. What matters it along which road each individual endeavors to find the ultimate truth? The riddle of existence is too great that there should be only one road leading to an answer.

QUINTUS AURELIUS SYMMACHUS.

TOLERANCE

BY
HENDRIK VAN LOON

BONI & LIVERIGHT
1927

First printing, September, 1925
Second printing, November, 1925
Third printing, December, 1925
Fourth printing, December, 1925
Fifth printing, January, 1926
Sixth printing, March, 1926
Seventh printing, August, 1926
Eighth printing, December, 1926
Ninth printing, September, 1927
(Illustrated Edition)

TO THE MEMORY OF
JOHN W. T. NICHOLS

CONTENTS

CONTENTS

PAGE

PROLOGUE 11

CHAPTER

I. THE TYRANNY OF IGNORANCE 18
II. THE GREEKS 28
III. THE BEGINNING OF RESTRAINT 66
IV. THE TWILIGHT OF THE GODS 76
V. IMPRISONMENT 98
VI. THE PURE OF LIFE 110
VII. THE INQUISITION 121
VIII. THE CURIOUS ONES 140
IX. THE WAR UPON THE PRINTED WORD . . 154
X. CONCERNING THE WRITING OF HISTORY IN
GENERAL AND THIS BOOK IN PARTICULAR . 162
XI. RENAISSANCE 165
XII. THE REFORMATION 173
XIII. ERASMUS 187
XIV. RABELAIS 203
XV. NEW SIGNBOARDS FOR OLD 214
XVI. THE ANABAPTISTS 235
XVII. THE SOZZINI FAMILY 245
XVIII. MONTAIGNE 255
XIX. ARMINIUS 261
XX. BRUNO 271
XXI. SPINOZA 277
XXII. THE NEW ZION 290
XXIII. THE SUN KING 303
XXIV. FREDERICK THE GREAT 307
XXV. VOLTAIRE 310
XXVI. THE ENCYCLOPEDIA 330
XXVII. THE INTOLERANCE OF REVOLUTION . . . 338

CHAPTER		PAGE
XXVIII.	LESSING	348
XXIX.	TOM PAINE	361
XXX.	THE LAST HUNDRED YEARS	367
XXXI.	. . . AND AFTER TWO YEARS	373

ILLUSTRATIONS

	PAGE
The Valley of Ignorance	11
The Lonely Wanderer	12
The New Home	13
The Winter of Horror	15
The Memorial Stone	16
The Meeting of East and West	20
Taboo	25
Greece	29
The Commercial City	31
The Philosopher	35
Greek Fairy Tales	37
The Astronomers	39
Protagoras	42
Socrates	46
The Death of Socrates	48
The Academy	52
Aristotle	54
The Rival Religions	58
Escape from a Sinful World	86
The Sinful City of the Seven Hills	93
Constantine the Great	96
The Deserted Temple	99
The New World Empire	103
The Rival Prisons	104
The Dissenter	107
The Fourth Crusade	117
The Provence	128
Peter Waldo	131
The Last of the Waldensians	134
Martyrdom	137

PAGE

The Old World Arises Anew 145
That Round, Round World 147
The Irrefutable Argument 149
The New Infallibility 151
Suppression 157
The Booklegger 160
The Protest 177
The Universal Prison 180
Two Prisons for One 183
Space to Breathe 185
Those Terrible Little Books 191
Rotterdam 194
The Cloister Steyn 195
"The Old Building Will Last Our Time" 204
Wholesale Methods of Persuasion 209
The World-Wide Ocean 214
Geneva 216
Loyola 218
The New Tyranny 225
The Anabaptists 235
The Sozzinis 245
"Our Lord of the Attick" 256
Montaigne 259
The Quarreling Professors 265
Arminius 266
Bruno Goes to Geneva 273
Bruno Goes to Venice 275
Spinoza 279
The New Zion 297
The Winter of a New World 298
The Foundation of Maryland 300
The Royal "Scrap of Paper" 305
Voltaire Goes to School in France 311
Voltaire Goes to School in England 314
Calas 325
The Encyclopedist 331

Illustrations

PAGE

Revolution 339
The Tolerance of Revolution 343
Robespierre 346
Lessing 351
Tom Paine 363
The Intolerance of the State 376
The Horizontal Revolution 378
The Vertical Revolution . . . . . . , . . 380

TOLERANCE

PROLOGUE

HAPPILY lived Mankind in the peaceful Valley of Ignorance.

To the north, to the south, to the west and to the east stretched the ridges of the Hills Everlasting.

A little stream of Knowledge trickled slowly through a deep worn gully.

It came out of the Mountains of the Past.

It lost itself in the Marshes of the Future.

It was not much, as rivers go. But it was enough for the humble needs of the villagers.

In the evening, when they had watered their cattle and had filled their casks, they were content to sit down to enjoy life.

The Old Men Who Knew were brought forth from the shady corners where they had spent their day, pondering over the mysterious pages of an old book.

They mumbled strange words to their grandchildren, who would have preferred to play with the pretty pebbles, brought down from distant lands.

Often these words were not very clear.

THE VALLEY OF IGNORANCE

But they were, writ a thousand years ago by a forgotten race. Hence they were holy.

For in the Valley of Ignorance, whatever was old was venerable.

11

And those who dared to gainsay the wisdom of the fathers were shunned by all decent people.

And so they kept their peace.

Fear was ever with them. What if they should be refused the common share of the products of the garden?

Vague stories there were, whispered at night among the narrow streets of the little town, vague stories of men and women who had dared to ask questions.

They had gone forth, and never again had they been seen.

A few had tried to scale the high walls of the rocky range that hid the sun.

Their whitened bones lay at the foot of the cliffs.

The years came and the years went by.

Happily lived Mankind in the peaceful Valley of Ignorance.

*   *   *   *   *

Out of the darkness crept a man.

THE LONELY WANDERER

The nails of his hands were torn.

His feet were covered with rags, red with the blood of long marches.

He stumbled to the door of the nearest hut and knocked.

Then he fainted. By the light of a frightened candle, he was carried to a cot.

In the morning throughout the village it was known: "He has come back."

The neighbors stood around and shook their heads. They had always known that this was to be the end.

Defeat and surrender awaited those who dared to stroll away from the foot of the mountains.

And in one corner of the village the Old Men shook their heads and whispered burning words.

They did not mean to be cruel, but the Law was the Law. Bitterly this man had sinned against the wishes of Those Who Knew.

As soon as his wounds were healed he must be brought to trial.

They meant to be lenient.

They remembered the strange, burning eyes of his mother. They recalled the tragedy of his father, lost in the desert these thirty years ago.

The Law, however, was the Law; and the Law must be obeyed.

The Men Who Knew would see to that.

*   *   *   *   *

They carried the wanderer to the Market Place, and the people stood around in respectful silence.

He was still weak from hunger and thirst and the Elders bade him sit down.

He refused.

They ordered him to be silent.

But he spoke.

THE NEW HOME

Upon the Old Men he turned his back and his eyes sought those who but a short time before had been his comrades.

"Listen to me," he implored. "Listen to me and be rejoiced. I have come back from beyond the mountains. My feet have trod a fresh soil. My hands have felt the touch of other races. My eyes have seen wondrous sights.

"When I was a child, my world was the garden of my father.

"To the west and to the east, to the south and to the north lay the ranges from the Beginning of Time.

"When I asked what they were hiding, there was a hush and a hasty shaking of heads. When I insisted, I was taken to the rocks and shown the bleached bones of those who had dared to defy the Gods.

"When I cried out and said, 'It is a lie! The Gods love those who are brave!' the Men Who Knew came and read to me from their sacred books. The Law, they explained, had ordained all things of Heaven and Earth. The Valley was ours to have and to hold. The animals and the flowers, the fruits and the fishes were ours, to do our bidding. But the mountains were of the Gods. What lay beyond was to remain unknown until the End of Time.

"So they spoke, and they lied. They lied to me, even as they have lied to you.

"There are pastures in those hills. Meadows, too, as rich as any. And men and women of our own flesh and blood. And cities resplendent with the glories of a thousand years of labor.

"I have found the road to a better home. I have seen the promise of a happier life. Follow me and I shall lead you thither. For the smile of the Gods is the same there as here and everywhere."

    *   *   *   *   *   *   *   *

He stopped and there went up a great cry of horror.

"Blasphemy!" cried the Old Men. "Blasphemy and sacrilege! A fit punishment for his crime! He has lost his reason. He dares to scoff at the Law as it was written down a thousand years ago. He deserves to die!"

And they took up heavy stones.

And they killed him.

And his body they threw at the foot of the cliffs, that it might lie there as a warning to all who questioned the wisdom of the ancestors.

    *   *   *   *   *   *   *   *

Then it happened a short time later that there was a great drought. The little Brook of Knowledge ran dry. The cattle died of thirst. The harvest perished in the fields, and there was hunger in the Valley of Ignorance.

The Old Men Who Knew, however, were not disheartened. Everything would all come right in the end, they prophesied, for so it was writ in their most Holy Chapters.

Besides, they themselves needed but little food. They were so very old.

* * * * * * * *

Winter came.
The village was deserted.
More than half of the populace died from sheer want.
The only hope for those who survived lay beyond the mountains.
But the Law said "No!"
And the Law must be obeyed.

* * * * *

One night there was a rebellion.
Despair gave courage to those whom fear had forced into silence.
Feebly the Old Men protested.
They were pushed aside. They

THE WINTER OF HORROR

complained of their lot. They bewailed the ingratitude of their children, but when the last wagon pulled out of the village, they stopped the driver and forced him to take them along.

The flight into the unknown had begun.

* * * * * * * *

It was many years since the Wanderer had returned. It was no easy task to discover the road he had mapped out.

THE MEMORIAL STONE

Thousands fell a victim to hunger and thirst before the first cairn was found.

From there on the trip was less difficult.

The careful pioneer had blazed a clear trail through the woods and amidst the endless wilderness of rock.

By easy stages it led to the green pastures of the new land.

Silently the people looked at each other.

"He was right after all," they said. "He was right, and the Old Men were wrong. . . .

"He spoke the truth, and the Old Men lied. . . .

"His bones lie rotting at the foot of the cliffs, but the Old Men sit in our carts and chant their ancient lays. . . .

"He saved us, and we slew him. . . .

"We are sorry that it happened, but of course, if we could have known at the time . . ."

Then they unharnessed their horses and their oxen and they drove their cows and their goats into the pastures and they built themselves houses and laid out their fields and they lived happily for a long time afterwards.

* * * * * * * *

A few years later an attempt was made to bury the brave pioneer in the fine new edifice which had been erected as a home for the Wise Old Men.

A solemn procession went back to the now deserted valley, but when the spot was reached where his body ought to have been, it was no longer there.

A hungry jackal had dragged it to his lair.

A small stone was then placed at the foot of the trail (now a magnificent highway). It gave the name of the man who had first defied the dark terror of the unknown, that his people might be guided into a new freedom.

And it stated that it had been erected by a grateful posterity.

*   *   *   *   *   *   *   *

As it was in the beginning—as it is now—and as some day (so we hope) it shall no longer be.

Chapter I

THE TYRANNY OF IGNORANCE

IN the year 527 Flavius Anicius Justinianus became ruler of the eastern half of the Roman Empire.

This Serbian peasant (he came from Uskub, the much disputed railroad junction of the late war) had no use for "book-learnin'." It was by his orders that the ancient Athenian school of philosophy was finally suppressed. And it was he who closed the doors of the only Egyptian temple that had continued to do business centuries after the valley of the Nile had been invaded by the monks of the new Christian faith.

This temple stood on a little island called Philæ, not far from the first great waterfall of the Nile. Ever since men could remember, the spot had been dedicated to the worship of Isis, and for some curious reason the Goddess had survived where all her African and Greek and Roman rivals had miserably perished. Until finally, in the sixth century, the island was the only spot where the old and most holy art of picture writing was still understood and where a small number of priests continued to practice a trade which had been forgotten in every other part of the land of Cheops.

And now, by order of an illiterate farmhand, known as His Imperial Majesty, the temple and the adjoining school were declared state property, the statues and images were sent to the museum of Constantinople and the priests and the writing-masters were thrown into jail. And when the last of them had died from hunger and neglect, the age-old trade of making hieroglyphics had become a lost art.

All this was a great pity.

If Justinian (a plague upon his head!) had been a little less thorough and had saved just a few of those old picture experts in a sort of literary Noah's Ark, he would have made the task of the historian a great deal easier. For while (owing to the genius of Champollion) we can once more spell out the strange Egyptian words, it remains exceedingly difficult for us to understand the inner meaning of their message to posterity.

And the same holds true for all other nations of the ancient world.

What did those strangely bearded Babylonians, who left us whole brickyards full of religious tracts, have in mind when they exclaimed piously, "Who shall ever be able to understand the counsel of the Gods in Heaven?" How did they feel towards those divine spirits which they invoked so continually, whose laws they endeavored to interpret, whose commands they engraved upon the granite shafts of their most holy city? Why were they at once the most tolerant of men, encouraging their priests to study the high heavens, and to explore the land and the sea, and at the same time the most cruel of executioners, inflicting hideous punishments upon those of their neighbors who had committed some breach of divine etiquette which to-day would pass unnoticed?

Until recently we did not know.

We sent expeditions to Nineveh, we dug holes in the sand of Sinai and deciphered miles of cuneiform tablets. And everywhere in Mesopotamia and Egypt we did our best to find the key that should unlock the front door of this mysterious storehouse of wisdom.

And then, suddenly and almost by accident, we discovered that the back door had been wide open all the time and that we could enter the premises at will.

But that convenient little gate was not situated in the neighborhood of Akkad or Memphis.

It stood in the very heart of the jungle.

And it was almost hidden by the wooden pillars of a pagan temple.

*   *   *   *   *   *   *   *

Our ancestors, in search of easy plunder, had come in contact with what they were pleased to call "wild men" or "savages."

The meeting had not been a pleasant one.

The poor heathen, misunderstanding the intentions of the white men, had welcomed them with a salvo of spears and arrows.

The visitors had retaliated with their blunderbusses.

After that there had been little chance for a quiet and unprejudiced exchange of ideas.

The savage was invariably depicted as a dirty, lazy, good-for-nothing loafer who worshiped crocodiles and dead trees and deserved all that was coming to him.

THE MEETING OF EAST AND WEST

Then came the reaction of the eighteenth century. Jean Jacques Rousseau began to contemplate the world through a haze of sentimental tears. His contemporaries, much impressed by his ideas, pulled out their handkerchiefs and joined in the weeping.

The benighted heathen was one of their most favorite subjects. In their hands (although they had never seen one) he became the unfortunate victim of circumstances and the true representative of all those manifold virtues of which the human race had been deprived by three thousand years of a corrupt system of civilization.

To-day, at least in this particular field of investigation, we know better.

We study primitive man as we study the higher domesticated animals, from which as a rule he is not so very far removed.

In most instances we are fully repaid for our trouble. The savage, but for the grace of God, is our own self under much less favorable conditions. By examining him carefully we begin to understand the early society of the valley of the Nile and of the peninsula of Mesopotamia and by knowing him thoroughly we get a glimpse of many of those strange hidden instincts which lie buried deep down beneath the thin crust of manners and customs which our own species of mammal has acquired during the last five thousand years.

This encounter is not always flattering to our pride. On the other hand, a realization of the conditions from which we have escaped, together with an appreciation of the many things that have actually been accomplished, can only tend to give us new courage for the work in hand and if anything it will make us a little more tolerant towards those among our distant cousins who have failed to keep up the pace.

This is not a handbook of anthropology.

It is a volume dedicated to the subject of tolerance.

But tolerance is a very broad theme.

The temptation to wander will be great. And once we leave the beaten track, Heaven alone knows where we will land.

I therefore suggest that I be given half a page to state exactly and specifically what I mean by tolerance.

Language is one of the most deceptive inventions of the human race and all definitions are bound to be arbitrary. It therefore behooves an humble student to go to that authority which is accepted as final by the largest number of those who speak the language in which this book is written.

I refer to the Encyclopedia Britannica.

There on page 1052 of volume XXVI stands written: "Tolerance (from Latin *tolerare*—to endure):—The allowance of freedom of action or judgment to other people, the patient and unprejudiced endurance of dissent from one's own or the generally received course or view."

There may be other definitions but for the purpose of this

book I shall let myself be guided by the words of the Britannica.

And having committed myself (for better or worse) to a definite policy, I shall return to my savages and tell you what I have been able to discover about tolerance in the earliest forms of society of which we have any record.

* * * * * * * *

It is still generally believed that primitive society was very simple, that primitive language consisted of a few simple grunts and that primitive man possessed a degree of liberty which was lost only when the world became "complex."

The investigations of the last fifty years made by explorers and missionaries and doctors among the aborigines of central Africa and the Polar regions and Polynesia show the exact opposite. Primitive society was exceedingly complicated, primitive language had more forms and tenses and declensions than Russian or Arabic, and primitive man was a slave not only to the present, but also to the past and to the future; in short, an abject and miserable creature who lived in fear and. died in terror.

This may seem far removed from the popular picture of brave red-skins merrily roaming the prairies in search of buffaloes and scalps, but it is a little nearer to the truth.

And how could it have been otherwise?

I have read the stories of many miracles.

But one of them was lacking; the miracle of the survival of man.

How and in what manner and why the most defenseless of all mammals should have been able to maintain himself against microbes and mastodons and ice and heat and eventually become master of all creation, is something I shall not try to solve in the present chapter.

One thing, however, is certain. He never could have accomplished all this alone.

In order to succeed he was obliged to sink his individuality in the composite character of the tribe.

* * * * * * * *

Primitive society, therefore, was dominated by a single idea, an all-overpowering desire to survive.

This was very difficult.

And as a result all other considerations were sacrificed to the one supreme demand—to live.

The individual counted for nothing, the community at large counted for everything, and the tribe became a roaming fortress which lived by itself and for itself and of itself and found safety only in exclusiveness.

But the problem was even more complicated than at first appears. What I have just said held good only for the visible world, and the visible world in those early times was a negligible quantity compared to the realm of the invisible.

In order to understand this fully we must remember that primitive people are different from ourselves. They are not familiar with the law of cause and effect.

If I sit me down among the poison ivy, I curse my negligence, send for the doctor and tell my young son to get rid of the stuff as soon as he can. My ability to recognize cause and effect tells me that the poison ivy has caused the rash, that the doctor will be able to give me something that will make the itch stop and that the removal of the vine will prevent a repetition of this painful experience.

The true savage would act quite differently. He would not connect the rash with the poison ivy at all. He lives in a world in which past, present and future are inextricably interwoven. All his dead leaders survive as Gods and his dead neighbors survive as spirits and they all continue to be invisible members of the clan and they accompany each individual member wherever he goes. They eat with him and sleep with him and they stand watch over his door. It is his business to keep them at arm's length or gain their friendship. If ever he fail to do this he will be immediately punished and as he cannot possibly know how to please all those spirits all the time, he is in constant fear of that misfortune which comes as the revenge of the Gods.

He therefore reduces every event that is at all out of the ordinary not to a primary cause but to interference on the part of an invisible spirit and when he notices a rash on his arms he does not say, "Damn that poison ivy!" but he mumbles, "I have offended a God. The God has punished me," and he runs to the medicine-man, not, however, to get a lotion to counteract the poison of the ivy but to get a "charm" that shall prove stronger than the charm which the irate God (and not the ivy) has thrown upon him.

As for the ivy, the primary cause of all his suffering, he lets it grow right there where it has always grown. And if perchance the white man comes with a can of kerosene and burns the shrub down, he will curse him for his trouble.

It follows that a society in which everything happens as the result of the direct personal interference on the part of an invisible being must depend for its continued existence upon a strict obedience of such laws as seem to appease the wrath of the Gods.

Such a law, according to the opinion of a savage, existed. His ancestors had devised it and had bestowed it upon him and it was his most sacred duty to keep that law intact and hand it over in its present and perfect form to his own children.

This, of course, seems absurd to us. We firmly believe in progress, in growth, in constant and uninterrupted improvement.

But "progress" is an expression that was coined only year before last, and it is typical of all low forms of society that the people see no possible reason why they should improve what (to them) is the best of all possible worlds because they never knew any other.

* * * * * * * *

Granted that all this be true, then how does one prevent a change in the laws and in the established forms of society?

The answer is simple.

By the immediate punishment of those who refuse to regard common police regulations as an expression of the divine will, or in plain language, by a rigid system of intolerance.

* * * * * * * *

If I hereby state that the savage was the most intolerant of human beings, I do not mean to insult him, for I hasten to add that given the circumstances under which he lived, it was his duty to be intolerant. Had he allowed any one to interfere with the thousand and one rules upon which his tribe depended for its continued safety and peace of mind, the life of the tribe would have been put in jeopardy and that would have been the greatest of all possible crimes.

But (and the question is worth asking) how could a group of people, relatively limited in number, protect a most complex system of verbal regulations when we in our own day with millions of soldiers and thousands of policemen find it difficult to enforce a few plain laws?

Again the answer is simple.

The savage was a great deal cleverer than we are. He accomplished by shrewd calculation what he could not do by force.

He invented the idea of "taboo."

Perhaps the word "invented" is not the right expression. Such things are rarely the product of a sudden inspiration. They are the result of long years of growth and experiment. Let that

TABOO

be as it may, the wild men of Africa and Polynesia devised the taboo, and thereby saved themselves a great deal of trouble.

The word taboo is of Australian origin. We all know more or less what it means. Our own world is full of taboos, things we simply must not do or say, like mentioning our latest operation at the dinner table, or leaving our spoon in our cup of coffee. But our taboos are never of a very serious nature. They are part of the handbook of etiquette and rarely interfere with our own personal happiness.

To primitive man, on the other hand, the taboo was of the utmost importance.

It meant that certain persons or inanimate objects had been "set apart" from the rest of the world, that they (to use the Hebrew equivalent) were "holy" and must not be discussed or touched on pain of instant death and everlasting torture. A fairly large order but woe unto him or her who dared to disobey the will of the spirit-ancestors.

* * * * * * * *

Whether the taboo was an invention of the priests or the priesthood was created to maintain the taboo is a problem which has not yet been solved. As tradition is much older than religion, it seems more than likely that taboos existed long before the world had heard of sorcerers and witch-doctors. But as soon as the latter had made their appearance, they became the staunch supporters of the idea of taboo and used it with such great virtuosity that the taboo became the "verboten" sign of prehistoric ages.

When we first heard the names of Babylon and Egypt, those countries were still in a state of development in which the taboo counted for a great deal. Not a taboo in the crude and primitive form as it was afterwards found in New Zealand, but solemnly transformed into negative rules of conduct, the sort of "thou-shalt-not" decrees with which we are all familiar through six of our Ten Commandments.

Needless to add that the idea of tolerance was entirely unknown in those lands at that early age.

What we sometimes mistake for tolerance was merely indifference caused by ignorance.

But we can find no trace of any willingness (however vague) on the part of either kings or priests to allow others to exercise that "freedom of action or judgment" or of that "patient and unprejudiced endurance of dissent from the generally received cause or view" which has become the ideal of our modern age.

*   *   *   *   *   *   *   *

Therefore, except in a very negative way, this book is not interested in prehistoric history or what is commonly called "ancient history."

The struggle for tolerance did not begin until after the discovery of the individual.

And the credit for this, the greatest of all modern revelations, belongs to the Greeks.

Chapter II

THE GREEKS

How it happened that a little rocky peninsula in a remote corner of the Mediterranean was able to provide our world in less than two centuries with the complete framework for all our present day experiments in politics, literature, drama, sculpture, chemistry, physics and Heaven knows what else, is a question which has puzzled a great many people for a great many centuries and to which every philosopher, at one time or another during his career, has tried to give an answer.

Respectable historians, unlike their colleagues of the chemical and physical and astronomical and medical faculties, have always looked with ill-concealed contempt upon all efforts to discover what one might call "the laws of history." What holds good of polliwogs and microbes and shooting stars seems to have no business within the realm of human beings.

I may be very much mistaken, but it seems to me that there must be such laws. It is true that thus far we have not discovered many of them. But then again we have never looked very hard. We have been so busy accumulating facts that we have had no time to boil them and liquefy them and evaporate them and extract from them the few scraps of wisdom which might be of some real value to our particular variety of mammal.

It is with considerable trepidation that I approach this new field of research and, taking a leaf out of the scientist's book, offer the following historical axiom.

According to the best knowledge of modern scientists, life (animate existence as differentiated from inanimate existence) began when for once all physical and chemical elements were present in the ideal proportion necessary for the creation of the first living cell.

Translate this into terms of history and you get this:

"A sudden and apparently spontaneous outbreak of a very high form of civilization is only possible when all the racial, climatic, economic and political conditions are present in an ideal proportion or in as nearly an ideal condition and proportion as they can be in this imperfect world."

Let me elaborate this statement by a few negative observations.

A race with the brain development of a cave-man would not prosper, even in Paradise.

Rembrandt would not have painted pictures, Bach would not have composed fugues, Praxiteles would not have made statues if they had been born in an igloo near Upernivik and had been obliged to spend most of their w a k i n g hours watching a seal-hole in an ice-field.

GREECE

Darwin would not have made his contributions to biology if he had been obliged to gain his livelihood in a cotton mill in Lancashire. And Alexander Graham Bell would not have invented the telephone if he had been a conscripted serf and had lived in a remote village of the Romanov domains.

In Egypt, where the first high form of civilization was found, the climate was excellent, but the original inhabitants were not very robust or enterprising, and political and economic conditions were decidedly bad. The same held true of Babylonia and Assyria. The Semitic races which afterwards moved into the valley between the Tigris and the Euphrates were strong and vigorous people. There was nothing the matter with the climate. But the political and economic environment remained far from good.

In Palestine the climate was nothing to boast of. Agriculture

was backward and there was little commerce outside of the cara-
van route which passed through the country from Africa to Asia
and vice versa. Furthermore, in Palestine politics were entirely
dominated by the priests of the temple of Jerusalem and this
of course did not encourage the development of any sort of
individual enterprise.

In Phœnicia, the climate was of little consequence. The race
was strong and trade conditions were good. The country, however, suffered from a badly balanced economic system. A small
class of ship owners had been able to get hold of all the wealth
and had established a rigid commercial monopoly. Hence the
government in Tyre and Sidon had at an early date fallen into
the hands of the very rich. The poor, deprived of all excuse
for the practice of a reasonable amount of industry, grew callous
and indifferent and Phœnicia eventually shared the fate of
Carthage and went to ruin through the short-sighted selfishness
of her rulers.

In short, in every one of the early centers of civilization, certain of the necessary elements for success were always lacking.

When the miracle of a perfect balance finally did occur, in
Greece in the fifth century before our era, it lasted only a very
short time, and strange to say, even then it did not take place
in the mother country but in the colonies across the Ægean Sea.

In another book I have given a description of those famous
island-bridges which connected the mainland of Asia with Europe
and across which the traders from Egypt and Babylonia and
Crete since time immemorial had traveled to Europe. The main
point of embarkation, both for merchandise and ideas bound from
Asia to Europe, was to be found on the western coast of Asia
Minor in a strip of land known as Ionia.

A few hundred years before the Trojan war, this narrow bit
of mountainous territory, ninety miles long and only a few miles
wide, had been conquered by Greek tribes from the mainland
who there had founded a number of colonial towns of which
Ephesus, Phocæa, Erythræa and Miletus were the best known,
and it was along those cities that at last the conditions of

THE COMMERCIAL CITY

success were present in such perfect proportion that civilization reached a point which has sometimes been equaled but never has been surpassed.

In the first place, these colonies were inhabited by the most active and enterprising elements from among a dozen different nations.

In the second place, there was a great deal of general wealth derived from the carrying trade between the old and the new world, between Europe and Asia.

In the third place, the form of government under which the colonists lived gave the majority of the freemen a chance to develop their talents to the very best of their ability.

If I do not mention the climate, the reason is this; that in countries devoted exclusively to commerce, the climate does not matter much. Ships can be built and goods can be unloaded, rain or shine. Provided it does not get so cold that the harbors freeze or so wet that the towns are flooded, the inhabitants will take very little interest in the daily weather reports.

But aside from this, the weather of Ionia was distinctly favorable to the development of an intellectual class. Before the existence of books and libraries, learning was handed down from man to man by word of mouth and the town-pump was the earliest of all social centers and the oldest of universities.

In Miletus it was possible to sit around the town-pump for 350 out of every 365 days. And the early Ionian professors made such excellent use of their climatic advantages that they became the pioneers of all future scientific development.

The first of whom we have any report, the real founder of modern science, was a person of doubtful origin. Not in the sense that he had robbed a bank or murdered his family and had fled to Miletus from parts unknown. But no one knew much about his antecedents. Was he a Bœotian or a Phœnician, a Nordic (to speak in the jargon of our learned racial experts) or a Semite?

It shows what an international center this little old city at the mouth of the Meander was in those days. Its population (like that of New York to-day) consisted of so many different elements that people accepted their neighbors at their face value and did not look too closely into the family antecedents.

Since this is not a history of mathematics or a handbook of philosophy, the speculations of Thales do not properly belong in these pages, except in so far as they tend to show the tolerance towards new ideas which prevailed among the Ionians at a time when Rome was a small market-town on a muddy river somewhere in a distant and unknown region, when the Jews were still captives in the land of Assyria and when northern and western Europe were naught but a howling wilderness.

In order that we may understand how such a development was possible, we must know something about the changes which had taken place since the days when Greek chieftains sailed across the Ægean Sea, intent upon the plunder of the rich fortress of Troy. Those far-famed heroes were still the product of an exceedingly primitive form of civilization. They were overgrown children who regarded life as one long, glorified roughhouse, full of excitement and wrestling matches and running races and all the many things which we ourselves would dearly love to do if we were not forced to stick to the routine jobs which provide us with bread and bananas.

The relationship between these boisterous paladins and their Gods was as direct and as simple as their attitude towards the serious problems of everyday existence. For the inhabitants of high Olympus, who ruled the world of the Hellenes in the tenth century before our era, were of this earth earthy, and not very far removed from ordinary mortals. Exactly where and when and how man and his Gods had parted company was a more or less hazy point, never clearly established. Even then the friendship which those who lived beyond the clouds had always felt towards their subjects who crawled across the face of the earth had in no way been interrupted and it had remained flavored with those personal and intimate touches which gave the religion of the Greeks its own peculiar charm.

Of course, all good little Greek boys were duly taught that Zeus was a very powerful and mighty potentate with a long beard who upon occasion would juggle so violently with his flashes of lightning and his thunderbolts that it seemed that the world was coming to an end. But as soon as they were a little older and were able to read the ancient sagas for themselves, they began to appreciate the limitations of those terrible personages of whom they had heard so much in their nursery and who now appeared in the light of a merry family-party—everlastingly playing practical jokes upon each other and taking such bitter sides in the political disputes of their mortal friends that every quarrel in Greece was immediately followed by a corresponding row among the denizens of the ether.

Of course, in spite of all these very human shortcomings, Zeus remained a very great God, the mightiest of all rulers and a personage whom it was not safe to displease. But he was "reasonable" in that sense of the word which is so well understood among the lobbyists of Washington. He was reasonable. He could be approached if one knew the proper way. And best of all, he had a sense of humor and did not take either himself or his world too seriously.

This was, perhaps, not the most sublime conception of a divine figure, but it offered certain very distinct advantages. Among the ancient Greeks there never was a hard and fast rule as to what people must hold true and what they must disregard as false. And because there was no "creed" in the modern sense of the word, with adamantine dogmas and a class of professional priests, ready to enforce them with the help of the secular gallows, the people in different parts of the country were able to reshape their religious ideas and ethical conceptions as best suited their own individual tastes.

The Thessalians, who lived within hailing distance of Mount Olympus, showed of course much less respect for their august neighbors than did the Asopians who dwelled in a distant village on the Laconian Gulf. The Athenians, feeling themselves under the direct protection of their own patron saint, Pallas Athene, felt that they could take great liberties with the lady's father, while the Arcadians, whose valleys were far removed from the main trade routes, clung tenaciously to a simpler faith and frowned upon all levity in the serious matter of religion, and as for the inhabitants of Phocis, who made a living from the pilgrims bound for the village of Delphi, they were firmly convinced that Apollo (who was worshiped at that profitable shrine) was the greatest of all divine spirits and deserved the special homage of those who came from afar and still had a couple of drachmas in their pocket.

The belief in only one God which soon afterwards was to set the Jews apart from all other nations, would never have been possible if the life of Judæa had not centered around a single city which was strong enough to destroy all rival places of pilgrimage and was able to maintain an exclusive religious monopoly for almost ten consecutive centuries.

In Greece such a condition did not prevail. Neither Athens nor Sparta ever succeeded in establishing itself as the recognized capital of a united Greek fatherland. Their efforts in this direction only led to long years of unprofitable civil war.

No wonder that a race composed of such sublime individualists offered great scope for the development of a very independent spirit of thought.

The Iliad and the Odyssey have sometimes been called the Bible of the Greeks. They were nothing of the sort. They were just books. They were never united into "The Book." They told the adventures of certain wonderful heroes who were fondly believed to be the direct ancestors of the generation then living. Incidentally they contained a certain amount of religious information because the Gods, without exception, had taken sides in the quarrel and had neglected all other business for the joy of watching the rarest prizefight that had ever been staged within their domain.

The idea, however, that the works of Homer might either directly or indirectly have been inspired by Zeus or Minerva or Apollo never even dawned upon the Greek mind. These were a fine piece of literature and made excellent reading during the long winter evenings. Furthermore they caused children to feel proud of their own race.

THE PHILOSOPHER

And that was all.

In such an atmosphere of intellectual and spiritual freedom, in a city filled with the pungent smell of ships from all the seven seas, rich with fabrics of the Orient, merry with the laughter of a well-fed and contented populace, Thales was born. In such a city he worked and taught and in such a city he died. If the conclusions which he reached differed greatly from the opinions held by most of his neighbors, remember that his ideas never penetrated beyond a very limited circle. The average Miletian may have heard the name of Thales, just as the average New Yorker has probably heard the name of Einstein. Ask him who Einstein is, and he will answer that he is a fellow with long hair who smokes a pipe and plays the fiddle and who wrote something about a man walking through a railroad train, about which there once was an article in a Sunday paper.

That this strange person who smokes a pipe and plays the fiddle has got hold of a little spark of truth which eventually may upset (or at least greatly modify) the scientific conclusions of the last sixty centuries, is a matter of profound indifference to the millions of easy-going citizens whose interest in mathematics does not reach beyond the conflict which arises when their favorite batsman tries to upset the law of gravity.

The text-books of ancient history usually get rid of the difficulty by printing "Thales of Miletus (640-546 B.C.), the founder of modern science." And we can almost see the headlines in the "Miletus Gazette" saying, "Local graduate discovers secret of true science."

But just how and where and when Thales left the beaten track and struck out for himself, I could not possibly tell you. This much is certain, that he did not live in an intellectual vacuum, nor did he develop his wisdom out of his inner consciousness. In the seventh century before Christ, a great deal of the pioneer work in the realm of science had already been done and there was quite a large body of mathematical and physical and astronomical information at the disposal of those intelligent enough to make use of it.

Babylonian star-gazers had searched the heavens.

Egyptian architects had done considerable figuring before
they dared to dump a couple of million tons of granite on top
of a little burial chamber in the heart of a pyramid.

The mathematicians of the Nile Valley had seriously studied
the behavior of the sun that they might predict the wet and

GREEK FAIRY TALES

dry seasons and give the peasants a calendar by which they
could regulate their work on the farms.

All these problems, however, had been solved by people who
still regarded the forces of nature as the direct and personal
expression of the will of certain invisible Gods who administered
the seasons and the course of the planets and the tides of the
ocean as the members of the President's Cabinet manage the
department of agriculture or the post-office or the treasury.

Thales rejected this point of view. But like most well-educated
people of his day, he did not bother to discuss it in public. If
the fruit vendors along the waterfront wanted to fall upon their
faces whenever there was an eclipse of the sun and invoke the
name of Zeus in fear of this unusual sight, that was their busi-

ness and Thales would have been the last man to try to convince
them that any schoolboy with an elementary knowledge of the
behavior of heavenly bodies would have foretold that on the
25th of May of the year 585 B.C., at such and such an hour,
the moon would find herself between the earth and the sun and
that therefore the town of Miletus would experience a few minutes
of comparative darkness.

Even when it appeared (as it did appear) that the Persians
and the Lydians had been engaged in battle on the afternoon
of this famous eclipse and had been obliged to cease killing each
other for lack of sufficient light, he refused to believe that the
Lydian deities (following a famous precedent established a few
years previously during a certain battle in the valley of Ajalon)
had performed a miracle, and had suddenly turned off the light
of Heaven that the victory might go to those whom they favored.

For Thales had reached the point (and that was his great
merit) where he dared to regard all nature as the manifestation
of one Eternal Will, subject to one Eternal Law and entirely
beyond the personal influence of those divine spirits which man
was forever creating after his own image. And the eclipse, so
he felt, would have taken place just the same if there had been
no more important engagement that particular afternoon than a
dog fight in the streets of Ephesus or a wedding feast in Hali-
carnassus.

Drawing the logical conclusions from his own scientific observations, he laid down one general and inevitable law for all creation
and guessed (and to a certain extent guessed correctly) that the
beginning of all things was to be found in the water which
apparently surrounded the world on all sides and which had
probably existed from the very beginning of time.

Unfortunately we do not possess anything that Thales himself
wrote. It is possible that he may have put his ideas into concrete
form (for the Greeks had already learned the alphabet from the
Phœnicians) but not a page which can be directly attributed to
him survives to-day. For our knowledge of himself and his ideas
we depend upon the scanty bits of information found in the
books of some of his contemporaries. From these, however, we

have learned that Thales, in private life, was a merchant with wide connections in all parts of the Mediterranean. That, by the way, was typical of most of the early philosophers. They were "lovers of wisdom." But they never closed their eyes to the fact that the secret of life is found among the living and that "wisdom for the sake of wisdom" is quite as dangerous as "art for art's sake" or a dinner for the sake of the food.

To them, man with all his human qualities, good and bad and indifferent, was the supreme measure of all things. Wherefore they spent their leisure time patiently studying this strange creature as he was and not as they thought that he ought to be.

This made it possible for them to remain on the most amicable terms with their fellow citizens and allowed them to wield a much greater power than if they had undertaken to show their neighbors a short cut to the Millennium.

They rarely laid down a hard and fast rule of conduct.

But by their own example they managed to show how a true understanding of the forces of nature must inevitably lead to that inner peace of the soul upon which all true happiness depends and having in this way gained the good-will of their community they were given full liberty to study and explore and investigate and were even permitted to v e n t u r e w i t h i n those domains which were popularly believed to be the exclusive

THE ASTRONOMERS

property of the Gods. And as one of the pioneers of this new gospel did Thales spend the long years of his useful career.

Although he had pulled the entire world of the Greeks apart, although he had examined each little piece separately, and had openly questioned all sorts of things which the majority of the people since the beginning of time had held to be established facts, he was allowed to die peacefully in his own bed, and if any one ever called him to account for his heresies, we fail to have a record of the fact.

And once he had shown the way, there were many others eager to follow.

There was, for example, Anaxagoras of Clazomenae, who left Asia Minor for Athens at the age of thirty-six and spent the following years as a "sophist" or private tutor in different Greek cities. He specialized in astronomy and among other things he taught that the sun was not a heavenly chariot, driven by a God, as was generally believed, but a red-hot ball of fire, thousands and thousands of times larger than the whole of Greece.

When nothing happened to him, when no bolt from Heaven killed him for his audacity, he went a little further in his theories and stated boldly that the moon was covered with mountains and valleys and finally he even hinted at a certain "original matter" which was the beginning and the end of all things and which had existed from the very beginning of time.

But here, as many other scientists after him were to discover, he trod upon dangerous ground, for he discussed something with which people were familiar. The sun and the moon were distant orbs. The average Greek did not care what names the philosopher wished to call them. But when the professor began to argue that all things had gradually grown and developed out of a vague substance called "original matter"—then he went decidedly too far. Such an assertion was in flat contradiction with the story of Deucalion and Pyrrha, who after the great flood had repopulated the world by turning bits of stone into men and women. To deny the truth of a most solemn tale which all little Greek boys and girls had been taught in their early childhood was most dangerous to the safety of established society. It would make the children doubt the wisdom of their elders and that would never do. Hence Anaxagoras was made the subject of a formidable attack on the part of the Athenian Parents' League.

During the monarchy and the early days of the republic, the rulers of the city would have been more than able to protect a teacher of unpopular doctrines from the foolish hostility of the illiterate Attic peasants. But Athens by this time had become a full-fledged democracy and the freedom of the individual was no longer what it used to be. Furthermore, Pericles, just then in disgrace with the majority of the people, was himself a favorite pupil of the great astronomer, and the legal prosecution of Anaxagoras was welcomed as an excellent political move against the city's old dictator.

A priest by the name of Diopheites, who also was a ward-leader in one of the most densely populated suburbs, got a law passed which demanded "the immediate prosecution of all those who disbelieved in the established religion or held theories of their own about certain divine things." Under this law, Anaxagoras was actually thrown into prison. Finally, however, the better elements in the city prevailed. Anaxagoras was allowed to go free after the payment of a small fine and move to Lampsacus in Asia Minor where he died, full of years and honor, in the year 428 B.C.

His case shows how little is ever accomplished by the official suppression of scientific theories. For although Anaxagoras was forced to leave Athens, his ideas remained behind and two centuries later they came to the notice of one Aristotle, who in turn used them as a basis for many of his own scientific speculations. Reaching merrily across a thousand years of darkness, he handed them on to one Abul-Walid Muhammad ibn-Ahmad (commonly known as Averroës), the great Arab physician who in turn popularized them among the students of the Moorish universities of southern Spain. Then, together with his own observations, he wrote them down in a number of books. These were duly carried across the Pyrenees until they reached the

universities of Paris and Boulogne. There they were translated
into Latin and French and English and so thoroughly were they
accepted by the people of western and northern Europe that
to-day they have become an integral part of every primer of
science and are considered as harmless as the tables of multiplication.

But to return to Anaxagoras. For almost an entire generation
after his trial, Greek scientists were allowed to teach doctrines
which were at variance with popular belief. And then, during
the last years of the fifth century, a second case took place.

The victim this time was a certain Protagoras, a wandering
teacher who hailed from the village of Abdera, an Ionian colony
in northern Greece. This spot already enjoyed a doubtful reputation as the birthplace of Democritus, the original "laughing
philosopher," who had laid down the law that "only that society

is worth while which offers to
the largest number of people the
greatest amount of happiness
obtainable with the smallest
amount of pain," and who therefore was regarded as a good deal
of a radical and a fellow who
should be under constant police
supervision.

Protagoras, deeply impressed
by this doctrine, went to Athens
and there, after many years of
study, proclaimed that man was
the measure of all things, that

PROTAGORAS

life was too short to waste valuable time upon an inquiry into the
doubtful existence of any Gods, and that all energies ought to
be used for the purpose of making existence more beautiful and
more thoroughly enjoyable.

This statement, of course, went to the very root of the matter
and it was bound to shock the faithful more than anything that
had ever been written or said. Furthermore, it was made during
a very serious crisis in the war between Athens and Sparta and

the people, after a long series of defeats and pestilence, were in a state of utter despair. Most evidently it was not the right moment to incur the wrath of the Gods by an inquiry into the scope of their supernatural powers. Protagoras was accused of atheism, of "godlessness," and was told to submit his doctrines to the courts.

Pericles, who could have protected him, was dead and Protagoras, although a scientist, felt little taste for martyrdom.

He fled.

Unfortunately, on the way to Sicily, his ship was wrecked, and it seems that he was drowned, for we never hear of him again.

As for Diagoras, another victim of Athenian malevolence, he was really not a philosopher at all but a young writer who harbored a personal grudge against the Gods because they had once failed to give him their support in a law-suit. He brooded so long upon his supposed grievance that finally his mind became affected and he went about saying all sorts of blasphemous things about the Holy Mysteries which just then enjoyed great popularity among the people of northern Hellas. For this unseemly conduct he was condemned to death. But ere the sentence was executed, the poor devil was given the opportunity to escape. He went to Corinth, continued to revile his Olympian enemies, and peacefully died of his own bad temper.

And this brings us at last to the most notorious and the most famous case of Greek intolerance of which we possess any record, the judicial murder of Socrates.

When it is sometimes stated that the world has not changed at all and that the Athenians were no more broad-minded than the people of later times, the name of Socrates is dragged into the debate as a terrible example of Greek bigotry. But to-day, after a very exhaustive study of the case, we know better and the long and undisturbed career of this brilliant but exasperating soap-box orator is a direct tribute to the spirit of intellectual liberty which prevailed throughout ancient Greece in the fifth century before our era.

For Socrates, at a time when the common people still firmly believed in a large number of divine beings, made himself the prophet of an only God. And although the Athenians may not always have known what he meant when he spoke of his "dæmon" (that inner voice of divine inspiration which told him what to do and say), they were fully aware of his very unorthodox attitude towards those ideals which most of his neighbors continued to hold in holy veneration and his utter lack of respect for the established order of things. In the end, however, politics killed the old man and theology (although dragged in for the benefit of the crowd) had really very little to do with the outcome of the trial.

Socrates was the son of a stone-cutter who had many children and little money. The boy therefore had never been able to pay for a regular college course, for most of the philosophers were practical fellows and often charged as much as two thousand dollars for a single course of instruction. Besides, the pursuit of pure knowledge and the study of useless scientific facts seemed to young Socrates a mere waste of time and energy. Provided a person cultivated his conscience, so he reasoned, he could well do without geometry, and a knowledge of the true nature of comets and planets was not necessary for the salvation of the soul.

All the same, the homely little fellow with the broken nose and the shabby cloak, who spent his days arguing with the loafers on the corner of the street and his nights listening to the harangues of his wife (who was obliged to provide for a large family by taking in washing, as her husband regarded the gaining of a livelihood as an entirely negligible detail of existence), this honorable veteran of many wars and expeditions and ex-member of the Athenian senate was chosen among all the many teachers of his day to suffer for his opinions.

In order to understand how this happened, we must know something about the politics of Athens in the days when Socrates rendered his painful but highly useful service to the cause of human intelligence and progress.

All his life long (and he was past seventy when he was executed) Socrates tried to show his neighbors that they were wasting their opportunities; that they were living hollow and shallow lives; that they devoted entirely too much time to empty pleasures and vain triumphs and almost invariably squandered the divine gifts with which a great and mysterious God had endowed them for the sake of a few hours of futile glory and self-satisfaction. And so thoroughly convinced was he of man's high destiny that he broke through the bounds of all old philosophies and went even further than Protagoras. For whereas the latter had taught that "man is the measure of all things," Socrates preached that "man's invisible conscience is (or ought to be) the ultimate measure of all things and that it is not the Gods but we ourselves who shape our destiny."

The speech which Socrates made before the judges who were to decide his fate (there were five hundred of them, to be precise, and they had been so carefully chosen by his political enemies that some of them could actually read and write) was one of the most delightful bits of common sense ever addressed to any audience, sympathetic or otherwise.

"No person on earth," so the philosopher argued, "has the right to tell another man what he should believe or to deprive him of the right to think as he pleases," and further, "Provided that man remain on good terms with his own conscience, he can well do without the approbation of his friends, without money, without a family or even a home. But as no one can possibly reach the right conclusions without a thorough examination of all the pros and cons of every problem, people must be given a chance to discuss all questions with complete freedom and without interference on the part of the authorities."

Unfortunately for the accused, this was exactly the wrong statement at the wrong moment. Ever since the Peloponnesian war there had been a bitter struggle in Athens between the rich and the poor, between capital and labor. Socrates was a "moderate"—a liberal who saw good and evil in both systems of government and who tried to find a compromise which should satisfy all reasonable people. This, of course, had made him thoroughly unpopular with both sides but thus far they had been too evenly balanced to take action against him.

When at last in the year 403 B.C. the one-hundred-per-cent

Democrats gained complete control of the state and expelled the aristocrats, Socrates was a doomed man.

His friends knew this. They suggested that he leave the city before it was too late and this would have been a very wise thing to do.

For Socrates had quite as many enemies as friends. During the greater part of a century he had been a sort of vocal "col-

SOCRATES

umnist," a terribly clever busybody who had made it his hobby to expose the shams and the intellectual swindles of those who regarded themselves as the pillars of Athenian society. As a result, every one had come to know him. His name had become a household word throughout eastern Greece. When he said something funny in the morning, by night the whole town had heard about it. Plays had been written about him and when he was finally arrested and taken to prison there was not a citizen in the whole of Attica who was not thoroughly familiar with all the details of his career.

Those who took the leading part in the actual trial (like that honorable grain merchant who could neither read nor write but who knew all about the will of the Gods and therefore was loudest in his accusations) were undoubtedly convinced that they were rendering a great service to the community by ridding the city of a highly dangerous member of the so-called "intelligentsia," a man whose teaching could only lead to laziness and crime and discontent among the slaves.

It is rather amusing to remember that even under those circumstances, Socrates pleaded his case with such tremendous virtuosity that a majority of the jury was all for letting him go free and suggested that he might be pardoned if only he would give up this terrible habit of arguing, of debating, of wrangling and moralizing, in short, if only he would leave his neighbors and their pet prejudices in peace and not bother them with his eternal doubts.

But Socrates would not hear of it.

"By no means," he exclaimed. "As long as my conscience, as long as the still small voice within me, bids me go forth and show men the true road to reason, I shall continue to buttonhole whomsoever I happen to meet and I shall say what is on my mind, regardless of consequences."

After that, there was no other course but to condemn the prisoner to death.

Socrates was given a respite of thirty days. The holy ship which made an annual pilgrimage to Delos had not yet returned from its voyage, and until then the Athenian law did not allow any executions. The whole of this month the old man spent quietly in his cell, trying to improve his system of logic. Although he was repeatedly given the opportunity to escape, he refused to go. He had lived his life and had done his duty. He was tired and ready to depart. Until the hour of his execution he continued to talk with his friends, trying to educate them in what he held to be right and true, asking them to turn their minds upon the things of the spirit rather than those of the material world.

Then he drank the beaker of hemlock, laid himself upon his couch and settled all further argument by sleep everlasting.

For a short time, his disciples, rather terrified by this terrible outburst of popular wrath, thought it wise to remove themselves from the scene of their former activities.

But when nothing happened, they returned and resumed their former occupations as public teachers, and within a dozen years after the death of the old philosopher, his ideas were more popular than ever.

The city meanwhile had gone through a very difficult period. It was five years since the struggle for the leadership of the Greek peninsula had ended with the defeat of Athens and the ultimate victory of the Spartans. This had been a complete triumph of brawn over brain. Needless to say that it did not last very long. The Spartans, who never wrote a line worth remembering or contributed a single idea to the sum total of human knowledge (with the exception of certain military tactics which survive in our modern game of football), thought that they had accomplished their task when the walls of their rival had been pulled down and the Athenian fleet had been reduced to a dozen ships. But the Athenian mind had lost none of its shrewd brilliancy. A decade after the end of the Peloponnesian war, the old harbor of the Piræus was once more filled with ships from all parts of the world and Athenian admirals were again fighting at the head of the allied Greek navies.

THE DEATH OF SOCRATES

Furthermore, the labor of Pericles, although not appreciated by his contemporaries, had made the city the intellectual capi-

tal of the world—the Paris of the fourth century before the
birth of Christ. Whosoever in Rome or Spain or Africa was
rich enough to give his sons a fashionable education, felt flattered if the boys were allowed to visit a school situated within
the shadow of the Acropolis.

For this ancient world, which we modern people find so difficult to understand properly, took the problem of existence
seriously.

Under the influence of the early Christian enemies of pagan
civilization, the impression has gained ground that the average
Roman or Greek was a highly immoral person who paid a shallow
homage to certain nebulous Gods and for the rest spent his
waking hours eating enormous dinners, drinking vast bumpers
of Salernian wine and listening to the pretty prattle of Egyptian
dancing girls, unless for a change he went to war and slaughtered
innocent Germans and Franks and Dacians for the pure sport
of shedding blood.

Of course, both in Greece and even more so in Rome, there
were a great many merchants and war contractors who had
accumulated their millions without much regard for those ethical
principles which Socrates had so well defined before his judges.
Because these people were very wealthy, they had to be put up
with. This, however, did not mean that they enjoyed the respect
of the community or were regarded as commendable representatives of the civilization of their day.

We dig up the villa of Epaphroditus, who amassed millions
as one of the gang who helped Nero plunder Rome and her
colonies. We look at the ruins of the forty-room palace which
the old profiteer built out of his ill-gotten gains. And we shake
our heads and say, "What depravity!"

Then we sit down and read the works of Epictetus, who was
one of the house slaves of the old scoundrel, and we find ourselves
in the company of a spirit as lofty and as exalted as ever lived.

I know that the making of generalizations about our neighbors
and about other nations is one of the most popular of indoor
sports, but let us not forget that Epictetus, the philosopher, was
quite as truly a representative of the time in which he lived as

Epaphroditus, the imperial flunkey, and that the desire for holiness was as great twenty centuries ago as it is to-day.

Undoubtedly it was a very different sort of holiness from that which is practiced to-day. It was the product of an essentially European brain and had nothing to do with the Orient. But the "barbarians" who established it as their ideal of what they held to be most noble and desirable were our own ancestors, and they were slowly developing a philosophy of life which was highly successful if we agree that a clear conscience and a simple, straightforward life, together with good health and a moderate but sufficient income, are the best guarantee for general happiness and contentment. The future of the soul did not interest these people overmuch. They accepted the fact that they were a special sort of mammal which by reason of its intellectual application had risen high above the other creatures which crawled upon this earth. If they frequently referred to the Gods, they used the word as we use "atoms" or "electrons" or "ether." The beginning of things has got to have a name, but Zeus in the mouth of Epictetus was as problematical a value as x or y in the problems of Euclid and meant just as much or as little.

Life it was which interested those men and next to living, art.

Life, therefore, in all its endless varieties, they studied and following the method of reasoning which Socrates had originated and made popular, they achieved some very remarkable results.

That sometimes in their zeal for a perfect spiritual world they went to absurd extremes was regrettable, but no more than human. But Plato is the only one among all the teachers of antiquity who from sheer love for a perfect world ever came to preach a doctrine of intolerance.

This young Athenian, as is well known, was the beloved disciple of Socrates and became his literary executor.

In this capacity he immediately gathered all that Socrates had ever said or thought into a series of dialogues which might be truthfully called the Socratian Gospels.

When this had been done, he began to elaborate certain of the more obscure points in his master's doctrines and explained them in a series of brilliant essays. And finally he conducted a num-

ber of lecture courses which spread the Athenian ideas of justice
and righteousness far beyond the confines of Attica.

In all these activities he showed such whole-hearted and unselfish devotion that we might almost compare him to St. Paul.
But whereas St. Paul had led a most adventurous and dangerous
existence, ever traveling from north to south and from west to
east that he might bring the Good Tidings to all parts of the
Mediterranean world, Plato never budged from his comfortable
garden chair and allowed the world to come to him.

Certain advantages of birth and the possession of independent
wealth allowed him to do this.

In the first place, he was an Athenian citizen and through his
mother could trace his descent to no one less than Solon. Then
as soon as he came of age he inherited a fortune more than sufficient for his simple needs.

And finally, his eloquence was such that people willingly traveled to the Ægean Sea if only they were allowed to follow a few
of the lectures in the Platonic University.

For the rest, Plato was very much like the other young men
of his time. He served in the army, but without any particular interest in military affairs. He went in for outdoor sports, became
a good wrestler, a fairly good runner, but never achieved any
particular fame in the stadium. Again, like most young men
of his time, he spent a great deal of his time in foreign travel
and crossed the Ægean Sea and paid a short visit to northern
Egypt, as his famous grandfather Solon had done before him.
After that, however, he returned home for good and during fifty
consecutive years he quietly taught his doctrines in the shadowy
corners of a pleasure garden which was situated on the banks
of the river Cephissus in the suburbs of Athens and was called
the Academy.

He had begun his career as a mathematician, but gradually
he switched over to politics and in this field he laid the foundations for our modern school of government. He was at heart
a confirmed optimist and believed in a steady process of human
evolution. The life of man, so he taught, rises slowly from a
lower plane to a higher one. From beautiful bodies, the world

proceeds to beautiful institutions and from beautiful institutions
to beautiful ideas.

This sounded well on parchment, but when Plato tried to lay
down certain definite principles upon which his perfect state was
to be founded, his zeal for righteousness and his desire for justice
were so great that they made him deaf and blind to all other

THE ACADEMY

considerations. His Republic, which has ever since been regarded
as the last word in human perfection by the manufacturers of
paper Utopias, was a very strange commonwealth and reflected
and continues to reflect with great nicety the prejudices of those
retired colonels who have always enjoyed the comforts of a private income, who like to move in polite circles and who have a
profound distrust of the lower classes, lest they forget "their
place" and want to have a share of those special privileges which
by right should go to the members of the "upper class."

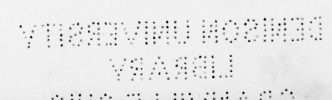

Unfortunately the books of Plato enjoyed great respect among the medieval scholars of western Europe and in their hands the famous Republic became a most formidable weapon in their warfare upon tolerance.

For these learned doctors were apt to forget that Plato had reached his conclusions from very different premises than those which were popular in the twelfth and thirteenth centuries.

For instance, Plato had been anything but a pious man in the Christian sense of the word. The Gods of his ancestors he had always regarded with deep contempt as ill-mannered rustics from distant Macedonia. He had been deeply mortified by their scandalous behavior as related in the chronicles of the Trojan War. But as he grew older and sat and sat and sat in his little olive grove and became more and more exasperated by the foolish quarrels of the little city-states of his native land, and witnessed the utter failure of the old democratic ideal, he grew convinced that some sort of religion was necessary for the average citizen, or his imaginary Republic would at once degenerate into a state of rampant anarchy. He therefore insisted that the legislative body of his model community should establish a definite rule of conduct for all citizens and should force both freemen and slaves to obey these regulations on pain of death or exile or imprisonment. This sounded like an absolute negation of that broad spirit of tolerance and of that liberty of conscience for which Socrates had so valiantly fought only a short time before, and that is exactly what it was meant to be.

The reason for this change in attitude is not hard to find. Whereas Socrates had been a man among men, Plato was afraid of life and escaped from an unpleasant and ugly world into the realm of his own day-dreams. He knew of course that there was not the slightest chance of his ideas ever being realized. The day of the little independent city-states, whether imaginary or real, was over. The era of centralization had begun and soon the entire Greek peninsula was to be incorporated into that vast Macedonian Empire which stretched from the shores of the Maritsa to the banks of the Indus River.

But ere the heavy hand of the conqueror descended upon the

unruly democracies of the old peninsula, the country had produced the greatest of those many benefactors who have put the
rest of the world under eternal obligation to the now defunct race
of the Greeks.

I refer of course to Aristotle, the wonder-child from Stagira,
the man who in his day and age knew everything that was to
be known and added so much to the sum total of human knowledge that his books became an intellectual quarry from which
fifty successive generations of Europeans and Asiatics were able
to steal to their hearts' content without exhausting that rich
vein of pure learning.

ARISTOTLE

At the age of eighteen, Aristotle had left his native village in Macedonia to go to Athens and follow the lectures in Plato's university. After his graduation he lectured in a number of places until the year 336 when he returned to Athens and opened a school of his own in a garden near the temple of Apollo Lyceus, which became known as the Lyceum and soon attracted pupils from all over the world.

Strangely enough, the Athenians were not at all in favor of increasing the number of academies within their walls. The town was at last beginning to lose its old commercial importance and all of her more energetic citizens were moving to Alexandria and to Marseilles and other cities of the south and the west. Those who remained behind were either too poor or too indolent to escape. They were the hide-bound remnant of those old, turbulent masses of free citizens, who had been at once the glory and the ruin of the long-suffering Republic. They had regarded the "goings on" in Plato's orchard with small favor. When, a dozen years after his death, his most notorious pupil came back and openly taught still more outrageous doctrines about the beginning of the world and the limited ability of the Gods, the old fogies shook their solemn heads and mumbled dark threats against the man who was making their city a by-word for free thinking and unbelief.

If they had had their own way, they would have forced him to leave their country. But they wisely kept these opinions to themselves. But this short-sighted, stoutish gentleman, famous for his good taste in books and in clothes, was no negligible quantity in the political life of that day, no obscure little professor who could be driven out of town by a couple of hired toughs. He was no one less than the son of a Macedonian court-physician and he had been brought up with the royal princes. And furthermore, as soon as he had finished his studies, he had been appointed tutor to the crown prince and for eight years he had been the daily companion of young Alexander. Hence he enjoyed the friendship and the protection of the most powerful ruler the world had ever seen and the regent who administered the Greek provinces during the monarch's absence on the Indian front watched carefully lest harm should befall one who had been the boon companion of his imperial master.

No sooner, however, had news of Alexander's death reached Athens than Aristotle's life was in peril. He remembered what had happened to Socrates and felt no desire to suffer a similar fate. Like Plato, he had carefully avoided mixing philosophy with practical politics. But his distaste for the democratic form of government and his lack of belief in the sovereign abilities of the common people were known to all. And when the Athenians, in a sudden outburst of fury, expelled the Macedonian garrison, Aristotle moved across the Euboean Sound and went to live in Calchis, where he died a few months before Athens was reconquered by the Macedonians and was duly punished for her disobedience.

At this far distance it is not easy to discover upon what positive grounds Aristotle was accused of impiety. But as usual in that nation of amateur orators, his case was inextricably mixed up with politics and his unpopularity was due to his disregard of the prejudices of a few local ward-bosses, rather than to the expression of any startlingly new heresies, which might have exposed Athens to the vengeance of Zeus.

Nor does it matter very much.

The days of the small independent republics were numbered.

Soon afterwards, the Romans fell heir to the European heritage of Alexander and Greece became one of their many provinces.

Then there was an end to all further bickering, for the Romans in most matters were even more tolerant than the Greeks of the Golden Age had been and they permitted their subjects to think as they pleased, provided they did not question certain principles of political expediency upon which the peace and prosperity of the Roman state had, since time immemorial, been safely builded.

All the same there existed a subtle difference between the ideals which animated the contemporaries of Cicero and those which had been held sacred by the followers of such a man as Pericles. The old leaders of Greek thought had based their tolerance upon certain definite conclusions which they had reached after centuries of careful experiment and meditation. The Romans felt that they could do without the preliminary study. They were merely indifferent, and were proud of the fact. They were interested in practical things. They were men of action and had a deep-seated contempt for words.

If other people wished to spend their afternoons underneath an old olive tree, discussing the theoretical aspects of government or the influence of the moon upon the tides, they were more than welcome to do so.

If furthermore their knowledge could be turned to some practical use, then it was worthy of further attention. Otherwise, together with singing and dancing and cooking, sculpture and science, this business of philosophizing had better be left to the Greeks and to the other foreigners whom Jupiter in his mercy had created to provide the world with those things which were unworthy of a true Roman's attention.

Meanwhile they themselves would devote their attention to the administration of their ever increasing domains; they would drill the necessary companies of foreign infantry and cavalry to protect their outlying provinces; they would survey the roads that were to connect Spain with Bulgaria; and generally they would devote their energies to the keeping of the peace between half a thousand different tribes and nations.

Let us give honor where honor is due.

The Romans did their job so thoroughly that they erected a structure which under one form or another has survived until our own time, and that in itself is no mean accomplishment. As long as the necessary taxes were paid and a certain outward homage was paid to the few rules of conduct laid down by their Roman masters, the subject-tribes enjoyed a very large degree of liberty. They could believe or disbelieve whatever they pleased. They could worship one God or a dozen Gods or whole temples full of Gods. It made no difference. But whatever religion they chose to profess, these strangely assorted members of a world-encircling empire were forever reminded that the "pax Romana" depended for its success upon a liberal applica-

THE RIVAL RELIGIONS

tion of the principle of "live and let live." They must under
no condition interfere either with their own neighbors or with
the strangers within their gates. And if perchance they thought
that their Gods had been insulted, they must not rush to the
magistrate for relief. "For," as the Emperor Tiberius remarked
upon one memorable occasion, "if the Gods think that they have
just claims for grievance, they can surely take care of themselves."

And with such scant words of consolation, all similar cases
were instantly dismissed and people were requested to keep their
private opinions out of the courts.

If a number of Cappadocian traders decided to settle down
among the Colossians, they had a right to bring their own Gods
with them and erect a temple of their own in the town of Colossæ.
But if the Colossians should for similar reasons move into the
land of the Cappadocians, they must be granted the same privileges and must be given an equal freedom of worship.

It has often been argued that the Romans could permit themselves the luxury of such a superior and tolerant attitude because they felt an equal contempt for both the Colossians and the Cappadocians and all the other savage tribes who dwelled outside of Latium. That may have been true. I don't know. But the fact remains that for half a thousand years, a form of almost complete religious tolerance was strictly maintained within the greater part of civilized and semi-civilized Europe, Asia and Africa and that the Romans developed a technique of statecraft which produced a maximum of practical results together with a minimum of friction.

To many people it seemed that the millennium had been achieved and that this condition of mutual forbearance would last forever.

But nothing lasts forever. Least of all, an empire built upon force.

Rome had conquered the world, but in the effort she had destroyed herself.

The bones of her young soldiers lay bleaching on a thousand battlefields.

For almost five centuries the brains of her most intelligent citizens had wasted themselves upon the gigantic task of administering a colonial empire that stretched from the Irish Sea to the Caspian.

At last the reaction set in.

Both the body and the mind of Rome had been exhausted by the impossible task of a single city ruling an entire world.

And then a terrible thing happened. A whole people grew tired of life and lost the zest for living.

They had come to own all the country-houses, all the town-houses, all the yachts and all the stage-coaches they could ever hope to use.

They found themselves possessed of all the slaves in the world.

They had eaten everything, they had seen everything, they had heard everything.

They had tried the taste of every drink, they had been everywhere, they had made love to all the women from Barcelona to

Thebes. All the books that had ever been written were in their libraries. The best pictures that had ever been painted hung on their walls. The cleverest musicians of the entire world had entertained them at their meals. And, as children, they had been instructed by the best professors and pedagogues who had taught them everything there was to be taught. As a result, all food and drink had lost its taste, all books had grown dull, all women had become uninteresting, and existence itself had developed into a burden which a good many people were willing to drop at the first respectable opportunity.

There remained only one consolation, the contemplation of the Unknown and the Invisible.

The old Gods, however, had died years before. No intelligent Roman any longer took stock in the silly nursery rhymes about Jupiter and Minerva.

There were the philosophic systems of the Epicureans and the Stoics and the Cynics, all of whom preached charity and self-denial and the virtues of an unselfish and useful life.

But they were so empty. They sounded well enough in the books of Zeno and Epicurus and Epictetus and Plutarch, which were to be found in every cornerstore library.

But in the long run, this diet of pure reason was found to lack the necessary nourishing qualities. The Romans began to clamor for a certain amount of "emotion" with their spiritual meals.

Hence the purely philosophical "religions" (for such they really were, if we associate the idea of religion with a desire to lead useful and noble lives) could only appeal to a very small number of people, and almost all of those belonged to the upper classes who had enjoyed the advantages of private instruction at the hands of competent Greek teachers.

To the mass of the people, these finely-spun philosophies meant less than nothing at all. They too had reached a point of development at which a good deal of the ancient mythology seemed the childish invention of rude and credulous ancestors. But they could not possibly go as far as their so-called intellectual superiors and deny the existence of any and all personal Gods.

Wherefore they did what all half-educated people do under such circumstances. They paid a formal and outward tribute of respect to the official Gods of the Republic and then betook themselves for real comfort and happiness to one of the many mystery religions which during the last two centuries had found a most cordial welcome in the ancient city on the banks of the Tiber.

The word "mystery" which I have used before was of Greek origin. It originally meant a gathering of "initiated people"— of men and women whose "mouth had been shut" against the betrayal of those most holy secrets which only the true members of the mystery were supposed to know and which bound them together like the hocus pocus of a college fraternity or the cabalistic incantations of the Independent Order of Sea-Mice.

During the first century of our era, however, a mystery was nothing more nor less than a special form of worship, a denomination, a church. If a Greek or a Roman (if you will pardon a little juggling with time) had left the Presbyterian church for the Christian Science church, he would have told his neighbors that he had gone to "another mystery." For the word "church," the "kirk," the "house of the Lord," is of comparatively recent origin and was not known in those days.

If you happen to be especially interested in the subject and wish to understand what was happening in Rome, buy a New York paper next Saturday. Almost any paper will do. Therein you will find four or five columns of announcements about new creeds, about new mysteries, imported from India and Persia and Sweden and China and a dozen other countries and all of them offering special promises of health and riches and salvation everlasting.

Rome, which so closely resembled our own metropolis, was just as full of imported and domestic religions. The international nature of the city had made this unavoidable. From the vine-covered mountain slopes of northern Asia Minor had come the cult of Cybele, whom the Phrygians revered as the mother of the Gods and whose worship was connected with such unseemly outbreaks of emotional hilarity that the Roman police had repeatedly been forced to close the Cybelian temples and had at last passed very drastic laws against the further propaganda of a faith which encouraged public drunkenness and many other things that were even worse.

Egypt, the old land of paradox and secrecy, had contributed half a dozen strange divinities and the names of Osiris, Serapis and Isis had become as familiar to Roman ears as those of Apollo, Demeter and Hermes.

As for the Greeks, who centuries before had given unto the world a primary system of abstract truth and a practical code of conduct, based upon virtue, they now supplied the people of foreign lands who insisted upon images and incense with the far-famed "mysteries" of Attis and Dionysus and Orpheus and Adonis, none of them entirely above suspicion as far as public morals were concerned, but nevertheless enjoying immense popularity.

The Phœnician traders, who for a thousand years had frequented the shores of Italy, had made the Romans familiar with their great God Baal (the arch-enemy of Jehovah) and with Astarte his wife, that strange creature to whom Solomon in his old age and to the great horror of all his faithful subjects had built a "high place" in the very heart of Jerusalem; the terrible Goddess who had been recognized as the official protector of the city of Carthage during her long struggle for the supremacy of the Mediterranean and who finally after the destruction of all her temples in Asia and Africa was to return to Europe in the shape of a most respectable and demure Christian saint.

But the most important of all, because highly popular among the soldiers of the army, was a deity whose broken images can still be found underneath every rubbish pile that marks the Roman frontier from the mouth of the Rhine to the source of the Tigris.

This was the great God Mithras.

Mithras, as far as we know, was the old Asiatic God of Light and Air and Truth, and he had been worshiped in the plains of the Caspian lowlands when our first ancestors took possession of those wonderful grazing fields and made ready to settle those valleys and hills which afterwards became known as Europe. To them he had been the giver of all good things and they believed that the rulers of this earth exercised their power only by the grace of his mighty will. Hence, as a token of his divine favor, he sometimes bestowed upon those called to high offices a bit of that celestial fire by which he himself was forever surrounded, and although he is gone and his name has been forgotten, the kindly saints of the Middle Ages, with their halo of light, remind us of an ancient tradition which was started thousands of years before the Church was ever dreamed of.

But although he was held in great reverence for an incredibly long time, it has been very difficult to reconstruct his life with any degree of accuracy. There was a good reason for this. The early Christian missionaries abhorred the Mithras myth with a hatred infinitely more bitter than that reserved for the common, everyday mysteries. In their heart of hearts they knew that the Indian God was their most serious rival. Hence they tried as hard as possible to remove everything that might possibly remind people of his existence. In this task they succeeded so well that all Mithras temples have disappeared and that not a scrap of written evidence remains about a religion which for more than half a thousand years was as popular in Rome as Methodism or Presbyterianism is in the United States of to-day.

However, with the help of a few Asiatic sources and by a careful perusal of certain ruins which could not be entirely destroyed in the days before the invention of dynamite, we have been able to overcome this initial handicap and now possess a fairly accurate idea about this interesting God and the things for which he stood.

Ages and ages ago, so the story ran, Mithras was mysteriously born of a rock. As soon as he lay in his cradle, several nearby shepherds came to worship him and make him happy with their gifts.

As a boy, Mithras had met with all sorts of strange adventures. Many of these remind us closely of the deeds which had made Hercules such a popular hero with the children of the Greeks. But whereas Hercules was often very cruel, Mithras was forever doing good. Once he had engaged in a wrestling match with the sun and had beaten him. But he was so generous in his victory, that the sun and he had become like brothers, and were often mistaken for each other.

When the God of all evil had sent a drought which threatened to kill the race of man, Mithras had struck a rock with his arrow, and behold! plentiful water had gushed forth upon the parched fields. When Ahriman (for that was the name of the arch-enemy) had thereupon tried to achieve his wicked purpose by a terrible flood, Mithras had heard of it, had warned one man, had told him to build a big boat and load it with his relatives and his flocks and in this way had saved the human race from destruction. Until finally, having done all he could to save the world from the consequences of its own follies, he had been taken to Heaven to rule the just and righteous for all time.

Those who wished to join the Mithras cult were obliged to go through an elaborate form of initiation and were forced to eat a ceremonious meal of bread and wine in memory of the famous supper eaten by Mithras and his friend the Sun. Furthermore, they were obliged to accept baptism in a font of water and do many other things which have no special interest for us, as that form of religion was completely exterminated more than fifteen hundred years ago.

Once inside the fold, the faithful were all treated upon a footing of absolute equality. Together they prayed before the same candle-lit altars. Together they chanted the same holy hymns and together they took part in the festivities which were held each year on the twenty-fifth of December to celebrate the birth of Mithras. Furthermore they obtained from all work on the first day of the week, which even to-day is called Sun-day in honor of the great God. And finally when they died, they were laid away in patient rows to await the day of resurrection when the good should enter into their just reward and the wicked should be cast into the fire everlasting.

The success of these different mysteries, the widespread influence of Mithraism among the Roman soldiers, points to a condition far removed from religious indifference. Indeed the early centuries of the empire were a period of restless search after something that should satisfy the emotional needs of the masses.

But early in the year 47 of our own era something happened. A small vessel left Phœnicia for the city of Perga, the starting point for the overland route to Europe. Among the passengers were two men not overburdened with luggage.

Their names were Paul and Barnabas.

They were Jews, but one of them carried a Roman passport and was well versed in the wisdom of the Gentile world.

It was the beginning of a memorable voyage.

Christianity had set out to conquer the world.

Chapter III

THE BEGINNING OF RESTRAINT

THE rapid conquest of the western world by the Church is sometimes used as proof definite that the Christian ideas must have been of divine origin. It is not my business to debate this point, but I would suggest that the villainous conditions under which the majority of the Romans were forced to live had as much to do with the success of the earliest missionaries as the sound common sense of their message.

Thus far I have shown you one side of the Roman picture— the world of the soldiers and statesmen and rich manufacturers and scientists, fortunate folks who lived in delightful and enlightened ease on the slopes of the Lateran Hill or among the valleys and hills of the Campania or somewhere along the bay of Naples.

But they were only part of the story.

Amidst the teeming slums of the suburbs there was little enough evidence of that plentiful prosperity which made the poets rave about the Millennium and inspired orators to compare Octavian to Jupiter.

There, in the endless and dreary rows of overcrowded and reeking tenement houses lived those vast multitudes to whom life was merely an uninterrupted sensation of hunger, sweat and pain. To those men and women, the wonderful tale of a simple carpenter in a little village beyond the sea, who had gained his daily bread by the labor of his own hands, who had loved the poor and downtrodden and who therefore had been killed by his cruel and rapacious enemies, meant something very real and tangible. Yes, they had all of them heard of Mithras and Isis and Astarte. But these Gods were dead, and they had died hundreds and thousands of years ago and what people knew

66

about them they only knew by hearsay from other people who had also died hundreds and thousands of years ago.

Joshua of Nazareth, on the other hand, the Christ, the anointed, as the Greek missionaries called him, had been on this earth only a short time ago. Many a man then alive might have known him, might have listened to him, if by chance he had visited southern Syria during the reign of the Emperor Tiberius.

And there were others, the baker on the corner, the fruit peddler from the next street, who in a little dark garden on the Appian Way had spoken with a certain Peter, a fisherman from the village of Capernaum, who had actually been near the mountain of Golgotha on that terrible afternoon when the Prophet had been nailed to the cross by the soldiers of the Roman governor.

We should remember this when we try to understand the sudden popular appeal of this new faith.

It was that personal touch, that direct and personal feeling of intimacy and near-by-ness which gave Christianity such a tremendous advantage over all other creeds. That and the love which Jesus had so incessantly expressed for the submerged and disinherited among all nations and which radiated from everything he had said. Whether he had put it into the exact terms used by his followers was of very slight importance. The slaves had ears to hear and they understood. And trembling before the high promise of a glorious future, they for the first time in their lives beheld the rays of a new hope.

At last the words had been spoken that were to set them free.

No longer were they poor and despised, an evil thing in the sight of the great of this world.

On the contrary, they were the predilected children of a loving Father.

They were to inherit the earth and the fullness thereof.

They were to partake of joys withheld from many of those proud masters who even then dwelled behind the high walls of their Samnian villas.

For that constituted the strength of the new faith. Christianity was the first concrete religious system which gave the average man a chance.

Of course I am now talking of Christianity as an experience of the soul—as a mode of living and thinking—and I have tried to explain how, in a world full of the dry-rot of slavery, the good tidings must spread with the speed and fury of an emotional prairie fire. But history, except upon rare occasions, does not concern itself with the spiritual adventures of private citizens, be they free or in bondage. When these humble creatures have been neatly organized into nations, guilds, churches, armies, brotherhoods and federations; when they have begun to obey a single directing head; when they have accumulated sufficient wealth to pay taxes and can be forced into armies for the purpose of national conquest, then at last they begin to attract the attention of our chroniclers and are given serious attention. Hence we know a great deal about the early Church, but exceedingly little about the people who were the true founders of that institution. That is rather a pity, for the early development of Christianity is one of the most interesting episodes in all history.

The Church which finally was built upon the ruins of the ancient empire was really a combination of two conflicting interests. On the one side it stood forth as the champion of those all-embracing ideals of love and charity which the Master himself had taught. But on the other side it found itself ineradicably bound up with that arid spirit of provincialism which since the beginning of time had set the compatriots of Jesus apart from the rest of the world.

In plain language, it combined Roman efficiency with Judaean intolerance and as a result it established a reign of terror over the minds of men which was as efficient as it was illogical.

To understand how this could have happened, we must go back once more to the days of Paul and to the first fifty years after the death of Christ, and we must firmly grasp the fact that Christianity had begun as a reform movement within the bosom of the Jewish church and had been a purely nationalistic movement which in the beginning had threatened the rulers of the Jewish state and no one else.

The Pharisees who had happened to be in power when Jesus lived had understood this only too clearly. Quite naturally they had feared the ultimate consequences of an agitation which boldly threatened to question a spiritual monopoly which was based upon nothing more substantial than brute force. To save themselves from being wiped out they had been forced to act in a spirit of panic and had sent their enemy to the gallows before the Roman authorities had had time to intervene and deprive them of their victim.

What Jesus would have done had he lived it is impossible to say. He was killed long before he was able to organize his disciples into a special sect nor did he leave a single word of writing from which his followers could conclude what he wanted them to do.

In the end, however, this had proved to be a blessing in disguise.

The absence of a written set of rules, of a definite collection of ordinances and regulations, had left the disciples free to follow the spirit of their master's words rather than the letter of his law. Had they been bound by a book, they would very likely have devoted all their energies to a theological discussion upon the ever enticing subject of commas and semicolons.

In that case, of course, no one outside of a few professional scholars could have possibly shown the slightest interest in the new faith and Christianity would have gone the way of so many other sects which begin with elaborate written programs and end when the police are called upon to throw the haggling theologians into the street.

At the distance of almost twenty centuries, when we realize what tremendous damage Christianity did to the Roman Empire, it is a matter of surprise that the authorities took practically no steps to quell a movement which was fully as dangerous to the safety of the state as an invasion by Huns or Goths. They knew of course that the fate of this eastern prophet had caused great excitement among their house slaves, that the women were forever telling each other about the imminent reappearance of the King of Heaven, and that quite a number of old men had solemnly predicted the impending destruction of this world by a ball of fire.

But it was not the first time that the poorer classes had gone into hysterics about some new religious hero. Most likely it would not be the last time, either. Meanwhile the police would see to it that these poor, frenzied fanatics did not disturb the peace of the realm.

And that was that.

The police did watch out, but found little occasion to act. The followers of the new mystery went about their business in a most exemplary fashion. They did not try to overthrow the government. At first, several slaves had expected that the common fatherhood of God and the common brotherhood of man would imply a cessation of the old relation between master and servant. The apostle Paul, however, had hastened to explain that the Kingdom of which he spoke was an invisible and intangible kingdom of the soul and that people on this earth had better take things as they found them, in expectation of the final reward which awaited them in Heaven.

Similarly, a good many wives, chafing at the bondage of matrimony as established by the harsh laws of Rome, had rushed to the conclusion that Christianity was synonymous with emancipation and full equality of rights between men and women. But again Paul had stepped forward and in a number of tactful letters had implored his beloved sisters to refrain from all those extremes which would make their church suspect in the eyes of the more conservative pagans and had persuaded them to continue in that state of semi-slavery which had been woman's share ever since Adam and Eve had been driven out of Paradise. All this showed a most commendable respect for the law and as far as the authorities were concerned, the Christian missionaries could therefore come and go at will and preach as best suited their own individual tastes and preferences.

But as has happened so often in history, the masses had shown themselves less tolerant than their rulers. Just because people are poor it does not necessarily follow that they are high-minded citizens who could be prosperous and happy if their conscience would only permit them to make those compromises which are held to be necessary for the accumulation of wealth.

And the Roman proletariat, since centuries debauched by free meals and free prizefights, was no exception to this rule. At first it derived a great deal of rough pleasure from those sober-faced groups of men and women who with rapt attention listened to the weird stories about a God who had ignominiously died on a cross, like any other common criminal, and who made it their business to utter loud prayers for the hoodlums who pelted their gatherings with stones and dirt.

The Roman priests, however, were not able to take such a detached view of this new development.

The religion of the empire was a state religion. It consisted of certain solemn sacrifices made upon certain specified occasions and paid for in cash. This money went toward the support of the church officers. When thousands of people began to desert the old shrines and went to another church which did not charge them anything at all, the priests were faced by a very serious reduction in their salary. This of course did not please them at all, and soon they were loud in their abuse of the godless heretics who turned their backs upon the Gods of their fathers and burned incense to the memory of a foreign prophet.

But there was another class of people in the city who had even better reason to hate the Christians. Those were the fakirs, who as Indian Yogis and Pooughies and hierophants of the great and only mysteries of Isis and Ishtar and Baal and Cybele and Attis had for years made a fat and easy living at the expense of the credulous Roman middle classes. If the Christians had set up a rival establishment and had charged a handsome price for their own particular revelations, the guild of spook-doctors and palmists and necromancers would have had no reason for complaint. Business was business and the soothsaying fraternity did not mind if a bit of their trade went elsewhere. But these Christians—a plague upon their silly notions!—refused to take any reward. Yea, they even gave away what they had, fed the hungry and shared their own roof with the homeless. And all that for nothing! Surely that was going too far and they never could have done this unless they were possessed of certain hidden sources of revenue, the origin of which no one thus far had been able to discover.

Rome by this time was no longer a city of free-born burghers. It was the temporary dwelling place of hundreds of thousands of disinherited peasants from all parts of the empire. Such a mob, obeying the mysterious laws that rule the behavior of crowds, is always ready to hate those who behave differently from themselves and to suspect those who for no apparent reason prefer to live a life of decency and restraint. The hail-fellow-well-met who will take a drink and (occasionally) will pay for one is a fine neighbor and a good fellow. But the man who holds himself aloof and refuses to go to the wild-animal show in the Coliseum, who does not cheer when batches of prisoners of war are being dragged through the streets of the Capitoline Hill, is a spoil-sport and an enemy of the community at large.

When in the year 64 a great conflagration destroyed that part of Rome inhabited by the poorer classes, the scene was set for the first organized attacks upon the Christians.

At first it was rumored that the Emperor Nero, in a fit of drunken conceit, had ordered his capital to be set on fire that he might get rid of the slums and rebuild the city according to his own plans. The crowd, however, knew better. It was the fault of those Jews and Christians who were forever telling each other about the happy day when large balls of fire would descend from Heaven and the homes of the wicked would go up in flames.

Once this story had been successfully started, others followed in rapid succession. One old woman had heard the Christians talk with the dead. Another knew that they stole little children and cut their throats and smeared their blood upon the altar of their outlandish God. Of course, no one had ever been able to detect them at any of these scandalous practices, but that was only because they were so terribly clever and had bribed the police. But now at last they had been caught red-handed and they would be made to suffer for their vile deeds.

Of the number of faithful who were lynched upon this occasion, we know nothing. Paul and Peter, so it seems, were among the victims for thereafter their names are never heard again.

That this terrible outbreak of popular folly accomplished nothing, it is needless to state. The noble dignity with which the martyrs accepted their fate was the best possible propaganda for the new ideas and for every Christian who perished, there were a dozen pagans, ready and eager to take his place. As soon as Nero had committed the only decent act of his short and useless life (he killed himself in the year 68), the Christians returned to their old haunts and everything was as it had been before.

By this time the Roman authorities were making a great discovery. They began to suspect that a Christian was not exactly the same thing as a Jew.

We can hardly blame them for having committed this error. The historical researches of the last hundred years have made it increasingly clear that the Synagogue was the clearing-house through which the new faith was passed on to the rest of the world.

Remember that Jesus himself was a Jew and that he had always been most careful in observing the ancient laws of his father and that he had addressed himself almost exclusively to Jewish audiences. Once, and then only for a short time, had he left his native country, but the task which he had set himself he had accomplished with and by and for his fellow Jews. Nor was there anything in what he had ever said which could have given the average Roman the impression that there was a deliberate difference between Christianity and Judaism.

What Jesus had actually tried to do was this. He had clearly seen the terrible abuses which had entered the church of his fathers. He had loudly and sometimes successfully protested against them. But he had fought his battles for reform from within. Never apparently had it dawned upon him that he might be the founder of a new religion. If some one had mentioned the possibility of such a thing to him, he would have rejected the idea as preposterous. But like many a reformer before his day and after, he had gradually been forced into a position where compromise was no longer possible. His un-

timely death alone had saved him from a fate like that of Luther
and so many other advocates of reform, who were deeply per-
plexed when they suddenly found themselves at the head of a
brand new party "outside" the organization to which they belonged, whereas they were merely trying to do some good from
the "inside."

For many years after the death of Jesus, Christianity (to use
the name long before it had been coined) was the religion of a
small Jewish sect which had a few adherents in Jerusalem and
in the villages of Judæa and Galilee and which had never been
heard of outside of the province of Syria.

It was Gaius Julius Paulus, a full-fledged Roman citizen of
Jewish descent, who had first recognized the possibilities of the
new doctrine as a religion for all the world. The story of his
suffering tells us how bitterly the Jewish Christians had been
opposed to the idea of a universal religion instead of a purely
national denomination, membership to which should only be
open to people of their own race. They had hated the man
who dared preach salvation to Jews and Gentiles alike so bitterly that on his last visit to Jerusalem Paul would undoubtedly
have suffered the fate of Jesus if his Roman passport had not
saved him from the fury of his enraged compatriots.

But it had been necessary for half a battalion of Roman soldiers to protect him and conduct him safely to the coastal town
from where he could be shipped to Rome for that famous trial
which never took place.

A few years after his death, that which he had so often feared
during his lifetime and which he had repeatedly foretold actually
occurred.

Jerusalem was destroyed by the Romans. On the place of
the temple of Jehovah a new temple was erected in honor of
Jupiter. The name of the city was changed to Ælia Capitolina
and Judæa itself had become part of the Roman province of
Syria Palæstina. As for the inhabitants, they were either killed
or driven into exile and no one was allowed to live within several
miles of the ruins on pain of death.

It was the final destruction of their holy city which had been so disastrous to the Jewish Christians. During several centuries afterwards, in the little villages of the Judæan hinterland colonies might have been found of strange people who called themselves "poor men" and who waited with great patience and amidst everlasting prayers for the end of the world which was at hand. They were the remnants of the old Jewish-Christian community in Jerusalem. From time to time we hear them mentioned in books written during the fifth and sixth centuries. Far away from civilization, they developed certain strange doctrines of their own in which hatred for the apostle Paul took a prominent place. After the seventh century, however, we no longer find any trace of these so-called Nazarenes and Ebionites. The victorious Mahometans had killed them all. And, anyway, if they had managed to exist a few hundred years longer, they would not have been able to avert the inevitable.

Rome, by bringing east and west and north and south into one large political union, had made the world ready for the idea of a universal religion. Christianity, because it was both simple and practical and full of a direct appeal, was predestined to succeed where Judaism and Mithraism and all of the other competing creeds were predestined to fail. But, unfortunately, the new faith never quite rid itself of certain rather unpleasant characteristics which only too clearly betrayed its origin.

The little ship which had brought Paul and Barnabas from Asia to Europe had carried a message of hope and mercy.

But a third passenger had smuggled himself on board.

He wore a mask of holiness and virtue.

But the face beneath bore the stamp of cruelty and hatred.

And his name was Religious Intolerance.

Chapter IV

THE TWILIGHT OF THE GODS

THE early Church was a very simple organization. As soon as it became apparent that the end of the world was not at hand, that the death of Jesus was not to be followed immediately by the last judgment and that the Christians might expect to dwell in this vale of tears for a good long time, the need was felt for a more or less definite form of government.

Originally the Christians (since all of them were Jews) had come together in the synagogue. When the rift had occurred between the Jews and the Gentiles, the latter had betaken themselves to a room in some one's house and if none could be found big enough to hold all the faithful (and the curious) they had met out in the open or in a deserted stone quarry.

At first these gatherings had taken place on the Sabbath, but when bad feeling between the Jewish Christians and the Gentile Christians increased, the latter began to drop the habit of keeping the Sabbath-day and preferred to meet on Sunday, the day on which the resurrection had taken place.

These solemn celebrations, however, had borne witness to the popular as well as to the emotional character of the entire movement. There were no set speeches or sermons. There were no preachers. Both men and women, whenever they felt themselves inspired by the Holy Fire, had risen up in meeting to give evidence of the faith that was in them. Sometimes, if we are to trust the letters of Paul, these devout brethren, "speaking with tongues," had filled the heart of the great apostle with apprehension for the future. For most of them were simple folk without much education. No one doubted the sincerity of their impromptu exhortations but very often they got so excited that they raved like maniacs and while a church may survive persecution, it is helpless against ridicule. Hence the efforts of Paul and Peter and their successors to bring some semblance of order into this chaos of spiritual divulgation and divine enthusiasm.

At first these efforts met with little success. A regular program seemed in direct contradiction to the democratic nature of the Christian faith. In the end, however, practical considerations supervened and the meetings became· subject to a definite ritual.

They began with the reading of one of the Psalms (to placate the Jewish Christians who might be present). Then the congregation united in a song of praise of more recent composition for the benefit of the Roman and the Greek worshipers.

The only prescribed form of oration was the famous prayer in which Jesus had summed up his entire philosophy of life. The preaching, however, for several centuries remained entirely spontaneous and the sermons were delivered only by those who felt that they had something to say.

But when the number of those gatherings increased, when the police, forever on the guard against secret societies, began to make inquiries, it was necessary that certain men be elected to represent the Christians in their dealings with the rest of the world. Already Paul had spoken highly of the gift of leadership. He had compared the little communities which he visited in Asia and Greece to so many tiny vessels which were tossed upon a turbulent sea and were very much in need of a clever pilot if they were to survive the fury of the angry ocean.

And so the faithful came together once more and elected deacons and deaconesses, pious men and women who were the "servants" of the community, who took care of the sick and the poor (an object of great concern to the early Christians) and who looked after the property of the community and took care of all the small daily chores.

Still later when the church continued to grow in membership and the business of administration had become too intricate for mere amateurs, it was entrusted to a small group of "elders." These were known by their Greek name of Presbyters and hence our word "priest."

After a number of years, when every village or city possessed a Christian church of its own, the need was felt for a common policy. Then an "overseer" (an Episkopos or Bishop) was elected to superintend an entire district and direct its dealings with the Roman government.

Soon there were bishops in all the principal towns of the empire, and those in Antioch and Constantinople and Jerusalem and Carthage and Rome and Alexandria and Athens were reputed to be very powerful gentlemen who were almost as important as the civil and military governors of their provinces.

In the beginning of course the bishop who presided over that part of the world where Jesus had lived and suffered and died enjoyed the greatest respect. But after Jerusalem had been destroyed and the generation which had expected the end of the world and the triumph of Zion had disappeared from the face of the earth, the poor old bishop in his ruined palace saw himself deprived of his former prestige.

And quite naturally his place as leader of the faithful was taken by the "overseer" who lived in the capital of the civilized world and who guarded the sites where Peter and Paul, the great apostles of the west, had suffered their martyrdom—the Bishop of Rome.

This bishop, like all others, was known as Father or Papa, the common expression of love and respect bestowed upon members of the clergy. In the course of centuries the title of Papa, however, became almost exclusively associated in people's minds with the particular "Father" who was the head of the metropolitan diocese. When they spoke of the Papa or Pope they meant just one Father, the Bishop of Rome, and not by any chance the Bishop of Constantinople or the Bishop of Carthage. This was an entirely normal development. When we read in our newspaper about "the President" it is not necessary to add "of the United States." We know that the head of our government is meant and not the President of the Pennsylvania Railroad or the President of Harvard University or the President of the League of Nations.

The first time the name occurred officially in a document was in the year 258. At that time Rome was still the capital of a

highly successful empire and the power of the bishops was entirely
overshadowed by that of the emperors. But during the next
three hundred years, under the constant menace of both foreign
and domestic invasions, the successors of Cæsar began to look
for a new home that would offer them greater safety. This they
found in a city in a different part of their domains. It was
called Byzantium, after a mythical hero by the name of Byzas
who was said to have landed there shortly after the Trojan war.
Situated on the straits which separated Europe from Asia and
dominating the trade route between the Black Sea and the Mediterranean, it controlled several important monopolies and was
of such great commercial importance that already Sparta and
Athens had fought for the possession of this rich fortress.

Byzantium, however, had held its own until the days of Alexander and after having been for a short while part of Macedonia
it had finally been incorporated into the Roman Empire.

And now, after ten centuries of increasing prosperity, its
Golden Horn filled with the ships from a hundred nations, it was
chosen to become the center of the empire.

The people of Rome, left to the mercy of Visigoths and Vandals
and Heaven knows what other sort of barbarians, felt that the
end of the world had come when the imperial palaces stood empty
for years at a time; when one department of state after another
was removed to the shores of the Bosporus and when the inhabitants of the capital were asked to obey laws made a thousand
miles away.

But in the realm of history, it is an ill wind that does not
blow some one good. With the emperors gone, the bishops remained behind as the most important dignitaries of the town, the
only visible and tangible successors to the glory of the imperial
throne.

And what excellent use they made of their new independence!
They were shrewd politicians, for the prestige and the influence
of their office had attracted the best brains of all Italy. They
felt themselves to be the representatives of certain eternal ideas.
Hence they were never in a hurry, but proceeded with the
deliberate slowness of a glacier and dared to take chances where

others, acting under the pressure of immediate necessity, made rapid decisions, blundered and failed.

But most important of all, they were men of a single purpose, who moved consistently and persistently towards one goal. In all they did and said and thought they were guided by the desire to increase the glory of God and the strength and power of the organization which represented the divine will on earth.

How well they wrought, the history of the next ten centuries was to show.

While everything else perished in the deluge of savage tribes which hurled itself across the European continent, while the walls of the empire, one after the other, came crumbling down, while a thousand institutions as old as the plains of Babylon were swept away like so much useless rubbish, the Church stood strong and erect, the rock of ages, but more particularly the rock of the Middle Ages.

The victory, however, which was finally won, was bought at a terrible cost.

For Christianity which had begun in a stable was allowed to end in a palace. It had been started as a protest against a form of government in which the priest as the self-appointed intermediary between the deity and mankind had insisted upon the unquestioning obedience of all ordinary human beings. This revolutionary body grew and in less than a hundred years it developed into a new supertheocracy, compared to which the old Jewish state had been a mild and liberal commonwealth of happy and carefree citizens.

And yet all this was perfectly logical and quite unavoidable, as I shall now try to show you.

Most of the people who visit Rome make a pilgrimage to the Coliseum and within those wind-swept walls they are shown the hallowed ground where thousands of Christian martyrs fell as victims of Roman intolerance.

But while it is true that upon several occasions there were persecutions of the adherents of the new faith, these had very little to do with religious intolerance.

They were purely political.

The Christian, as a member of a religious sect, enjoyed the greatest possible freedom.

But the Christian who openly proclaimed himself a conscientious objector, who bragged of his pacifism even when the country was threatened with foreign invasion and openly defied the laws of the land upon every suitable and unsuitable occasion, such a Christian was considered an enemy of the state and was treated as such.

That he acted according to his most sacred convictions did not make the slightest impression upon the mind of the average police judge. And when he tried to explain the exact nature of his scruples, that dignitary looked puzzled and was entirely unable to follow him.

A Roman police judge after all was only human. When he suddenly found himself called upon to try people who made an issue of what seemed to him a very trivial matter, he simply did not know what to do. Long experience had taught him to keep clear of all theological controversies. Besides, he remembered many imperial edicts, admonishing public servants to use "tact" in their dealings with the new sect. Hence he used tact and argued. But as the whole dispute boiled down to a question of principles, very little was ever accomplished by an appeal to logic.

In the end, the magistrate was placed before the choice of surrendering the dignity of the law or insisting upon a complete and unqualified vindication of the supreme power of the state. But prison and torture meant nothing to people who firmly believed that life did not begin until after death and who shouted with joy at the idea of being allowed to leave this wicked world for the joys of Heaven.

The guerilla warfare, therefore, which finally broke out between the authorities and their Christian subjects was long and painful. We possess very few authentic figures upon the total number of victims. According to Origen, the famous church father of the third century, several of whose own relatives had been killed in Alexandria during one of the persecutions, "the number of true Christians who died for their convictions could easily be enumerated."

On the other hand, when we peruse the lives of the early saints we find ourselves faced by such incessant tales of bloodshed that we begin to wonder how a religion exposed to these constant and murderous persecutions could ever have survived at all.

No matter what figures I shall give, some one is sure to call me a prejudiced liar. I will therefore keep my opinion to myself and let my readers draw their own conclusions. By studying the lives of the Emperors Decius (249-251) and Valerian (253-260) they will be able to form a fairly accurate opinion as to the true character of Roman intolerance during the worst era of persecution.

Furthermore, if they will remember that as wise and liberal minded a ruler as Marcus Aurelius confessed himself unable to handle the problem of his Christian subjects successfully, they will derive some idea about the difficulties which beset obscure little officials in remote corners of the empire, who tried to do their duty and must either be unfaithful to their oath of office or execute those of their relatives and neighbors who could not or would not obey those few and very simple ordinances upon which the imperial government insisted as a matter of self-preservation.

Meanwhile the Christians, not hindered by false sentimentality towards their pagan fellow citizens, were steadily extending the sphere of their influence.

Late in the fourth century, the Emperor Gratian at the request of the Christian members of the Roman senate who complained that it hurt their feelings to gather in the shadow of a heathenish idol, ordered the removal of the statue of Victory which for more than four hundred years had stood in the hall built by Julius Cæsar. Several senators protested. This did very little good and only caused a number of them to be sent into exile.

It was then that Quintus Aurelius Symmachus, a devoted

patriot of great personal distinction, wrote his famous letter in which he tried to suggest a compromise.

"Why," so he asked, "should we pagans and our Christian neighbors not live in peace and harmony? We look up to the same stars, we are fellow passengers on the same planet and dwell beneath the same sky. What matters it along which road each individual endeavors to find ultimate truth? The riddle of existence is too great that there should be only one path leading to an answer."

He was not the only man who felt that way and saw the danger which threatened the old Roman tradition of a broad-minded religious policy. Simultaneously with the removal of the statue of Victory in Rome a violent quarrel had broken out between two contending factions of the Christians who had found a refuge in Byzantium. This dispute gave rise to one of the most intelligent discussions of tolerance to which the world had ever listened. Themistius the philosopher, who was the author, had remained faithful to the Gods of his fathers. But when the Emperor Valens took sides in the fight between his orthodox and his non-orthodox Christian subjects, Themistius felt obliged to remind him of his true duty.

"There is," so he said, "a domain over which no ruler can hope to exercise any authority. That is the domain of the virtues and especially that of the religious beliefs of individuals. Compulsion within that field causes hypocrisy and conversions that are based upon fraud. Hence it is much better for a ruler to tolerate all beliefs, since it is only by toleration that civic strife can be averted. Moreover, tolerance is a divine law. God himself has most clearly demonstrated his desire for a number of different religions. And God alone can judge the methods by which humanity aspires to come to an understanding of the Divine Mystery. God delights in the variety of homage which is rendered to him. He likes the Christians to use certain rites, the Greeks others, the Egyptians again others."

Fine words, indeed, but spoken in vain.

The ancient world together with its ideas and ideals was dead and all efforts to set back the clock of history were doomed beforehand. Life means progress, and progress means suffering. The old order of society was rapidly disintegrating. The army was a mutinous mob of foreign mercenaries. The frontier was in open revolt. England and the other outlying districts had long since been surrendered to the barbarians.

When the final catastrophe took place, those brilliant young men who in centuries past had entered the service of the state found themselves deprived of all but one chance for advancement. That was a career in the Church. As Christian archbishop of Spain, they could hope to exercise the power formerly held by the proconsul. As Christian authors, they could be certain of a fairly large public if they were willing to devote themselves exclusively to theological subjects. As Christian diplomats, they could be sure of rapid promotion if they were willing to represent the bishop of Rome at the imperial court of Constantinople or undertake the hazardous job of gaining the good will of some barbarous chieftain in the heart of Gaul or Scandinavia. And finally, as Christian financiers, they could hope to make fortunes administering those rapidly increasing estates which had made the occupants of the Lateran Palace the largest landowners of Italy and the richest men of their time.

We have seen something of the same nature during the last five years. Up to the year 1914 the young men of Europe who were ambitious and did not depend upon manual labor for their support almost invariably entered the service of the state. They became officers of the different imperial and royal armies and navies. They filled the higher judicial positions, administered the finances or spent years in the colonies as governors or military commanders. They did not expect to grow very rich, but the social prestige of the offices which they held was very great and by the application of a certain amount of intelligence, industry and honesty, they could look forward to a pleasant life and an honorable old age.

Then came the war and swept aside these last remnants of the old feudal fabric of society. The lower classes took hold of the government. Some few among the former officials were too old to change the habits of a lifetime. They pawned their orders and died. The vast majority, however, surrendered to the inevitable. From childhood on they had been educated to regard business as a low profession, not worthy of their attention. Perhaps business was a low profession, but they had to choose between an office and the poorhouse. The number of people who will go hungry for the sake of their convictions is always relatively small. And so within a few years after the great upheaval, we find most of the former officers and state officials doing the sort of work which they would not have touched ten years ago and doing it not unwillingly. Besides, as most of them belonged to families which for generations had been trained in executive work and were thoroughly accustomed to handle men, they have found it comparatively easy to push ahead in their new careers and are to-day a great deal happier and decidedly more prosperous than they had ever expected to be.

What business is to-day, the Church was sixteen centuries ago.

It may not always have been easy for young men who traced their ancestry back to Hercules or to Romulus or to the heroes of the Trojan war to take orders from a simple cleric who was the son of a slave, but the simple cleric who was the son of a slave had something to give which the young men who traced their ancestry back to Hercules and Romulus and the heroes of the Trojan war wanted and wanted badly. And therefore, if they were both bright fellows (as they well may have been) they soon learned to appreciate the other fellow's good qualities and got along beautifully. For it is one of the other strange laws of history that the more things appear to be changing, the more they remain the same.

Since the beginning of time it has seemed inevitable that there shall be one small group of clever men and women who do the ruling and a much larger group of not-quite-so-bright men and women who shall do the obeying. The stakes for which these two groups play are at different periods known by different names. Invariably they represent Strength and Leadership on the one hand and Weakness and Compliance on the other. They have been called Empire and Church and Knighthood and Monarchy and Democracy and Slavery and Serfdom and Proletariat.

But the mysterious law which governs human development works the same in Moscow as it does in London or Madrid or Washington, for it is bound to neither time nor place. It has often manifested itself under strange forms and disguises. More than once it has worn a lowly garb and has loudly proclaimed its love for humanity, its devotion to God, its humble desire to bring about the greatest good for the greatest number. But underneath such pleasant exteriors it has always hidden and continues to hide the grim truth of that primeval law which insists that the first duty of man is to keep alive. People who resent the fact that they were born in a world of mammals are apt to get

ESCAPE FROM A SINFUL WORLD

angry at such statements. They call us "materialistics" and "cynics" and what not. Because they have always regarded history as a pleasant fairy tale, they are shocked to discover that it is a science which obeys the same iron rules which govern the rest of the universe. They might as well fight against the habits of parallel lines or the results of the tables of multiplication.

Personally I would advise them to accept the inevitable.

For then and only then can history some day be turned into something that shall have a practical value to the human race and cease to be the ally and confederate of those who profit by racial prejudice, tribal intolerance and the ignorance of the vast majority of their fellow citizens.

And if any one doubts the truth of this statement, let him look for the proof in the chronicles of those centuries of which I was writing a few pages back.

Let him study the lives of the great leaders of the Church during the first four centuries.

Almost without exception he will find that they came from the ranks of the old pagan society, that they had been trained in the schools of the Greek philosophers and had only drifted into the Church afterwards, when they had been obliged to choose a career. Several of them of course were attracted by the new ideas and accepted the words of Christ with heart and soul. But the great majority changed its allegiance from a worldly master to a Heavenly ruler because the chances for advancement with the latter were infinitely greater.

The Church from her side, always very wise and very understanding, did not look too closely into the motives which had impelled many of her new disciples to take this sudden step. And most carefully she endeavored to be all things to all men. Those who felt inclined towards a practical and worldly existence were given a chance to make good in the field of politics and economics. While those of a different temperament, who took their faith more emotionally, were offered every possible opportunity to escape from the crowded cities that they might cogitate in silence upon the evils of existence and so might acquire that degree of personal holiness which they deemed necessary for the eternal happiness of their souls.

In the beginning it had been quite easy to lead such a life of devotion and contemplation.

The Church during the first centuries of her existence had been merely a loose spiritual bond between humble folks who dwelled far away from the mansions of the mighty. But when the Church succeeded the empire as ruler of the world, and became a strong political organization with vast real-estate holdings in Italy and France and Africa, there were less opportunities for a life of solitude. Many pious men and women began to hark back to the "good old days" when all true Christians had spent their waking hours in works of charity and in prayer. That they might again be happy, they now artificially recreated what once had been a natural development of the times.

This movement for a monastic form of life which was to exercise such an enormous influence upon the political and economic development of the next thousand years and which was to give the Church a devoted group of very useful shock-troops in her warfare upon heathen and heretics was of Oriental origin.

This need not surprise us.

In the countries bordering upon the eastern shores of the Mediterranean, civilization was very, very old and the human race was tired to the point of exhaustion. In Egypt alone, ten different and separate cycles of culture had succeeded each other since the first settlers had occupied the valley of the Nile. The same was true of the fertile plain between the Tigris and the Euphrates. The vanity of life, the utter futility of all human effort, lay visible in the ruins of thousands of bygone temples and palaces. The younger races of Europe might accept Christianity as an eager promise of life, a constant appeal to their newly regained energy and enthusiasm. But Egyptians and Syrians took their religious experiences in a different mood.

To them it meant the welcome prospect of relief from the curse of being alive. And in anticipation of the joyful hour of death, they escaped from the charnel-house of their own memories and they fled into the desert that they might be alone with their grief and their God and nevermore look upon the reality of existence.

For some curious reason the business of reform always seems to have had a particular appeal to soldiers. They, more than all other people, have come into direct contact with the cruelty and the horrors of civilization. Furthermore they have learned that nothing can be accomplished without discipline. The greatest of all modern warriors to fight the battles of the Church was a former captain in the army of the Emperor Charles V. And the man who first gathered the spiritual stragglers into a single organization had been a private in the army of the Emperor Constantine. His name was Pachomius and he was an Egyptian. When he got through with his military service, he joined a small group of hermits who under the leadership of a certain Anthony, who hailed from his own country, had left the cities and were living peacefully among the jackals of the desert. But as the solitary life seemed to lead to all sorts of strange afflictions of the mind and caused certain very regrettable excesses of devotion which made people spend their days on the top of an old pillar or at the bottom of a deserted grave (thereby giving cause for great mirth to the pagans and serious reason for grief to the true believers), Pachomius decided to put the whole movement upon a more practical basis and in this way he became the founder of the first religious order. From that day on (the middle of the fourth century) hermits living together in small groups obeyed one single commander who was known as the "superior general" and who in turn appointed the abbots who were responsible for the different monasteries which they held as so many fortresses of the Lord.

Before Pachomius died in 346 his monastic idea had been carried from Egypt to Rome by the Alexandrian bishop Athanasius and thousands of people had availed themselves of this opportunity to flee the world, its wickedness and its too insistent creditors.

The climate of Europe, however, and the nature of the people made it necessary that the original plans of the founder be slightly changed. Hunger and cold were not quite so easy to bear under a wintry sky as in the valley of the Nile. Besides, the more practical western mind was disgusted rather than edified by that display of dirt and squalor which seemed to be an integral part of the Oriental ideal of holiness.

"What," so the Italians and the Frenchmen asked themselves, "is to become of those good works upon which the early Church has laid so much stress? Are the widows and the orphans and the sick really very much benefited by the self-mortification of small groups of emaciated zealots who live in the damp caverns of a mountain a million miles away from everywhere?"

The Western mind therefore insisted upon a modification of the monastic institution along more reasonable lines, and credit for this innovation goes to a native of the town of Nursia in the Apennine mountains. His name was Benedict and he is invariably spoken of as Saint Benedict. His parents had sent him to Rome to be educated, but the city had filled his Christian soul with horror and he had fled to the village of Subiaco in the Abruzzi mountains to the deserted ruins of an old country palace that once upon a time had belonged to the Emperor Nero.

There he had lived for three years in complete solitude. Then the fame of his great virtue began to spread throughout the countryside and the number of those who wished to be near him was soon so great that he had enough recruits for a dozen full-fledged monasteries.

He therefore retired from his dungeon and became the lawgiver of European monasticism. First of all he drew up a constitution. In every detail it showed the influence of Benedict's Roman origin. The monks who swore to obey his rules could not look forward to a life of idleness. Those hours which they did not devote to prayer and meditation were to be filled with work in the fields. If they were too old for farm work, they were expected to teach the young how to become good Christians and useful citizens and so well did they acquit themselves of this task that the Benedictine monasteries for almost a thousand years had a monopoly of education and were allowed to train most of the young men of exceptional ability during the greater part of the Middle Ages.

In return for their labors, the monks were decently clothed, received a sufficient amount of eatable food and were given a bed upon which they could sleep the two or three hours of each day that were not devoted to work or to prayer.

But most important, from an historical point of view, was the fact that the monks ceased to be laymen who had merely run away from this world and their obligations to prepare their souls for the hereafter. They became the servants of God. They were obliged to qualify for their new dignity by a long and most painful period of probation and furthermore they were expected to take a direct and active part in spreading the power and the glory of the kingdom of God.

The first elementary missionary work among the heathen of Europe had already been done. But lest the good accomplished by the Apostles come to naught, the labors of the individual preachers must be followed up by the organized effort of permanent settlers and administrators. The monks now carried their spade and their ax and their prayer-book into the wilderness of Germany and Scandinavia and Russia and far-away Iceland. They plowed and they harvested and they preached and they taught school and brought unto those distant lands the first rudimentary elements of a civilization which most people only knew by hearsay.

In this way did the Papacy, the executive head of the entire Church, make use of all the manifold forces of the human spirit.

The practical man of affairs was given quite as much of an opportunity to distinguish himself as the dreamer who found happiness in the silence of the woods. There was no lost motion. Nothing was allowed to go to waste. And the result was such an increase of power that soon neither emperor nor king could afford to rule his realm without paying humble attention to the wishes of those of his subjects who confessed themselves the followers of the Christ.

The way in which the final victory was gained is not without interest. For it shows that the triumph of Christianity was due to practical causes and was not (as is sometimes believed) the result of a sudden and overwhelming outburst of religious ardor.

The last great persecution of the Christians took place under the Emperor Diocletian.

Curiously enough, Diocletian was by no means one of the worst among those many potentates who ruled Europe by the grace of their body-guards. But he suffered from a complaint which alas! is quite common among those who are called upon to govern the human race. He was densely ignorant upon the subject of elementary economics.

He found himself possessed of an empire that was rapidly going to pieces. Having spent all his life in the army, he believed the weak point lay in the organization of the Roman military system, which entrusted the defenses of the outlying districts to colonies of soldiers who had gradually lost the habit of fighting and had become peaceful rustics, selling cabbages and carrots to the very barbarians whom they were supposed to keep at a safe distance from the frontiers.

It was impossible for Diocletian to change this venerable system. He therefore tried to solve the difficulty by creating a new field army, composed of young and agile men who at a few weeks' notice could be marched to any particular part of the empire that was threatened with an invasion.

This was a brilliant idea, but like all brilliant ideas of a military nature, it cost an awful lot of money. This money had to be produced in the form of taxes by the people in the interior of the country. As was to be expected, they raised a great hue and cry and claimed that they could not pay another denarius without going stone broke. The emperor answered that they were mistaken and bestowed upon his tax-gatherers certain powers thus far only possessed by the hangman. But all to no avail. For the subjects, rather than work at a regular trade which assured them a deficit at the end of a year's hard work, deserted house and home and family and herds and flocked to the cities or became hobos. His Majesty, however, did not believe in half-way measures and he solved the difficulty by a decree which shows how completely the old Roman Republic had degenerated into an Oriental despotism. By a stroke of his pen he made all government offices and all forms of handicraft and commerce heredi-

THE SINFUL CITY OF THE SEVEN HILLS

tary professions. That is to say, the sons of officers were supposed to become officers, whether they liked it or not. The sons of bakers must themselves become bakers, although they might have greater aptitude for music or pawn-broking. The sons of sailors were foredoomed to a life on shipboard, even if they were sea-sick when they rowed across the Tiber. And finally, the day laborers, although technically they continued to be freemen, were constrained to live and die on the same piece of soil on which they had been born and were henceforth nothing but a very ordinary variety of slaves.

To expect that a ruler who had such supreme confidence in his own ability either could or would tolerate the continued existence of a relatively small number of people who only obeyed such parts of his regulations and edicts as pleased them would be absurd. But in judging Diocletian for his harshness in dealing with the Christians, we must remember that he was fighting with his back against the wall and that he had good cause to suspect the loyalty of several million of his subjects who profited by the measures he had taken for their protection but refused to carry their share of the common burden.

You will remember that the earliest Christians had not taken the trouble to write anything down. They expected the world to come to an end at almost any moment. Therefore why waste time and money upon literary efforts which in less than ten years would be consumed by the fire from Heaven? But when the new Zion failed to materialize and when the story of Christ (after a hundred years of patient waiting) was beginning to be repeated with such strange additions and variations that a true disciple hardly knew what to believe and what not, the need was felt for some authentic book upon the subject and a number of short biographies of Jesus and such of the original letters of the Apostles as had been preserved were combined into one large volume which was called the New Testament.

This book contained among others a chapter called the Book of Revelation and therein were to be found certain references and certain prophecies about and anent a city built on "seven mountains." That Rome was built on seven hills had been a commonly known fact ever since the days of Romulus. It is true that the anonymous author of this curious chapter carefully called the city of his abomination Babylon. But it took no great degree of perspicacity on the part of the imperial magistrate to understand what was meant when he read these pleasant references to the "Mother of Harlots" and the "Abomination of the Earth," the town that was drunk with the blood of the saints and the martyrs, foredoomed to become the habitation of all devils, the home of every foul spirit, the cage of every unclean and hateful bird, and more expressions of a similar and slightly uncomplimentary nature.

Such sentences might have been explained away as the ravings of a poor fanatic, blinded by pity and rage as he thought of his many friends who had been killed during the last fifty years. But they were part of the solemn services of the Church. Week after week they were repeated in those places where the Christians came together and it was no more than natural that outsiders should think that they represented the true sentiments of all Christians towards the mighty city on the Tiber. I do not mean to imply that the Christians may not have had excellent reason to feel the way they did, but we can hardly blame Diocletian because he failed to share their enthusiasm.

But that was not all.

The Romans were becoming increasingly familiar with an expression which the world thus far had never heard. That was the word "heretics." Originally the name "heretic" was given only to those people who had "chosen" to believe certain doctrines, or, as we would say, a "sect." But gradually the meaning had narrowed down to those who had chosen to believe certain doctrines which were not held "correct" or "sound" or "true" or "orthodox" by the duly established authorities of the Church and which therefore, to use the language of the Apostles, were "heretical, unsound, false and eternally wrong."

The few Romans who still clung to the ancient faith were technically free from the charge of heresy because they had remained outside of the fold of the Church and therefore could not, strictly speaking, be held to account for their private opinions. All the same, it did not flatter the imperial pride to read in certain parts of the New Testament that "heresy was as terrible an evil as adultery, uncleanness, lasciviousness, idolatry, witchcraft, wrath, strife, murder, sedition and drunkenness" and a few other things which common decency prevents me from repeating on this page.

All this led to friction and misunderstanding and friction and misunderstanding led to persecution and once more Roman jails were filled with Christian prisoners and Roman executioners added to the number of Christian martyrs and a great deal of blood was shed and nothing was accomplished and finally Diocletian, in utter despair, went back to his home town of Salonæ on the Dalmatian coast, retired from the business of ruling and devoted himself exclusively to the even more exciting pastime of raising great big cabbages in his back yard.

His successor did not continue the policy of repression. On the contrary, since he could not hope to eradicate the Christian evil by force, he decided to make the best of a bad bargain and gain the good will of his enemies by offering them some special favors.

This happened in the year 313 and the honor of having been the first to "recognize" the Christian church officially belongs to a man by the name of Constantine.

Some day we shall possess an International Board of Revisioning Historians before whom all emperors, kings, pontiffs, presidents and mayors who now enjoy the title of the "great" shall have to submit their claims for this specific qualification. One of the candidates who will have to be watched very carefully when he appears before this tribunal is the aforementioned Emperor Constantine.

CONSTANTINE THE GREAT

This wild Serbian who had wielded a spear on every battlefield of Europe, from York in England to Byzantium on the shores of the Bosporus, was among other things the murderer of his wife, the murderer of his brother-in-law, the murderer of his nephew (a boy of seven) and the executioner of several other relatives of minor degree and importance. Nevertheless and notwithstanding, because in a moment of panic just before he marched against his most dangerous rival, Maxentius, he had made a bold bid for Christian support, he gained great fame as the "second Moses" and was ultimately elevated to sainthood both by the Armenian and by the Russian churches. That he lived and died a barbarian who had outwardly accepted Christianity, yet until the end of his days tried to read the riddle of the future from the steaming entrails of sacrificial sheep, all this was most considerately overlooked in view of the famous Edict of Tolerance by which the Emperor guaranteed unto his beloved Christian subjects the right to "freely profess their private opinions and to assemble in their meeting place without fear of molestation."

For the leaders of the Church in the first half of the fourth century, as I have repeatedly stated before, were practical politicians and when they had finally forced the Emperor to sign this ever memorable decree, they elevated Christianity from the rank of a minor sect to the dignity of the official church of the state. But they knew how and in what manner this had been accomplished and the successors of Constantine knew it, and although they tried to cover it up by a display of oratorical fireworks the arrangement never quite lost its original character.

* * * * * * * *

"Deliver me, oh mighty ruler," exclaimed Nestor the Patriarch unto Theodosius the Emperor, "deliver me of all the enemies of my church and in return I will give thee Heaven. Stand by me in putting down those who disagree with our doctrines and we in turn will stand by thee in putting down thine enemies."

There have been other bargains during the history of the last twenty centuries.

But few have been so brazen as the compromise by which Christianity came to power.

Chapter V

IMPRISONMENT

JUST before the curtain rings down for the last time upon the ancient world, a figure crosses the stage which had deserved a better fate than an untimely death and the unflattering appellation of "the Apostate."

The Emperor Julian, to whom I refer, was a nephew of Constantine the Great and was born in the new capital of the empire in the year 331. In 337 his famous uncle died. At once his three sons fell upon their common heritage and upon each other with the fury of famished wolves.

To rid themselves of all those who might possibly lay claim to part of the spoils, they ordered that those of their relatives who lived in or near the city be murdered. Julian's father was one of the victims. His mother had died a few years after his birth. In this way, at the age of six, the boy was left an orphan. An older half-brother, an invalid, shared his loneliness and his lessons. These consisted mostly of lectures upon the advantages of the Christian faith, given by a kindly but uninspired old bishop by the name of Eusebius.

But when the children grew older, it was thought wiser to send them a little farther away where they would be less conspicuous and might possibly escape the usual fate of junior Byzantine princes. They were removed to a little village in the heart of Asia Minor. It was a dull life, but it gave Julian a chance to learn many useful things. For his neighbors, the Cappadocian mountaineers, were a simple people and still believed in the Gods of their ancestors.

There was not the slightest chance that the boy would ever hold a responsible position and when he asked permission to devote himself to a life of study, he was told to go ahead.

First of all he went to Nicomedia, one of the few places where

THE DESERTED TEMPLE

the old Greek philosophy continued to be taught. There he crammed his head so full of literature and science that there was no space left for the things he had learned from Eusebius.

Next he obtained leave to go to Athens, that he might study on the very spot hallowed by the recollections of Socrates and Plato and Aristotle.

Meanwhile, his half-brother too had been assassinated and Constantius, his cousin and the one and only remaining son of Constantine, remembering that he and his cousin, the boy philosopher, were by this time the only two surviving male members of the imperial family, sent for Julian, received him kindly, married him, still in the kindest of spirits, to his own sister, Helena, and ordered him to proceed to Gaul and defend that province against the barbarians.

It seems that Julian had learned something more practical from his Greek teachers than an ability to argue. When in the year 357 the Alamanni threatened France, he destroyed their army near Strassburg, and for good measure added all the country between the Meuse and the Rhine to his own province and went to live in Paris, filled his library with a fresh supply of books by his favorite authors and was as happy as his serious nature allowed him to be.

When news of these victories reached the ears of the Emperor, little Greek fire was wasted in celebration of the event. On the contrary, elaborate plans were laid to get rid of a competitor who might be just a trifle too successful.

But Julian was very popular with his soldiers. When they heard that their commander-in-chief had been ordered to return home (a polite invitation to come and have one's head cut off), they invaded his palace and then and there proclaimed him emperor. At the same time they let it be known that they would kill him if he should refuse to accept.

Julian, like a sensible fellow, accepted.

Even at that late date, the Roman roads must have been in a remarkably good state of preservation. Julian was able to break all records by the speed with which he marched his troops from the heart of France to the shores of the Bosporus. But ere he reached the capital, he heard that his cousin Constantius had died.

And in this way, a pagan once more became ruler of the western world.

Of course the thing which Julian had undertaken to do was impossible. It is a strange thing indeed that so intelligent a man should have been under the impression that the dead past could ever be brought back to life by the use of force; that the age of Pericles could be revived by reconstructing an exact replica of the Acropolis and populating the deserted groves of the Academy with professors dressed up in togas of a bygone age and talking to each other in a tongue that had disappeared from the face of the earth more than five centuries before.

And yet that is exactly what Julian tried to do.

All his efforts during the two short years of his reign were directed towards the reëstablishment of that ancient science which was now held in profound contempt by the majority of his people; towards the rekindling of a spirit of research in a world ruled by illiterate monks who felt certain that everything worth knowing was contained in a single book and that independent study and investigation could only lead to unbelief and hell fire; towards the requickening of the joy-of-living among those who had the vitality and the enthusiasm of ghosts.

Many a man of greater tenacity than Julian would have been driven to madness and despair by the spirit of opposition which met him on all sides. As for Julian, he simply went to pieces under it. Temporarily at least he clung to the enlightened principles of his great ancestors. The Christian rabble of Antioch might pelt him with stones and mud, yet he refused to punish the city. Dull-witted monks might try to provoke him into another era of persecution, yet the Emperor persistently continued to instruct his officials "not to make any martyrs."

In the year 363 a merciful Persian arrow made an end to this strange career.

It was the best thing that could have happened to this, the last and greatest of the pagan rulers.

Had he lived any longer, his sense of tolerance and his hatred of stupidity would have turned him into the most intolerant man of his age. Now, from his cot in the hospital, he could reflect that during his rule, not a single person had suffered death for his private opinions. For this mercy, his Christian subjects rewarded him with their undying hatred. They boasted that an arrow from one of his own soldiers (a Christian legionary) had killed the Emperor and with rare delicacy they composed eulogies in praise of the murderer. They told how, just before he collapsed, Julian had confessed the errors of his ways and had acknowledged the power of Christ. And they emptied the arsenal of foul epithets with which the vocabulary of the fourth century was so richly stocked to disgrace the fame of an honest man who had lived a life of ascetic simplicity and had devoted all his energies to the happiness of the people who had been entrusted to his care.

When he had been carried to his grave the Christian bishops could at last consider themselves the veritable rulers of the

Empire and immediately began the task of destroying whatever opposition to their domination might remain in isolated corners of Europe, Asia and Africa.

Under Valentinian and Valens, two brothers who ruled from 364 to 378, an edict was passed forbidding all Romans to sacrifice animals to the old Gods. The pagan priests were thereby deprived of their revenue and forced to look for other employment.

But the regulations were mild compared to the law by which Theodosius ordered all his subjects not only to accept the Christian doctrines, but to accept them only in the form laid down by the "universal" or "Catholic" church of which he had made himself the protector and which was to have a monopoly in all matters spiritual.

All those who after the promulgation of this ordinance stuck to their "erroneous opinions"—who persisted in their "insane heresies"—who remained faithful to their "scandalous doctrines" —were to suffer the consequences of their willful disobedience and were to be exiled or put to death.

From then on the old world marched rapidly to its final doom. In Italy and Gaul and Spain and England hardly a pagan temple remained. They were either wrecked by the contractors who needed stones for new bridges and streets and city-walls and water-works, or they were remodeled to serve as meeting places for the Christians. The thousands of golden and silver images which had been accumulated since the beginning of the Republic were publicly confiscated and privately stolen and such statues as remained were made into mortar.

The Serapeum of Alexandria, a temple which Greeks and Romans and Egyptians alike had held in the greatest veneration for more than six centuries, was razed to the ground. There remained the university, famous all over the world ever since it had been founded by Alexander the Great. It had continued to teach and explain the old philosophies and as a result attracted a large number of students from all parts of the Mediterranean. When it was not closed at the behest of the Bishop of Alexandria, the monks of his diocese took the matter into their own hands.

They broke into the lecture rooms, lynched Hypatia, the last of the great Platonic teachers, and threw her mutilated body into the streets where it was left to the mercy of the dogs.

In Rome things went no better.

The temple of Jupiter was closed, the Sibylline books, the very basis of the old Roman faith, were burned. The capitol was left a ruin.

THE NEW WORLD EMPIRE

THE RIVAL PRISONS

In Gaul, under the leadership of the famous Bishop of Tours, the old Gods were declared to be the predecessors of the Christian devils and their temples were therefore ordered to be wiped off the face of the earth.

If, as sometimes happened in remote country districts, the peasants rushed forth to the defense of their beloved shrines, the soldiers were called out and by means of the ax and the gallows made an end to such "insurrections of Satan."

In Greece, the work of destruction proceeded more slowly. But finally in the year 394, the Olympic games were abolished. As soon as this center of Greek national life (after an uninterrupted existence of eleven hundred and seventy years) had come to an end, the rest was comparatively easy. One after the other, the philosophers were expelled from the country. Finally, by order of the Emperor Justinian, the University of Athens was closed. The funds established for its maintenance were confiscated. The last seven professors, deprived of their livelihood, fled to Persia where King Chosroes received them hospitably and allowed them to spend the rest of their days peacefully playing the new and mysterious Indian game called "chess."

In the first half of the fifth century, Archbishop Chrysos-
tomus could truthfully state that the works of the old authors
and philosophers had disappeared from the face of the earth.
Cicero and Socrates and Virgil and Homer (not to mention the
mathematicians and the astronomers and the physicians who
were an object of special abomination to all good Christians)
lay forgotten in a thousand attics and cellars. Six hundred
years were to go by before they were called back to life, and in
the meantime the world would be obliged to subsist on such
literary fare as it pleased the theologians to place before it.

A strange diet, and not exactly (in the jargon of the medical
faculty) a balanced one.

For the Church, although triumphant over its pagan enemies,
was beset by many and serious tribulations. The poor peasant
in Gaul and Lusitania, clamoring to burn incense in honor of
his ancient Gods, could be silenced easily enough. He was a
heathen and the law was on the side of the Christian. But the
Ostrogoth or the Alaman or the Longobard who declared that
Arius, the priest of Alexandria, was right in his opinion upon
the true nature of Christ and that Athanasius, the bishop of
that same city and Arius' bitter enemy, was wrong (or vice
versa)—the Longobard or Frank who stoutly maintained that
Christ was not "of the same nature" but of a "like nature only"
with God (or vice versa)—the Vandal or the Saxon who insisted
that Nestor spoke the truth when he called the Virgin Mary
the "mother of Christ" and not the "mother of God" (or vice
versa)—the Burgundian or Frisian who denied that Jesus was
possessed of two natures, one human and one divine (or vice
versa)—all these simple-minded but strong-armed barbarians
who had accepted Christianity and were, outside of their unfortunate errors of opinion, staunch friends and supporters of the
Church—these indeed could not be punished with a general
anathema and a threat of perpetual hell fire. They must be
persuaded gently that they were wrong and must be brought
within the fold with charitable expressions of love and devotion.
But before all else they must be given a definite creed that they

might know for once and for all what they must hold to be true
and what they must reject as false.

It was that desire for unity of some sort in all matters pertaining to the faith which finally caused those famous gatherings
which have become known as Ecumenical or Universal Councils,
and which since the middle of the fourth century have been called
together at irregular intervals to decide what doctrine is right
and what doctrine contains the germ of heresy and should therefore be adjudged erroneous, unsound, fallacious and heretical.

The first of those Ecumenical councils was held in the town
of Nicæa, not far from the ruins of Troy, in the year 325. The
second one, fifty-six years later, was held in Constantinople.
The third one in the year 431 in Ephesus. Thereafter they
followed each other in rapid succession in Chalcedon, twice again
in Constantinople, once more in Nicæa and finally once again in
Constantinople in the year 869.

After that, however, they were held in Rome or in some
particular town of western Europe designated by the Pope.
For it was generally accepted from the fourth century on that,
although the emperor had the technical right to call together
such meetings (a privilege which incidentally obliged him to
pay the traveling expenses of his faithful bishops), very serious attention should be paid to the suggestions made by the
powerful Bishop of Rome. And although we do not know
with any degree of certainty who occupied the chair in Nicæa,
all later councils were dominated by the Popes and the decisions
of these holy gatherings were not regarded as binding unless they
had obtained the official approval of the supreme pontiff himself or one of his delegates.

Hence we can now say farewell to Constantinople and travel
to the more congenial regions of the West.

The field of Tolerance and Intolerance has been fought over
so repeatedly by those who hold tolerance the greatest of all
human virtues and those who denounce it as an evidence of moral
weakness, that I shall pay very little attention to the purely
theoretical aspects of the case. Nevertheless it must be confessed that the champions of the Church follow a plausible line of

THE DISSENTER

reasoning when they try to explain away the terrible punishments which were inflicted upon all heretics.

"A church," so they argue, "is like any other organization. It is almost like a village or a tribe or a fortress. There must be a commander-in-chief and there must be a definite set of laws and by-laws, which all members are forced to obey. It follows that those who swear allegiance to the Church make a tacit vow both to respect the commander-in-chief and to obey the law. And if they find it impossible to do this, they must suffer the consequences of their own decisions and get out."

All of which, so far, is perfectly true and reasonable.

If to-day a minister feels that he can no longer believe in the articles of faith of the Baptist Church, he can turn Methodist, and if for some reason he ceases to believe in the creed as laid down by the Methodist Church, he can become a Unitarian or a Catholic or a Jew, or for that matter, a Hindoo or a Turk. The world is wide. The door is open. There is no one outside his own hungry family to say him nay.

But this is an age of steamships and railroad trains and unlimited economic opportunities.

The world of the fifth century was not quite so simple. It was far from easy to discover a region where the influence of the Bishop of Rome did not make itself felt. One could of course go to Persia or to India, as a good many heretics did, but the voyage was long and the chances of survival were small. And this meant perpetual banishment for oneself and for one's children.

And finally, why should a man surrender his good right to believe what he pleased if he felt sincerely that his conception of the idea of Christ was the right one and that it was only a question of time for him to convince the Church that its doctrines needed a slight modification?

For that was the crux of the whole matter.

The early Christians, both the faithful and the heretics, dealt with ideas which had a relative and not a positive value.

A group of mathematicians, sending each other to the gallows because they cannot agree upon the absolute value of x would be

no more absurd than a council of learned theologians trying to
define the undefinable and endeavoring to reduce the substance
of God to a formula.

But so thoroughly had the spirit of self-righteousness and
intolerance got hold of the world that until very recently all
those who advocated tolerance upon the basis that "we cannot
ever possibly know who is right and who is wrong" did so at
the risk of their lives and usually couched their warnings in such
careful Latin sentences that not more than one or two of their
most intelligent readers ever knew what they meant.

Chapter VI

THE PURE OF LIFE

HERE is a little problem in mathematics which is not out of place in a book of history.

Take a piece of string and make it into a circle, like this:

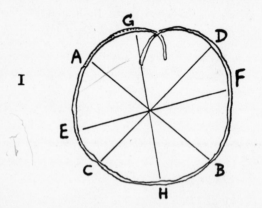

I

In this circle all diameters will of course be equal.

AB = CD = EF = GH and so on, ad infinitum.

But turn the circle into an ellipse by slightly pulling two sides. Then the perfect balance is at once disturbed. The diameters are thrown out of gear. A few like AB and EF have been

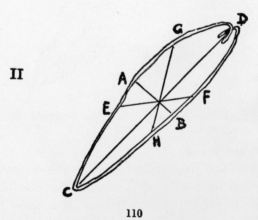

II

greatly shortened. Others, and especially **CD**, have been lengthened.

Now transfer the problem from mathematics to history. Let us for the sake of argument suppose that

AB represents politics
CD   "   trade
EF   "   art
GH   "   militarism

In the figure **I**, the perfectly balanced state, all lines are equally long and quite as much attention is paid to politics as to trade and art and militarism.

But in figure **II** (which is no longer a perfect circle) trade has got an undue advantage at the expense of politics and art has almost entirely disappeared, while militarism shows a gain.

Or make **GH** (militarism) the longest diameter, and the others will tend to disappear altogether.

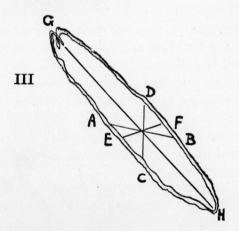

III

You will find this a handy key to a great many historical problems.

Try it on the Greeks.

For a short time the Greeks had been able to maintain a perfect circle of all-around accomplishments. But the foolish quarrels between the different political parties soon grew to such proportions that all the surplus energy of the nation was being absorbed by the incessant civil wars. The soldiers were no longer used for the purpose of defending the country against foreign aggression. They were turned loose upon their own neighbors, who had voted for a different candidate, or who believed in a slightly modified form of taxation.

Trade, that most important diameter of all such circles, at first became difficult, then became entirely impossible and fled to other parts of the world, where business enjoyed a greater degree of stability.

The moment poverty entered through the front gate of the city, the arts escaped by way of the back door, never to be seen again. Capital sailed away on the fastest ship it could find within a hundred miles, and since intellectualism is a very expensive luxury, it was henceforth impossible to maintain good schools. The best teachers hastened to Rome and to Alexandria.

What remained was a group of second-rate citizens who subsisted upon tradition and routine.

And all this happened because the line of politics had grown out of all proportion, because the perfect circle had been destroyed, and the other lines, art, science, philosophy, etc., etc., had been reduced to nothing.

If you apply the circular problem to Rome, you will find there the particular line called "political power" grew and grew and grew until there was nothing left of any of the others. The circle which had spelled the glory of the Republic disappeared. All that remained was a straight, narrow line, the shortest distance between success and failure.

And if, to give you still another example, you reduce the history of the medieval Church to this sort of mathematics, this is what you will find.

The earliest Christians had tried very hard to maintain a circle of conduct that should be perfect. Perhaps they had rather neglected the diameter of science, but since they were not interested in the life of the world, they could not very well be expected to pay much attention to medicine or physics or astronomy, useful subjects, no doubt, but of small appeal to men and women who were making ready for the last judgment and who regarded this world merely as the anteroom to Heaven.

But for the rest, these sincere followers of Christ endeavored (however imperfectly) to lead the good life and to be as industrious as they were charitable and as kindly as they were honest.

As soon, however, as their little communities had been united into a single powerful organization, the perfect balance of the old spiritual circle was rudely upset by the obligations and duties of the new international responsibilities. It was easy enough for small groups of half-starved carpenters and quarry workers to follow those principles of poverty and unselfishness upon which their faith was founded. But the heir to the imperial throne of Rome, the Pontifex Maximus of the Western World, the richest landowner of the entire continent, could not live as simply as if he were a sub-deacon in a provincial town somewhere in Pomerania or Spain.

Or, to use the circular language of this chapter, the diameter representing "worldliness" and the diameter representing "foreign policy" were lengthened to such an extent that the diameters representing "humility" and "poverty" and "self-negation" and the other elementary Christian virtues were being reduced to the point of extinction.

It is a pleasant habit of our time to speak patronizingly of the benighted people of the Middle Ages, who, as we all know, lived in utter darkness. It is true they burned wax tapers in their churches and went to bed by the uncertain light of a sconce, they possessed few books, they were ignorant of many things which are now being taught in our grammar schools and in our better grade lunatic asylums. But knowledge and intelligence are two very different things and of the latter, these excellent burghers, who constructed the political and social structure in which we ourselves continue to live, had their full share.

If a good deal of the time they seemed to stand apparently helpless before the many and terrible abuses in their Church, let us judge them mercifully. They had at least the courage of their convictions and they fought whatever they considered wrong with such sublime disregard for personal happiness and

comfort that they frequently ended their lives on the scaffold.
More than that we can ask of no one.

It is true that during the first thousand years of our era,
comparatively few people fell as victims to their ideas. Not,
however, because the Church felt less strongly about heresy than
she did at a later date, but because she was too much occupied
with more important questions to have any time to waste upon
comparatively harmless dissenters.

In the first place, there remained many parts of Europe where
Odin and the other heathen Gods still ruled supreme.

And in the second place, something very unpleasant had happened, which had wellnigh threatened the whole of Europe with
destruction.

This "something unpleasant" was the sudden appearance of
a brand-new prophet by the name of Mahomet, and the conquest of western Asia and northern Africa by the followers of
a new God who was called Allah.

The literature which we absorb in our childhood full of "infidel
dogs" and Turkish atrocities is apt to leave us under the impression that Jesus and Mahomet represented ideals which were
as mutually antagonistic as fire and water.

But as a matter of fact, the two men belonged to the same
race, they spoke dialects which belonged to the same linguistic
group, they both claimed Abraham as their great-great-grand-
father and they both looked back upon a common ancestral home,
which a thousand years before had stood on the shores of the
Persian Gulf.

And yet, the followers of those two great teachers who were
such close relatives have always regarded each other with bitter
scorn and have fought a war which has lasted more than twelve
centuries and which has not yet come to an end.

At this late day and age it is useless to speculate upon what
might have happened, but there was a time when Mecca, the
arch-enemy of Rome, might have easily been gained for the
Christian faith.

The Arabs, like all desert people, spent a great deal of their
time tending their flocks and therefore were much given to

meditation. People in cities can drug their souls with the pleasures of a perennial county-fair. But shepherds and fisher folk and farmers lead solitary lives and want something a little more substantial than noise and excitement.

In his quest for salvation, the Arab had tried several religions, but had shown a distinct preference for Judaism. This is easily explained, as Arabia was full of Jews. In the tenth century B.C., a great many of King Solomon's subjects, exasperated by the high taxes and the despotism of their ruler, had fled into Arabia and again, five hundred years later in 586 B.C., when Nebuchadnezzar conquered Judah, there had been a second wholesale exodus of Jews towards the desert lands of the south.

Judaism, therefore, was well known and furthermore the quest of the Jews after the one and only true God was entirely in line with the aspirations and ideals of the Arabian tribes.

Any one in the least familiar with the work of Mahomet will know how much the Medinite had borrowed from the wisdom contained in some of the books of the Old Testament.

Nor were the descendants of Ishmael (who together with his mother Hagar lay buried in the Holy of Holies in the heart of Arabia) hostile to the ideas expressed by the young reformer from Nazareth. On the contrary, they followed Jesus eagerly when he spoke of that one God who was a loving father to all men. They were not inclined to accept those miracles of which the followers of the Nazarene carpenter made so much. And as for the resurrection, they flatly refused to believe in it. But generally speaking, they felt very kindly disposed towards the new faith and were willing to give it a chance.

But Mahomet suffered considerable annoyance at the hands of certain Christian zealots who with their usual lack of discretion had denounced him as a liar and a false prophet before he had fairly opened his mouth. That and the impression which was rapidly gaining ground that the Christians were idol worshipers who believed in three Gods instead of one, made the people of the desert finally turn their backs upon Christianity and declare themselves in favor of the Medinese camel driver who spoke to them of one and only one God and did not confuse them with references to three deities that were "one" and yet were not one, but were one or three as it might please the convenience of the moment and the interests of the officiating priest.

Thus the Western World found itself possessed of two religions, each of which proclaimed its own God to be the One True God and each of which insisted that all other Gods were impostors.

Such conflicts of opinion are apt to lead to warfare.

Mahomet died in 632.

Within less than a dozen years, Palestine, Syria, Persia and Egypt had been conquered and Damascus had become the capital of a great Arab empire.

Before the end of 656 the entire coast of northern Africa had accepted Allah as its divine ruler and in less than a century after the flight of Mahomet from Mecca to Medina, the Mediterranean had been turned into a Moslem lake, all communications between Europe and Asia had been cut off and the European continent was placed in a state of siege which lasted until the end of the seventeenth century.

Under those circumstances it had been impossible for the Church to carry her doctrines eastward. All she could hope to do was to hold on to what she already possessed. Germany and the Balkans and Russia and Denmark and Sweden and Norway and Bohemia and Hungary had been chosen as a profitable field for intensive spiritual cultivation and on the whole the work was done with great success. Occasionally a hardy Christian of the variety of Charlemagne, well-intentioned but not yet entirely civilized, might revert to strong-arm methods and might butcher those of his subjects who preferred their own Gods to those of the foreigner. By and large, however, the Christian missionaries were well received, for they were honest men who told a simple and straightforward story which all the people could understand and because they introduced certain elements of order and neatness and mercy into a world full of bloodshed and strife and highway robbery.

But while this was happening along the frontier, things had not gone so well in the heart of the pontifical empire. Incessantly (to revert to the mathematics explained in the first pages of this

THE FOURTH CRUSADE

chapter) the line of worldliness had been lengthened until at last the spiritual element in the Church had been made entirely subservient to considerations of a purely political and economic nature and though Rome was to grow in power and exercise a tremendous influence upon the development of the next twelve centuries, certain elements of disintegration had already made their appearance and were being recognized as such by the more intelligent among the laity and the clergy.

We modern people of the Protestant north think of a "church" as a building which stands empty six days out of every seven and a place where people go on a Sunday to hear a sermon and sing a few hymns. We know that some of our churches have bishops and occasionally these bishops hold a convention in our town and then we find ourselves surrounded by a number of kindly old gentlemen with their collars turned backwards and we read in the papers that they have declared themselves in favor of dancing or against divorce, and then they go home again and nothing has happened to disturb the peace and happiness of our community.

We rarely associate this church (even if it happens to be our own) with the sum total of all our experiences, both in life and in death.

The State, of course, is something very different. The State may take our money and may kill us if it feels that such a course is desirable for the public good. The State is our owner, our master, but what is now generally called "the Church" is either our good and trusted friend or, if we happen to quarrel with her, a fairly indifferent enemy.

But in the Middle Ages this was altogether different. Then, the Church was something visible and tangible, a highly active organization which breathed and existed, which shaped man's destiny in many more ways than the State would ever dream of doing. Very likely those first Popes who accepted pieces of land from grateful princes and renounced the ancient ideal of poverty did not foresee the consequences to which such a policy was bound to lead. In the beginning it had seemed harmless enough and quite appropriate that faithful followers of Christ should bestow upon the successor of the Apostle Peter a share of their own worldly goods. Besides, there was the overhead of a complicated administration which reached all the way from John O'Groat's to Trebizond and from Carthage to Upsala. Think of all the thousands of secretaries and clerks and scribes, not to mention the hundreds of heads of the different departments, that had to be housed and clothed and fed. Think of the amount spent upon a courier service across an entire continent; the traveling expenses of diplomatic agents now going to London, then returning from Novgorod; the sums necessary to keep the papal courtiers in the style that was expected of people who foregathered with worldly princes on a footing of complete equality.

All the same, looking back upon what the Church came to stand for and contemplating what it might have been under slightly more favorable circumstances, this development seems a great pity. For Rome rapidly grew into a gigantic superstate with a slight religious tinge and the pope became an international autocrat who held all the nations of western Europe in a bondage compared to which the rule of the old emperors had been mild and generous.

And then, when complete success seemed within certain reach, something happened which proved fatal to the ambition for world dominion.

The true spirit of the Master once more began to stir among the masses and that is one of the most uncomfortable things that can happen to any religious organization.

Heretics were nothing new.

There had been dissenters as soon as there had been a single rule of faith from which people could possibly dissent, and disputes, which had divided Europe and Africa and western Asia into hostile camps for centuries at a time, were almost as old as the Church herself.

But these sanguinary quarrels between Donatists and Sabellianists and Monophysites and Manichæans and Nestorians hardly come within the scope of this book. As a rule, one party was quite as narrow-minded as the other and there was little to choose between the intolerance of a follower of Arius and the intolerance of a follower of Athanasius.

Besides, these quarrels were invariably based upon certain obscure points of theology which are gradually beginning to be forgotten. Heaven forbid that I should drag them out of their parchment graves. I am not wasting my time upon the fabrication of this volume to cause a fresh outbreak of theological fury. Rather, I am writing these pages to tell our children of certain ideals of intellectual liberty for which some of their ancestors fought at the risk of their lives and to warn them against that attitude of doctrinary arrogance and cock-sureness which has caused such a terrible lot of suffering during the last two thousand years.

But when I reach the thirteenth century, it is a very different story.

Then a heretic ceases to be a mere dissenter, a disputatious fellow with a pet hobby of his own based upon the wrong translation of an obscure sentence in the Apocalyse or the misspelling of a holy word in the gospel of St. John.

Instead he becomes the champion of those ideas for which during the reign of Tiberius a certain carpenter from the village of Nazareth went to his death, and behold! he stands revealed as the only true Christian!

Chapter VII

THE INQUISITION

In the year 1198 a certain Lotario, Count of Segni, succeeded to the high honors which his uncle Paolo had held only a few years before and as Innocent III took possession of the papal chair.

He was one of the most remarkable men who ever resided in the Lateran Palace. Thirty-seven years old at the time of his ascension. An honor-student in the universities of Paris and Boulogne. Rich, clever, full of energy and high ambition, he used his office so well that he could rightly claim to exercise the "government not of the Church alone but of the entire world."

He set Italy free from German interference by driving the imperial governor of Rome from that city; by reconquering those parts of the peninsula which were held by imperial troops; and finally by excommunicating the candidate to the imperial throne until that poor prince found himself beset by so many difficulties that he withdrew entirely from his domains on the other side of the Alps.

He organized the famous fourth Crusade which never even came within sight of the Holy Land but sailed for Constantinople, murdered a goodly number of the inhabitants of that town, stole whatever could be carried away and generally behaved in such a way that thereafter no crusader could show himself in a Greek port without running the chance of being hanged as an outlaw. It is true that Innocent expressed his disapproval of these proceedings which shrieked to high Heaven and filled the respectable minority of Christendom with disgust and despair. But Innocent was a practical man of affairs. He soon accepted the inevitable and appointed a Venetian to the vacant post of Patriarch of Constantinople. By this clever stroke he brought the Eastern Church once more under Roman jurisdiction and at the same

time gained the good will of the Venetian Republic which henceforth regarded the Byzantine domains as part of her eastern
colonies and treated them accordingly.

In spiritual matters too His Holiness showed himself a most
accomplished and tactful person.

The Church, after almost a thousand years of hesitation, had
at last begun to insist that marriage was not merely a civil con-
tract between a man and a woman but a most holy sacrament
which needed the public blessing of a priest to be truly valid.
When Philip August of France and Alphonso IX of León undertook to regulate their domestic affairs according to their own
particular preferences, they were speedily reminded of their
duties and being men of great prudence they hastened to comply
with the papal wishes.

Even in the high north, gained only recently for Christianity,
people were shown in unmistakable manner who was their master. King Haakon IV (known familiarly among his fellow
pirates as Old Haakon) who had just conquered a neat little
empire including besides his own Norway, part of Scotland and
all of Iceland, Greenland, the Orkneys and the Hebrides, was
obliged to submit the somewhat tangled problem of his birth to
a Roman tribunal before he could get himself crowned in his
old cathedral of Trondhjem.

And so it went.

The king of Bulgaria, who invariably murdered his Greek
prisoners of war, and was not above torturing an occasional
Byzantine emperor, who therefore was not the sort of person
one might expect to take a deep interest in religious matters,
traveled all the way to Rome and humbly asked that he be recognized as vassal of His Holiness. While in England certain
barons who had undertaken to discipline their sovereign master
were rudely informed that their charter was null and void because "it had been obtained by force" and next found themselves
excommunicated for having given unto this world the famous
document known as Magna Charta.

From all this it will appear that Innocent III was not the
sort of person who would deal lightly with the pretensions of a

few simple linen-weavers and illiterate shepherds who undertook to question the laws of his Church.

And yet, some there were found who had the courage to do this very thing as we shall now see.

The subject of all heresies is extremely difficult.

Heretics, almost invariably, are poor people who have small gift for publicity. The occasional clumsy little pamphlets they write to explain their ideas and to defend themselves against their enemies fall an easy prey to the ever watchful detectives of whatever inquisition happens to be in force at that particular moment and are promptly destroyed. Hence we depend for our knowledge of most heresies upon such information as we are able to glean from the records of their trials and upon such articles as have been written by the enemies of the false doctrines for the express purpose of exposing the new "conspiracy of Satan" to the truly faithful that all the world may be duly scandalized and warned against doing likewise.

As a result we usually get a composite picture of a long-haired individual in a dirty shirt, who lives in an empty cellar somewhere in the lowest part of the slums, who refuses to touch decent Christian food but subsists entirely upon vegetables, who drinks naught but water, who keeps away from the company of women and mumbles strange prophecies about the second coming of the Messiah, who reproves the clergy for their worldliness and wickedness and generally disgusts his more respectable neighbors by his ill-guided attacks upon the established order of things.

Undoubtedly a great many heretics have succeeded in making a nuisance of themselves, for that seems to be the fate of people who take themselves too seriously.

Undoubtedly a great many of them, driven by their almost unholy zeal for a holy life, were dirty, looked like the devil and did not smell pleasantly and generally upset the quiet routine of their home town by their strange ideas anent a truly Christian existence.

But let us give them credit for their courage and their honesty.

They had mighty little to gain and everything to lose.

As a rule, they lost it.

Of course, everything in this world tends to become organized. Eventually even those who believe in no organization at all must form a Society for the Promotion of Disorganization, if they wish to accomplish anything. And the medieval heretics, who loved the mysterious and wallowed in emotions, were no exception to this rule. Their instinct of self-preservation made them flock together and their feeling of insecurity forced them to surround their sacred doctrines by a double barrier of mystic rites and esoteric ceremonials.

But of course the masses of the people, who remained faithful to the Church, were unable to make any distinction between these different groups and sects. And they bunched them all together and called them dirty Manichæans or some other unflattering name and felt that that solved the problem.

In this way did the Manichæans become the Bolshevists of the Middle Ages. Of course I do not use the latter name as indicating membership in a certain well-defined political party which a few years ago established itself as the dominant factor in the old Russian Empire. I refer to a vague and ill-defined term of abuse which people nowadays bestow upon all their personal enemies from the landlord who comes to collect the rent down to the elevator boy who neglects to stop at the right floor.

A Manichæan, to a medieval super-Christian, was a most objectionable person. But as he could not very well try him upon any positive charges, he condemned him upon hearsay, a method which has certain unmistakable advantages over the less spectacular and infinitely slower procedure followed by the regular courts of law but which sometimes suffers from a lack of accuracy and is responsible for a great many judicial murders.

What made this all the more reprehensible in the case of the poor Manichæans was the fact that the founder of the original sect, a Persian by the name of Mani, had been the very incarnation of benevolence and charity. He was an historical figure and was born during the first quarter of the third century in the town of Ecbatana where his father, Patak, was a man of considerable wealth and influence.

He was educated in Ctesiphon, on the river Tigris, and spent the years of his youth in a community as international, as polyglot, as pious, as godless, as material and as idealistically-spiritual as the New York of our own day. Every heresy, every religion, every schism, every sect of east and west and south and north had its followers among the crowds that visited the great commercial centers of Mesopotamia. Mani listened to all the different preachers and prophets and then distilled a philosophy of his own which was a *mixtum-compositum* of Buddhism, Christianity, Mithraism and Judaism, with a slight sprinkling of half a dozen old Babylonian superstitions.

Making due allowance for certain extremes to which his followers sometimes carried his doctrines, it can be stated that Mani merely revived the old Persian myth of the Good God and the Evil God who are eternally fighting for the soul of man and that he associated the ancient God of Evil with the Jehovah of the Old Testament (who thus became his Devil) and the God of All Good Things with that Heavenly Father whom we find revealed within the pages of the Four Gospels. Furthermore (and that is where Buddhistic influence made itself felt) Mani believed that the body of man was by nature a vile and despicable thing; that all people should try to rid themselves of their worldly ambitions by the constant mortification of the flesh and should obey the strictest rules of diet and behavior lest they fall into the clutches of the Evil God (the Devil) and burn in Hell. As a result he revived a large number of taboos about things that must not be eaten or drunk and prescribed for his followers a menu composed exclusively of cold water, dried vegetables and dead fish. This latter ordinance may surprise us, but the inhabitants of the sea, being cold-blooded animals, have always been regarded as less harmful to man's immortal soul than their warm-blooded brethren of the dry land, and the self-same people who would rather suffer death than eat a veal chop cheerfully consume quantities of fish and never feel a qualm of conscience.

Mani showed himself a true Oriental in his contempt for women. He forbade his disciples to marry and advocated the slow extinction of the human race.

As for baptism and the other ceremonies instituted originally by the Jewish sect of which John the Baptist had been the exponent, Mani regarded them all with horror and instead of being submerged in water, his candidates for holy orders were initiated by the laying on of hands.

At the age of twenty-five, this strange man undertook to explain his ideas unto all mankind. First he visited India and China where he was fairly successful. Then he turned homeward to bring the blessings of his creed to his own neighbors.

But the Persian priests who began to find themselves deprived of much secret revenue by the success of these unworldly doctrines turned against him and asked that he be killed. In the beginning, Mani enjoyed the protection of the king, but when this sovereign died and was succeeded by some one else who had no interest whatsoever in religious questions, Mani was surrendered to the priestly class. They took him to the walls of the town and crucified him and flayed his corpse and publicly exposed his skin before the city gate as an example to all those who might feel inclined to take an interest in the heresies of the Ecbatanian prophet.

By this violent conflict with the authorities, the Manichæan church itself was broken up. But little bits of the prophet's ideas, like so many spiritual meteors, were showered far and wide upon the landscape of Europe and Asia and for centuries afterwards continued to cause havoc among the simple and the poor who inadvertently had picked them up, had examined them and had found them singularly to their taste.

Exactly how and when Manichæism entered Europe, I do not know.

Most likely it came by way of Asia Minor, the Black Sea and the Danube. Then it crossed the Alps and soon enjoyed immense popularity in Germany and France. There the followers of the new creed called themselves by the Oriental name of the Cathari, or "the people who lead a pure life," and so widespread was the affliction that all over western Europe the word "Ketzer" or "Ketter" came to mean the same as "heretic."

But please don't think of the Cathari as members of a definite

religious denomination. No effort was made to establish a new
sect. The Manichæan ideas exercised great influence upon a
large number of people who would have stoutly denied that they
were anything but most devout sons of the Church. And that
made this particular form of heresy so dangerous and so difficult
of detection.

It is comparatively easy for the average doctor to diagnose
a disease caused by microbes of such gigantic structure that their
presence can be detected by the microscope of a provincial board-
of-health.

But Heaven protect us against the little creatures who can
maintain their incognito in the midst of an ultra-violet illumina-
tion, for they shall inherit the. earth.

Manichæism, from the point of view of the Church, was therefore the most.dangerous expression of all social epidemics and it
filled the higher authorities of that organization with a terror
not felt before the more common varieties of spiritual afflictions.

It was rarely mentioned above a whisper, but some of the
staunchest supporters of the early Christian faith had shown
unmistakable symptoms of the disease. Yea, great Saint
Augustine, that most brilliant and indefatigable warrior of the
Cross, who had done more than any one else to destroy the last
stronghold of heathenism, was said to have been at heart considerable of a Manichæan.

Priscillian, the Spanish bishop who was burned at the stake
in the year 385 and who gained the distinction of being the first
victim of the law against heretics, was accused of Manichæan
tendencies.

Even the heads of the Church seemed gradually to have fallen
under the spell of the abominable Persian doctrines.

They were beginning to discourage laymen from reading the
Old Testament and finally, during the twelfth century, promul-
gated that famous order by which all clergymen were henceforth
condemned to a state of celibacy. Not to forget the deep impression which these Persian ideals of abstinence were soon to make
upon one of the greatest leaders of spiritual reform, causing that
most lovable of men, good Francis of Assisi, to establish a new

monastic order of such strict Manichæan purity that it rightly earned him the title of the Buddha of the West.

But when these high and noble ideals of voluntary poverty and humility of soul began to filter down to the common people, at the very moment when the world was filled with the din of yet another war between emperor and pope, when foreign mercenaries, bearing the banners of the cross and the eagle, were fighting each other for the most valuable bits of territory along the Mediterranean shores, when hordes of crusaders were rushing home with the ill-gotten plunder they had taken from friend and enemy alike, when abbots lived in luxurious palaces and maintained a staff of courtiers, when priests galloped through the morning's mass that they might hurry to the hunting breakfast, then indeed something very unpleasant was bound to happen, and it did.

Little wonder that the first symptoms of open discontent with the state of the Church made themselves felt in that part of France where the old Roman tradition of culture had survived

THE PROVENCE

longest and where civilization had never been quite absorbed by barbarism.

You will find it on the map. It is called the Provence and consists of a small triangle situated between the Mediterranean, the Rhone and the Alps. Marseilles, a former colony of the Phœnicians, was and still is its most important harbor and it possessed no mean number of rich towns and villages. It had always been a very fertile land and it enjoyed an abundance of sunshine and rain.

While the rest of medieval Europe still listened to the barbaric deeds of hairy Teuton heroes, the troubadours, the poets of the Provence, had already invented that new form of literature which in time was to give birth to our modern novel. Furthermore, the close commerical relations of these Provençals with their neighbors, the Mahometans of Spain and Sicily, were making the people familiar with the latest publications in the field of science at a time when the number of such books in the northern part of Europe could be counted on the fingers of two hands.

In this country, the back-to-early-Christianity movement had begun to make itself manifest as early as the first decade of the eleventh century.

But there had not been anything which, however remotely, could be construed into open rebellion. Here and there in certain small villages certain people were beginning to hint that their priests might live as simply and as unostentatiously as their parishioners; who refused (oh, memory of the ancient martyrs!) to fight when their lords went forth to war; who tried to learn a little Latin that they might read and study the Gospels for themselves; who let it be known that they did not approve of capital punishment; who denied the existence of that Purgatory which six centuries after the death of Christ had been officially proclaimed as part of the Christian Heaven; and who (a most important detail) refused to surrender a tenth of their income to the Church.

Whenever possible the ring leaders of such rebellions against clerical authority were sought out and sometimes, if they were deaf to persuasion, they were discreetly put out of the way.

But the evil continued to spread and finally it was deemed necessary to call together a meeting of all the bishops of the Provence to discuss what measures should be taken to put a stop to this very dangerous and highly seditious agitation. They duly convened and continued their debates until the year 1056.

By that time it had been plainly shown that the ordinary forms of punishment and excommunication did not produce any noticeable results. The simple country folk who desired to lead a "pure life" were delighted whenever they were given a chance to demonstrate their principles of Christian charity and forgiveness behind the locked doors of a jail and if perchance they were condemned to death, they marched to the stake with the meekness of a lamb. Furthermore, as always happens in such cases, the place left vacant by a single martyr was immediately occupied by a dozen fresh candidates for holiness.

Almost an entire century was spent in the quarrels between the papal delegates who insisted upon more severe persecutions and the local nobility and clergy who (knowing the true nature of their subjects) refused to comply with the orders from Rome and protested that violence only encouraged the heretics to harden their souls against the voice of reason and therefore was a waste of both time and energy.

And then, late in the twelfth century, the movement received a fresh impetus from the north.

In the town of Lyons, connected with the Provence by way of the Rhone, there lived a merchant by the name of Peter Waldo. A very serious man, a good man, a most generous man, almost fanatically obsessed by his eagerness to follow the example of his Saviour. Jesus had taught that it was easier for a camel to pass through the eye of a needle than for a rich young man to enter the kingdom of Heaven. Thirty generations of Christians had tried to explain just what Jesus had actually meant when he uttered these words. Not so Peter Waldo. He read and he believed. He divided whatever he had among the poor, retired from business and refused to accumulate fresh wealth.

John had written, "Search ye the scriptures."

Twenty popes had commented upon this sentence and had carefully stipulated under what conditions it might perhaps be desirable for the laity to study the holy books directly and without the assistance of a priest.

Peter Waldo did not see it that way.

John had said, "Search ye the scriptures."

Very well. Then Peter Waldo would search.

And when he discovered that the things he found did not

PETER WALDO

tally with the conclusions of Saint Jerome, he translated the New Testament into his own language and spread copies of his manuscript throughout the good land of Provence.

At first his activities did not attract much attention. His enthusiasm for poverty did not seem dangerous. Most likely he could be persuaded to found some new and very ascetic monastic order for the benefit of those who wished to lead a life of real hardships and who complained that the existing monasteries were a bit too luxurious and too comfortable.

Rome had always been very clever at finding fitting outlets

for those people whose excess of faith might make them troublesome.

But all things must be done according to rule and precedent. And in that respect the "pure men" of the Provence and the "poor men" of Lyons were terrible failures. Not only did they neglect to inform their bishops of what they were doing, they even went further and boldly proclaimed the startling doctrine that one could be a perfectly good Christian without the assistance of a professional member of the priesthood and that the Bishop of Rome had no more right to tell people outside of his jurisdiction what to do and what to believe than the Grand Duke of Tartary or the Caliph of Bagdad.

The Church was placed before a terrible dilemma and truth compels me to state that she waited a long time before she finally decided to exterminate this heresy by force.

But an organization based upon the principle that there is only one right way of thinking and living and that all other ways are infamous and damnable is bound to take drastic measures whenever its authority is being openly questioned.

If it failed to do so it could not possibly hope to survive and this consideration at last compelled Rome to take definite action and devise a series of punishments that should put terror into the hearts of all future dissenters.

The Albigenses (the heretics were called after the city of Albi which was a hotbed of the new doctrine) and the Waldenses (who bore the name of their founder, Peter Waldo) living in countries without great political value and therefore not well able to defend themselves, were selected as the first of her victims.

The murder of a papal delegate who for several years had ruled the Provence as if it were so much conquered territory, gave Innocent III an excuse to interfere.

He preached a formal crusade against both the Albigenses and the Waldenses.

Those who for forty consecutive days would join the expedition against the heretics would be excused from paying interest on their debts; they would be absolved from all past and future sins and for the time being they would be exempted from the jurisdiction of the ordinary courts of law. This was a fair offer and it greatly appealed to the people of northern Europe.

Why should they bother about going all the way to Palestine when a campaign against the rich cities of the Provence offered the same spiritual and economic rewards as a trip to the Orient and when a man could gain an equal amount of glory in exchange for a much shorter term of service?

For the time being the Holy Land was forgotten and the worst elements among the nobility and gentry of northern France and southern England, of Austria, Saxony and Poland came rushing southward to escape the local sheriff and incidentally replenish their depleted coffers at the expense of the prosperous Provençals.

The number of men, women and children hanged, burned, drowned, decapitated and quartered by these gallant crusaders is variously given. I have not any idea how many thousands perished. Here and there, whenever a formal execution took place, we are provided with a few concrete figures, and these vary between two thousand and twenty thousand, according to the size of each town.

After the city of Béziers had been captured, the soldiers were in a quandary how to know who were heretics and who were not. They placed their problem before the papal delegate, who followed the army as a sort of spiritual adviser.

"My children," the good man answered, "go ahead and kill them all. The Lord will know his own people."

But it was an Englishman by the name of Simon de Montfort, a veteran of the real crusades, who distinguished himself most of all by the novelty and the ingenuity of his cruelties. In return for his valuable services, he afterwards received large tracts of land in the country which he had just pillaged and his subordinates were rewarded in proportion.

As for the few Waldenses who survived the massacre, they fled to the more inaccessible valleys of Piedmont and there maintained a church of their own until the days of the Reformation.

The Albigenses were less fortunate. After a century of flogging and hanging, their name disappears from the court reports

of the Inquisition.　But three centuries later, in a slightly modified form, their doctrines were to crop up again and, propagated
by a Saxon priest called Martin Luther, they were to cause that
reform which was to break the monopoly which the papal superstate had enjoyed for almost fifteen hundred years.

All that, of course, was hidden to the shrewd eyes of Innocent III.　As far as he was concerned, the difficulty was at an
end and the principle of absolute obedience had been trium-
phantly reasserted.　The famous command in Luke xiv: 23

THE LAST OF THE WALDENSIANS

where Christ tells how a certain man who wished to give a party,
finding that there still was room in his banqueting hall and that
several of the guests had remained away, had said unto his
servant, "Go out into the highways and compel them to come
in," had once more been fulfilled.

"They," the heretics, had been compelled to come in.

The problem how to make them stay in still faced the Church
and this was not solved until many years later.

Then, after many unsuccessful experiments with local tribunals, special courts of inquiry, such as had been used for the
first time during the Albigensian uprising, were instituted in the
different capitals of Europe.　They were given jurisdiction over
all cases of heresy and they came to be known simply as the
Inquisition.

Even to-day when the Inquisition has long since ceased to function, the mere name fills our hearts with a vague feeling of unrest. We have visions of dark dungeons in Havana, of torture chambers in Lisbon, of rusty cauldrons and branding irons in the museum of Cracow, of yellow hoods and black masks, of a king with a heavy lower jaw leering at an endless row of old men and women, slowly shuffling to the gibbet.

Several popular novels written during the latter half of the nineteenth century have undoubtedly had something to do with this impression of sinister brutality. Let us therefore deduct twenty-five per cent for the phantasy of our romantic scribes and another twenty-five for Protestant prejudice and we shall find that enough horror remains to justify those who claim that all secret tribunals are an insufferable evil and should never again be tolerated in a community of civilized people.

Henry Charles Lea has treated the subject of the Inquisition in eight ponderous volumes. I shall have to reduce these to two or three pages, and it will be quite impossible to give a concise account of one of the most complicated problems of medieval history within so short a space. For there never was an Inquisition as there is a Supreme Court or an International Court of Arbitration.

There were all sorts of Inquisitions in all sorts of countries and created for all sorts of purposes.

The best known of these was the Royal Inquisition of Spain and the Holy Inquisition of Rome. The former was a local affair which watched over the heretics in the Iberian peninsula and in the American colonies.

The latter had its ramifications all over Europe and burned Joan of Arc in the northern part of the continent as it burned Giordano Bruno in the southern.

It is true that the Inquisition, strictly speaking, never killed any one.

After sentence had been pronounced by the clerical judges, the convicted heretic was surrendered to the secular authorities. These could then do with him what they thought fit. But if they failed to pronounce the death penalty, they exposed themselves to a great deal of inconvenience and might even find themselves excommunicated or deprived of their support at the papal court. If, as sometimes happened, the prisoner escaped this fate and was not given over to the magistrates his sufferings only increased. For he then ran the risk of solitary confinement for the rest of his natural life in one of the inquisitorial prisons.

As death at the stake was preferable to the slow terror of going insane in a dark hole in a rocky castle, many prisoners confessed all sorts of crimes of which they were totally innocent that they might be found guilty of heresy and thus be put out of their misery.

It is not easy to write upon this subject without appearing to be hopelessly biased.

It seems incredible that for more than five centuries hundreds of thousands of harmless people in all parts of the world were overnight lifted from their beds at the mere whispered hearsay of some loquacious neighbors; that they were held for months or for years in filthy cells awaiting an opportunity to appear bebefore a judge whose name and qualifications were unknown to them; that they were never informed of the nature of the accusation that was brought against them; that they were not allowed to know the names of those who had acted as witnesses against them; that they were not permitted to communicate with their relatives or consult a lawyer; that if they continued to protest their innocence, they could be tortured until all the limbs of their body were broken; that other heretics could testify against them but were not listened to if they offered to tell something favorable of the accused; and finally that they could be sent to their death without the haziest notion as to the cause of their terrible fate.

It seems even more incredible that men and women who had been buried for fifty or sixty years could be dug out of their graves, could be found guilty "in absentia" and that the heirs of people who were condemned in this fashion could be deprived of their worldly possessions half a century after the death of the offending parties.

But such was the case and as the inquisitors depended for

MARTYRDOM

their maintenance upon a liberal share of all the goods that were confiscated, absurdities of this sort were by no means an uncommon occurrence and frequently the grandchildren were driven to beggary on account of something which their grandfather was supposed to have done two generations before.

Those of us who followed the newspapers twenty years ago when Czarist Russia was in the heyday of its power, remember the agent provocateur. As a rule the agent provocateur was a former burglar or a retired gambler with a winning personality and a "grievance." He let it be secretly known that his sorrow had made him join the revolution and in this way he often gained the confidence of those who were genuinely opposed to the imperial government. But as soon as he had learned the secrets of his new friends, he betrayed them to the police, pocketed the reward and went to the next city, there to repeat his vile practices.

During the thirteenth, fourteenth and fifteenth centuries, southern and western Europe was overrun by this nefarious tribe of private spies.

They made a living denouncing those who were supposed to have criticized the Church or who had expressed doubts upon certain points of doctrine.

If there were no heretics in the neighborhood, it was the business of such an agent provocateur to manufacture them.

As he could rest assured that torture would make his victims confess, no matter how innocent they might be, he ran no risks and could continue his trade ad infinitum.

In many countries a veritable reign of terror was introduced by this system of allowing anonymous people to denounce those whom they suspected of spiritual deficiencies. At last, no one dared trust his nearest and dearest friends. Members of the same family were forced to be on their guard against each other.

The mendicant friars who handled a great deal of the inquisitorial work made excellent use of the panic which their methods created and for almost two centuries they lived on the fat of the land.

Yes, it is safe to say that one of the main underlying causes of the Reformation was the disgust which a large number of people felt for those arrogant beggars who under a cloak of piety forced themselves into the homes of respectable citizens, who slept in the most comfortable beds, who partook of the best dishes, who insisted that they be treated as honored guests and who were able to maintain themselves in comfort by the mere threat that they would denounce their benefactors to the Inquisition if ever they were deprived of any of those luxuries which they had come to regard as their just due.

The Church of course could answer to all this that the Inquisition merely acted as a spiritual health officer whose sworn duty it was to prevent contagious errors from spreading among the masses. It could point to the leniency shown to all heathen who acted in ignorance and therefore could not be held responsible for their opinions. It could even claim that few people ever suffered the penalty of death unless they were apostates and were caught in a new offense after having forsworn their former errors.

But what of it?

The same trick by which an innocent man was changed into a desperate criminal could afterwards be used to place him in an apparent position of recantation.

The agent provocateur and the forger have ever been close friends.

And what are a few faked documents between spies?

Chapter VIII

THE CURIOUS ONES

MODERN intolerance, like ancient Gaul, is divided into three parts; the intolerance of laziness, the intolerance of ignorance and the intolerance of self-interest.

The first of these is perhaps the most general. It is to be met with in every country and among all classes of society. It is most common in small villages and old-established towns, and it is not restricted to human beings.

Our old family horse, having spent the first twenty-five years of his placid life in a warm stable in Coley Town, resents the equally warm barn of Westport for no other reason than that he has always lived in Coley Town, is familiar with every stick and stone in Coley Town and knows that no new and unfamiliar sights will frighten him on his daily ambles through that pleasant part of the Connecticut landscape.

Our scientific world has thus far spent so much time learning the defunct dialects of Polynesian islands that the language of dogs and cats and horses and donkeys has been sadly neglected. But could we know what Dude says to his former neighbors of Coley Town, we would hear an outburst of the most ferocious equine intolerance. For Dude is no longer young and therefore is "set" in his ways. His horsey habits were all formed years and years ago and therefore all the Coley Town manners, customs and habits seem right to him and all the Westport customs and manners and habits will be declared wrong until the end of his days.

It is this particular variety of intolerance which makes parents shake their heads over the foolish behavior of their children, which has caused the absurd myth of "the good old days"; which makes savages and civilized creatures wear uncomfortable clothes; which fills the world with a great deal of superfluous nonsense

140

and generally turns all people with a new idea into the supposed enemies of mankind.

Otherwise, however, this sort of intolerance is comparatively harmless.

We are all of us bound to suffer from it sooner or later. In ages past it has caused millions of people to leave home, and in this way it has been responsible for the permanent settlement of vast tracts of uninhabited land which otherwise would still be a wilderness.

The second variety is much more serious.

An ignorant man is by the very fact of his ignorance, a very dangerous person.

But when he tries to invent an excuse for his own lack of mental faculties, he becomes a holy terror. For then he erects within his soul a granite bulwark of self-righteousness and from the high pinnacle of this formidable fortress, he defies all his enemies (to wit, those who do not share his own prejudices) to show cause why they should be allowed to live.

People suffering from this particular affliction are both uncharitable and mean. Because they live constantly in a state of fear, they easily turn to cruelty and love to torture those against whom they have a grievance. It was among people of this ilk that the strange notion of a predilected group of a "chosen people" first took its origin. Furthermore, the victims of this delusion are forever trying to bolster up their own courage by an imaginary relationship which exists between themselves and the invisible Gods. This, of course, in order to give a flavor of spiritual approbation to their intolerance.

For instance, such citizens never say, "We are hanging Danny Deever because we consider him a menace to our own happiness, because we hate him with a thousand hates and because we just love to hang him." Oh, no! They get together in solemn conclave and deliberate for hours and for days and for weeks upon the fate of said Danny Deever. When finally sentence is read, poor Danny, who has perhaps committed some petty sort of larceny, stands solemnly convicted as a most terrible person who has dared to offend the Divine Will (as privately communicated

to the elect who alone can interpret such messages) and whose
execution therefore becomes a sacred duty, bringing great credit
upon the judges who have the courage to convict such an ally
of Satan.

That good-natured and otherwise kind-hearted people are
quite as apt to fall under the spell of this most fatal delusion
as their more brutal and blood-thirsty neighbors is a commonplace both of history and of psychology.

The crowds that gaped delightedly at the sad plight of a
thousand poor martyrs were most assuredly not composed of
criminals. They were decent, pious folk and they felt sure that
they were doing something very creditable and pleasing in the
sight of their own particular Divinity.

Had one spoken to them of tolerance, they would have rejected the idea as an ignoble confession of moral weakness.
Perhaps they were intolerant, but in that case they were proud
of the fact and with good right. For there, out in the cold
dampness of early morning, stood Danny Deever, clad in a
saffron colored shirt and in a pair of pantaloons adorned with
little devils, and he was going, going slowly but surely, to be
hanged in the Market Place. While they themselves, as soon as
the show was over, would return to a comfortable home and a
plentiful meal of bacon and beans.

Was not that in itself proof enough that they were acting
and thinking correctly?

Otherwise would they be among the spectators? Would not
the rôles be reversed?

A feeble argument, I confess, but a very common one and
hard to answer when people feel sincerely convinced that their
own ideas are the ideas of God and are unable to understand how
they could possibly be mistaken.

There remains as a third category the intolerance caused by
self-interest. This, of course, is really a variety of jealousy and
as common as the measles.

When Jesus came to Jerusalem, there to teach that the favor
of Almighty God could not be bought by the killing of a dozen
oxen or goats, all those who made a living from the ceremonial

sacrifices in the temple decried him as a dangerous revolutionist and caused him to be executed before he could do any lasting damage to their main source of income.

When Saint Paul, a few years later, came to Ephesus and there preached a new creed which threatened to interfere with the prosperity of the jewelers who derived great profit from the sale of little images of the local Goddess Diana, the Guild of the Goldsmiths almost lynched the unwelcome intruder.

And ever since there has been open warfare between those who depend for their livelihood upon some established form of worship and those whose ideas threaten to take the crowd away from one temple in favor of another.

When we attempt to discuss the intolerance of the Middle Ages, we must constantly remember that we have to deal with a very complicated problem. Only upon very rare occasions do we find ourselves confronted with only one manifestation of these three separate forms of intolerance. Most frequently we can discover traces of all three varieties in the cases of persecution which are brought to our attention.

That an organization, enjoying great wealth, administering thousands of square miles of land and owning hundreds of thousands of serfs, should have turned the full vigor of its anger against a group of peasants who had undertaken to reëstablish a simple and unpretentious Kingdom-of-Heaven-on-Earth was entirely natural.

And in that case, the extermination of heretics became a matter of economic necessity and belonged to class C, the intolerance of self-interest.

But when we begin to consider another group of men who were to feel the heavy hand of official disapprobation, the scientists, the problem becomes infinitely more complicated.

And in order to understand the perverse attitude of the Church authorities towards those who tried to reveal the secrets of nature, we must go back a good many centuries and study what had actually happened in Europe during the first six centuries of our era.

The invasion of the Barbarians had swept across the continent with the ruthless thoroughness of a flood. Here and there a few pieces of the old Roman fabric of state had remained standing erect amidst the wastes of the turbulent waters. But the society that had once dwelled within these walls had perished. Their books had been carried away by the waves. Their art lay forgotten in the deep mud of a new ignorance. Their collections, their museums, their laboratories, their slowly accumulated mass of scientific facts, all these had been used to stoke the camp-fires of uncouth savages from the heart of Asia.

We possess several catalogues of libraries of the tenth century. Of Greek books (outside of the city of Constantinople, then almost as far removed from central Europe as the Melbourne of to-day) the people of the west possessed hardly any. It seems incredible, but they had completely disappeared. A few translations (badly done) of a few chapters from the works of Aristotle and Plato were all the scholar of that time could find when he wanted to familiarize himself with the thoughts of the ancients. If he desired to learn their language, there was no one to teach it to him, unless a theological dispute in Byzantium had driven a handful of Greek monks from their customary habitats and had forced them to find a temporary asylum in France or Italy.

Latin books there were in great quantity, but most of those dated from the fourth and fifth centuries. The few manuscripts of the classics that survived had been copied so often and so indifferently that their contents were no longer understandable to any one who had not made a life study of paleography.

As for books of science, with the possible exception of some of the simplest problems of Euclid, they were no longer to be found in any of the available libraries and what was much more regrettable, they were no longer wanted.

For the people who now ruled the world regarded science with a hostile eye and discouraged all independent labor in the field of mathematics, biology and zoölogy, not to mention medicine and astronomy, which had descended to such a low state of neglect that they were no longer of the slightest practical value.

It is exceedingly difficult for a modern mind to understand such a state of affairs.

We men and women of the twentieth century, whether rightly or wrongly, profoundly believe in the idea of progress. Whether we ever shall be able to make this world perfect, we do not know. In the meantime we feel it to be our most sacred duty to try.

Yea, sometimes this faith in the unavoidable destiny of progress seems to have become the national religion of our entire country.

But the people of the Middle Ages did not and could not share such a view.

The Greek dream of a world filled with beautiful and interesting things had lasted such a lamentably short time! It had been so rudely disturbed by the political cataclysm that had over-

THE OLD WORLD ARISES ANEW

taken the unfortunate country that most Greek writers of the later centuries had been confirmed pessimists who, contemplating the ruins of their once happy fatherland, had become abject believers in the doctrine of the ultimate futility of all worldly endeavor.

The Roman authors, on the other hand, who could draw their conclusions from almost a thousand years of consecutive history, had discovered a certain upward trend in the development of the human race and their philosophers, notably the Epicureans, had cheerfully undertaken the task of educating the younger generation for a happier and better future.

Then came Christianity.

The center of interest was moved from this world to the other. Almost immediately people fell back into a deep and dark abyss of hopeless resignation.

Man was evil. He was evil by instinct and by preference. He was conceived in sin, born in sin, he lived in sin and he died repenting of his sins.

But there was a difference between the old despair and the new.

The Greeks were convinced (and perhaps rightly so) that they were more intelligent and better educated than their neighbors and they felt rather sorry for those unfortunate barbarians. But they never quite reached the point at which they began to consider themselves as a race that had been set apart from all others because it was the chosen people of Zeus.

Christianity on the other hand was never able to escape from its own antecedents. When the Christians adopted the Old Testament as one of the Holy Books of their own faith, they fell heir to the incredible Jewish doctrine that their race was "different" from all others and that only those who professed a belief in certain officially established doctrines could hope to be saved while the rest were doomed to perdition.

This idea was, of course, of enormous direct benefit to those who were lacking sufficiently in humility of spirit to believe themselves predilected favorites among millions and millions of their fellow creatures. During many highly critical years it had turned the Christians into a closely-knit, self-contained little community which floated unconcernedly upon a vast ocean of paganism.

What happened elsewhere on those waters that stretched far and wide towards the north and the south and the east and the west was a subject of the most profound indifference to Tertullian or St. Augustine, or any of those other early writers who were busily engaged in putting the ideas of their Church into the concrete form of written books. Eventually they hoped to reach a safe shore and there to build their city of God. Meanwhile, what those in other climes hoped to accomplish and to achieve was none of their concern.

Hence they created for themselves entirely new conceptions about the origin of man and about the limits of time and space. What the Egyptians and Babylonians and the Greeks and the Romans had discovered about these mysteries did not interest them in the least. They were sincerely convinced that all the old values had been destroyed with the birth of Christ.

THAT ROUND, ROUND WORLD

There was for example the problem of our earth.

The ancient scientists held it to be one among a couple of billion of other stars.

The Christians flatly rejected this idea. To them, the little round disk on which they lived was the heart and center of the universe.

It had been created for the special purpose of providing one particular group of people with a temporary home. The way in which this had been brought about was very simple and was fully described in the first chapter of Genesis.

When it became necessary to decide just how long this group of predilected people had been on this earth, the problem became a little more complicated. On all sides there were evidences of great antiquity, of buried cities, of extinct monsters and of fossilized plants. But these could be reasoned away or overlooked or denied or shouted out of existence. And after this had been done, it was a very simple matter to establish a fixed date for the beginning of time.

In a universe like that, a universe which was static, which had begun at a certain hour of a certain day in a certain year, and would end at another certain hour of a certain day in a certain year, which existed for the exclusive benefit of one and only one denomination, in such a universe there was no room for the prying curiosity of mathematicians and biologists and chemists and all sorts of other people who only cared for general principles and juggled with the idea of eternity and unlimitedness both in the field of time and in the realm of space.

True enough, many of those scientific people protested that at heart they were devout sons of the Church. But the true Christians knew better. No man, who was sincere in his protestations of love and devotion for the faith, had any business to know so much or to possess so many books.

One book was enough.

That book was the Bible, and every letter in it, every comma, every semicolon and exclamation point had been written down by people who were divinely inspired.

A Greek of the days of Pericles would have been slightly amused if he had been told of a supposedly holy volume which contained scraps of ill-digested national history, doubtful love poems, the inarticulate visions of half-demented prophets and whole chapters devoted to the foulest denunciation of those who for some reason or another were supposed to have incurred the displeasure of one of Asia's many tribal deities.

But the barbarian of the third century had a most humble respect for the "written word" which to him was one of the great

THE IRREFUTABLE ARGUMENT

mysteries of civilization, and when this particular book, by successive councils of his Church, was recommended to him as being without error, flaw or slip, he willingly enough accepted, this extraordinary document as the sum total of everything that man had ever known, or ever could hope to know, and joined in the denunciation and persecution of those who defied Heaven by extending their researches beyond the limits indicated by Moses and Isaiah.

The number of people willing to die for their principles has always been necessarily limited.

At the same time the thirst for knowledge on the part of certain people is so irrepressible that some outlet must be found for their pent up energy. As a result of this conflict between curiosity and repression there grew up that stunted and sterile intellectual sapling which came to be known as Scholasticism.

It dated back to the middle of the eighth century. It was then that Bertha, wife to Pépin the Short, king of the Franks, gave birth to a son who has better claims to be considered the patron saint of the French nation than that good King Louis who cost his countrymen a ransom of eight hundred thousand Turkish gold pieces and who rewarded his subjects' loyalty by giving them an inquisition of their own.

When the child was baptized it was given the name of Carolus, as you may see this very day at the bottom of many an ancient charter. The signature is a little clumsy. But Charles was never much of a hand at spelling. As a boy he learned to read Frankish and Latin, but when he took up writing, his fingers were so rheumatic from a life spent fighting the Russians and the Moors that he had to give up the attempt and hired the best scribes of his day to act as his secretaries and do his writing for him.

For this old frontiersman, who prided himself upon the fact that only twice within fifty years had he worn "city clothes" (the toga of a Roman nobleman), had a most genuine appreciation of the value of learning, and turned his court into a private university for the benefit of his own children and for the sons and daughters of his officials.

There, surrounded by the most famous men of his time, the new imperator of the west loved to spend his hours of leisure. And so great was his respect for academic democracy that he dropped all etiquette and as simple Brother David took an active share in the conversation and allowed himself to be contradicted by the humblest of his professors.

But when we come to examine the problems that interested this goodly company and the questions they discussed, we are reminded of the list of subjects chosen by the debating teams of a rural high school in Tennessee.

THE NEW INFALLIBILITY

They were very naïve, to say the least. And what was true in the year 800 held equally good for 1400. This was not the fault of the medieval scholar, whose brain was undoubtedly quite as good as that of his successors of the twentieth century. But he found himself in the position of a modern chemist or doctor who is given complete liberty of investigation, provided he does not say or do anything at variance with the chemical and medical information contained in the volumes of the first edition of the Encyclopedia Britannica of the year 1768 when chemistry was practically an unknown subject and surgery was closely akin to butchery.

As a result (I am mixing my metaphors anyway) the medieval scientist with his tremendous brain capacity and his very limited field of experimentation reminds one somewhat of a Rolls-Royce motor placed upon the chassis of a flivver. Whenever he stepped on the gas, he met with a thousand accidents. But when he played safe and drove his strange contraption according to the rules and regulations of the road he became slightly ridiculous and wasted a terrible lot of energy without getting anywhere in particular.

Of course the best among these men were desperate at the rate of speed which they were forced to observe.

They tried in every possible way to escape from the everlasting observation of the clerical policemen. They wrote ponderous volumes, trying to prove the exact opposite of what they held to be true, in order that they might give a hint of the things that were uppermost in their minds.

They surrounded themselves with all sorts of hocus pocus; they wore strange garments; they had stuffed crocodiles hanging from their ceilings; they displayed shelves full of bottled monsters and threw evil smelling herbs in the furnace that they might frighten their neighbors away from their front door and at the same time establish a reputation of being the sort of harmless lunatics who could be allowed to say whatever they liked without being held too closely responsible for their ideas. And gradually they developed such a thorough system of scientific camouflage that even to-day it is difficult for us to decide what they actually meant.

That the Protestants a few centuries later showed themselves quite as intolerant towards science and literature as the Church of the Middle Ages had done is quite true, but it is beside the point.

The great reformers could fulminate and anathematize to their hearts' content, but they were rarely able to turn their threats into positive acts of repression.

The Roman Church on the other hand not only possessed the power to crush its enemies but it made use of it, whenever the occasion presented itself.

The difference may seem trivial to those of us who like to indulge in abstract cogitations upon the theoretical values of tolerance and intolerance.

But it was a very real issue to those poor devils, who were placed before the choice of a public recantation or an equally public flogging.

And if they sometimes lacked the courage to say what they held to be true, and preferred to waste their time on cross-word

puzzles made up exclusively from the names of the animals mentioned in the Book of Revelation, let us not be too hard on
them.

I am quite certain that I never would have written the present
volume, six hundred years ago.

Chapter IX

THE WAR UPON THE PRINTED WORD

I FIND it increasingly difficult to write history. I am rather like a man who has been trained to be a fiddler and then at the age of thirty-five is suddenly given a piano and ordered to make his living as a virtuoso of the Klavier, because that too "is music." I learned my trade in one sort of a world and I must practice it in an entirely different one. I was taught to look upon all events of the past in the light of a definitely established order of things; a universe more or less competently managed by emperors and kings and arch-dukes and presidents, aided and abetted by congressmen and senators and secretaries of the treasury. Furthermore, in the days of my youth, the good Lord was still tacitly recognized as the ex-officio head of everything, and a personage who had to be treated with great respect and decorum.

Then came the war.

The old order of things was completely upset, emperors and kings were abolished, responsible ministers were superseded by irresponsible secret committees, and in many parts of the world, Heaven was formally closed by an order in council and a defunct economic hack-writer was officially proclaimed successor and heir to all the prophets of ancient times.

Of course all this will not last. But it will take civilization several centuries to catch up and by then I shall be dead.

Meanwhile I have to make the best of things, but it will not be easy.

Take the question of Russia. When I spent some time in that Holy Land, some twenty years ago, fully one quarter of the pages of the foreign papers that reached us were covered with a smeary black substance, known technically as "caviar." This stuff was rubbed upon those items which a careful government wished to hide from its loving subjects.

The world at large regarded this sort of supervision as an insufferable survival of the Dark Ages and we of the great republic of the west saved copies of the American comic papers, duly "caviared," to show the folks at home what backward barbarians those far famed Russians actually were.

Then came the great Russian revolution.

For the last seventy-five years the Russian revolutionist had howled that he was a poor, persecuted creature who enjoyed no "liberty" at all and as evidence thereof he had pointed to the strict supervision of all journals devoted to the cause of socialism. But in the year 1918, the under-dog turned upper-dog. And what happened? Did the victorious friends of freedom abolish censorship of the press? By no means. They padlocked all papers and magazines which did not comment favorably upon the acts of the new masters, they sent many unfortunate editors to Siberia or Archangel (not much to choose) and in general showed themselves a hundred times more intolerant than the much maligned ministers and police sergeants of the Little White Father.

It happens that I was brought up in a fairly liberal community, which heartily believed in the motto of Milton that the "liberty to know, to utter and to argue freely according to our own conscience, is the highest form of liberty."

"Came the war," as the movies have it, and I was to see the day when the Sermon on the Mount was declared to be a dangerous pro-German document which must not be allowed to circulate freely among a hundred million sovereign citizens and the publication of which would expose the editors and the printers to fines and imprisonment.

In view of all this it would really seem much wiser to drop the further study of history and to take up short story writing or real estate.

But this would be a confession of defeat. And so I shall stick to my job, trying to remember that in a well regulated state, every decent citizen is supposed to have the right to say and think and utter whatever he feels to be true, provided he does not interfere with the happiness and comfort of his neighbors, does not act against the good manners of polite society or break one of the rules of the local police.

This places me, of course, on record as an enemy of all official censorship. As far as I can see, the police ought to watch out for certain magazines and papers which are being printed for the purpose of turning pornography into private gain. But for the rest, I would let every one print whatever he liked.

I say this not as an idealist or a reformer, but as a practical person who hates wasted efforts, and is familiar with the history of the last five hundred years. That period shows clearly that violent methods of suppression of the printed or spoken word have never yet done the slightest good.

Nonsense, like dynamite, is only dangerous when it is contained in a small and hermetically closed space and subjected to a violent impact from without. A poor devil, full of half-baked economic notions, when left to himself will attract no more than a dozen curious listeners and as a rule will be laughed at for his pains.

The same creature handcuffed to a crude and illiterate sheriff, dragged to jail and condemned to thirty-five years of solitary confinement, will become an object of great pity and in the end will be regarded and honored as a martyr.

But it will be well to remember one thing.

There have been quite as many martyrs for bad causes as martyrs for good causes. They are tricky people and one never can tell what they will do next.

Hence I would say, let them talk and let them write. If they have anything to say that is good, we ought to know it, and if not, they will soon be forgotten. The Greeks seem to have felt that way, and the Romans did until the days of the Empire. But as soon as the commander-in-chief of the Roman armies had become an imperial and semi-divine personage, a second-cousin to Jupiter and a thousand miles removed from all ordinary mortals, this was changed.

The crime of "læsa majestas," the heinous offense of "offer-

SUPPRESSION

ing insult to his Majesty," was invented. It was a purely political misdemeanor and from the time of Augustus until the days of Justinian, many people were sent to prison because they had been a little too outspoken in their opinions about their rulers. But if one let the person of the emperor alone, there was practically no other subject of conversation which the Roman must avoid.

This happy condition came to an end when the world was brought under the domination of the Church. The line between good and bad, between orthodox and heretical, was definitely drawn before Jesus had been dead more than a few years. During the second half of the first century, the Apostle Paul spent quite a long time in the neighborhood of Ephesus in Asia Minor, a place famous for its amulets and charms. He went about preaching and casting out devils, and with such great success that he convinced many people of the error of their heathenish ways. As a token of repentance they came together one fine day with all their books of magic and burned more than ten thousand dollars worth of secret formulas, as you may read in the nineteenth chapter of the Acts of the Apostles.

This, however, was an entirely voluntary act on the part of a group of repentant sinners and it is not stated that Paul made an attempt to forbid the other Ephesians from reading or owning similar books.

Such a step was not taken until a century later.

Then, by order of a number of bishops convened in this same city of Ephesus, a book containing the life of St. Paul was condemned and the faithful were admonished not to read it.

During the next two hundred years, there was very little censorship. There also were very few books.

But after the Council of Nicæa (325) when the Christian Church had become the official church of the Empire, the supervision of the written word became part of the routine duty of the clergy. Some books were absolutely forbidden. Others were described as "dangerous" and the people were warned that they must read them at their own risk. Until authors found it more convenient to assure themselves of the approval of the authorities before they published their works and made it a rule to send their manuscripts to the local bishops for their approbation.

Even then, a writer could not always be sure that his works would be allowed to exist. A book which one Pope had pronounced harmless might be denounced as blasphemous and indecent by his successor.

On the whole, however, this method protected the scribes quite effectively against the risk of being burned together with their parchment offspring and the system worked well enough as long as books were copied by hand and it took five whole years to get out an edition of three volumes.

All this of course was changed by the famous invention of Johann Gutenberg, alias John Gooseflesh.

After the middle of the fifteenth century, an enterprising publisher was able to produce as many as four or five hundred copies in less than two weeks' time and in the short period between 1453 and 1500 the people of western and southern Europe were presented with not less than forty thousand different editions of books that had thus far been obtainable only in some of the better stocked libraries.

The Church regarded this unexpected increase in the number of available books with very serious misgivings. It was difficult enough to catch a single heretic with a single home-made copy of the Gospels. What then of twenty million heretics with twenty million copies of cleverly edited volumes? They became a direct menace to all idea of authority and it was deemed necessary to appoint a special tribunal to inspect all forthcoming publications at their source and say which could be published and which must never see the light of day.

Out of the different lists of books which from time to time were published by this committee as containing "forbidden knowledge" grew that famous Index which came to enjoy almost as nefarious a reputation as the Inquisition.

But it would be unfair to create the impression that such a supervision of the printing-press was something peculiar to the Catholic Church. Many states, frightened by the sudden avalanche of printed material that threatened to upset the peace of the realm, had already forced their local publishers to submit their wares to the public censor and had forbidden them to print anything that did not bear the official mark of approbation.

But nowhere, except in Rome, has the practice been continued until to-day. And even there it has been greatly modified since the middle of the sixteenth century. It had to be. The presses worked so fast and furiously that even that most industrious Commission of Cardinals, the so-called Congregation of the Index, which was supposed to inspect all printed works, was soon years behind in its task. Not to mention the flood of rag-pulp and printers-ink which was poured upon the landscape in the form of newspapers and magazines and tracts and which no group of men, however diligent, could hope to read, let alone inspect and classify, in less than a couple of thousand years.

THE BOOKLEGGER

But rarely has it been shown in a more convincing fashion how terribly this sort of intolerance avenges itself upon the rulers who force it upon their unfortunate subjects.

Already Tacitus, during the first century of the Roman Empire, had declared himself against the persecution of authors as "a foolish thing which tended to advertise books which otherwise would never attract any public attention."

The Index proved the truth of this statement. No sooner had the Reformation been successful than the list of forbidden books was promoted to a sort of handy guide for those who wished to keep themselves thoroughly informed upon the subject of current literature. More than that. During the seventeenth century, enterprising publishers in Germany and in the Low Countries maintained special agents in Rome whose business it was to get hold of advance copies of the Index Expurgatorius. As soon as they had obtained these, they entrusted them to special couriers who raced across the Alps and down the valley of the Rhine that the valuable information might be delivered to their patrons with the least possible loss of time. Then the German and the Dutch printing shops would set to work and would get out hastily printed special editions which were sold at an exorbitant profit and were smuggled into the forbidden territory by an army of professional bookleggers.

But the number of copies that could be carried across the frontier remained necessarily very small and in such countries as Italy and Spain and Portugal, where the Index was actually enforced until a short time ago, the results of this policy of repression became very noticeable.

If such nations gradually dropped behind in the race for progress, the reason was not difficult to find. Not only were the students in their universities deprived of all foreign text-books, but they were forced to use a domestic product of very inferior quality.

And worst of all, the Index discouraged people from occupying themselves seriously with literature or science. For no man in his senses would undertake to write a book when he ran the risk of seeing his work "corrected" to pieces by an incompetent censor or emendated beyond recognition by the inconsequential secretary of an Inquisitorial Board of Investigators.

Instead, he went fishing or wasted his time playing dominoes in a wine-shop.

Or he sat down and in sheer despair of himself and his people, he wrote the story of Don Quixote.

Chapter X

CONCERNING THE WRITING OF HISTORY IN GENERAL AND THIS BOOK IN PARTICULAR

In the correspondence of Erasmus, which I recommend most eagerly to those who are tired of modern fiction, there occurs a stereotype sort of warning in many of the letters sent unto the learned Desiderius by his more timid friends.

"I hear that you are thinking of a pamphlet upon the Lutheran controversy," writes Magister X. "Please be very careful how you handle it, because you might easily offend the Pope, who wishes you well."

Or again: "Some one who has just returned from Cambridge tells me that you are about to publish a book of short essays. For Heaven's sake, do not incur the displeasure of the Emperor, who might be in a position to do you great harm."

Now it is the Bishop of Louvain, then the King of England or the faculty of the Sorbonne or that terrible professor of theology in Cambridge who must be treated with special consideration, lest the author be deprived of his income or lose the necessary official protection or fall into the clutches of the Inquisition or be broken on the wheel.

Nowadays the wheel (except for purposes of locomotion) is relegated to the museum of antiquities. The Inquisition has closed its doors these hundred years, protection is of little practical use in a career devoted to literature and the word "income" is hardly ever mentioned where historians come together.

But all the same, as soon as it was whispered that I intended to write a "History of Tolerance," a different sort of letters of admonition and advice began to find their way to my cloistered cell.

"Harvard has refused to admit a negro to her dormitories,"

writes the secretary of the S.P.C.C.P. "Be sure that you mention this most regrettable fact in your forthcoming book."

Or again: "The local K.K.K. in Framingham, Mass., has started to boycott a grocer who is a professed Roman Catholic. You will want to say something about this in your story of tolerance."

And so on.

No doubt all these occurrences are very stupid, very silly and altogether reprehensible. But they hardly seem to come within the jurisdiction of a volume on tolerance. They are merely manifestations of bad manners and a lack of decent public spirit. They are very different from that official form of intolerance which used to be incorporated into the laws of the Church and the State and which made persecution a holy duty on the part of all good citizens.

History, as Bagehot has said, ought to be like an etching by Rembrandt. It must cast a vivid light upon certain selected causes, on those which are best and most important, and leave all the rest in the shadow and unseen.

Even in the midst of the most idiotic outbreaks of the modern spirit of intolerance which are so faithfully chronicled in our news sheets, it is possible to discern signs of a more hopeful future.

For nowadays many things which previous generations would have accepted as self-evident and which would have been passed by with the remark that "it has always been that way," are cause for serious debate. Quite often our neighbors rush to the defense of ideas which would have been regarded as preposterously visionary and unpractical by our fathers and our grandfathers and not infrequently they are successful in their warfare upon some particularly obnoxious demonstration of the mob spirit.

This book must be kept very short.

I can't bother about the private snobbishness of successful pawn-brokers, the somewhat frayed glory of Nordic supremacy, the dark ignorance of backwoods evangelists, the bigotry of peasant priests or Balkan rabbis. These good people and their bad ideas have always been with us.

But as long as they do not enjoy the official support of the State, they are comparatively harmless and in most civilized countries such a possibility is entirely precluded.

Private intolerance is a nuisance which can cause more discomfort in any given community than the combined efforts of measles, smallpox and a gossiping woman. But private intolerance does not possess executioners of its own. If, as sometimes happens in this and other countries, it assumes the rôle of the hangman, it places itself outside the law and becomes a proper subject for police supervision.

Private intolerance does not dispose of jails and cannot prescribe to an entire nation what it shall think and say and eat and drink. If it tries to do this, it creates such terrific resentment among all decent folk, that the new ordinance becomes a dead letter and cannot be carried out even in the District of Columbia.

In short, private intolerance can go only as far as the indifference of the majority of the citizens of a free country will allow it to go, and no further. Whereas official intolerance is practically almighty.

It recognizes no authority beyond its own power.

It provides no mode of redress for the innocent victims of its meddlesome fury. It will listen to no argument. And ever again it backs up its decisions by an appeal to the Divine Being and then undertakes to explain the will of Heaven as if the key to the mysteries of existence were an exclusive possession of those who had been successful at the most recent elections.

If in this book the word intolerance is invariably used in the sense of official intolerance, and if I pay little attention to the private variety, have patience with me.

I can only do one thing at a time.

Chapter XI

RENAISSANCE

THERE is a learned cartoonist in our land who takes pleasure in asking himself, what do billiard-balls and cross-word puzzles and bull-fiddles and boiled shirts and door-mats think of this world?

But what I would like to know is the exact psychological reaction of the men who are ordered to handle the big modern siege guns. During the war a great many people performed a great many strange tasks, but was there ever a more absurd job than firing dicke Berthas?

All other soldiers knew more or less what they were doing.

A flying man could judge by the rapidly spreading red glow whether he had hit the gas factory or not.

The submarine commander could return after a couple of hours to judge by the abundance of flotsam in how far he had been successful.

The poor devil in his dug-out had the satisfaction of realizing that by his mere continued presence in a particular trench he was at least holding his own.

Even the artillerist, working his field-piece upon an invisible object, could take down the telephone and could ask his colleague, hidden in a dead tree seven miles away, whether the doomed church tower was showing signs of deterioration or whether he should try again at a different angle.

But the brotherhood of the big guns lived in a strange and unreal world of their own. Even with the assistance of a couple of full-fledged professors of ballistics, they were unable to foretell what fate awaited those projectiles which they shot so blithely into space. Their shells might actually hit the object for which they were destined. They might land in the midst of a powder factory or in the heart of a fortress. But then again they might strike a church or an orphan asylum or they might bury themselves peacefully in a river or in a gravel pit without doing any harm whatsoever.

Authors, it seems to me, have much in common with the siege-gunners. They too handle a sort of heavy artillery. Their literary missiles may start a revolution or a conflagration in the most unlikely spots. But more often they are just poor duds and lie harmless in a nearby field until they are used for scrap iron or converted into an umbrella-stand or a flower pot.

Surely there never was a period in history when so much rag-pulp was consumed within so short a space as the era commonly known as the Renaissance.

Every Tomasso, Ricardo and Enrico of the Italian peninsula, every Doctor Thomasius, Professor Ricardus and Dominus Heinrich of the great Teuton plain rushed into print with at least a dozen duodecimos. Not to mention the Tomassinos who wrote pretty little sonnets in imitation of the Greeks, the Ricardinos who reeled off odes after the best pattern of their Roman grandfathers, and the countless lovers of coins, statuary, images, pictures, manuscripts and ancient armor who for almost three centuries kept themselves busy classifying, ordering, tabulating, listing, filing and codifying what they had just dug out of the ancestral ruins and who then published their collections in countless folios illuminated with the most beautiful of copper engravings and the most ponderous of wood-cuts.

This great intellectual curiosity was very lucrative for the Frobens and the Alduses and the Etiennes and the other new firms of printers who were making a fortune out of the invention which had ruined Gutenberg, but otherwise the literary output of the Renaissance did not very greatly affect the state of that world in which the authors of the fifteenth and sixteenth centuries happened to find themselves. The distinction of having contributed something new was restricted to only a very few heroes of the quill and they were like our friends of the big guns. They rarely discovered during their own lifetime in how far they had been successful and how much damage their writings had actually done. But first and last they managed to demolish a great many of the obstacles which stood in the way of progress. And they deserve our everlasting gratitude for the thoroughness with which they cleaned up a lot of rubbish which otherwise would continue to clutter our intellectual front yard.

Strictly speaking, however, the Renaissance was not primarily a forward-looking movement. It turned its back in disgust upon the recent past, called the works of its immediate predecessors "barbaric" (or "Gothic" in the language of the country where the Goths had enjoyed the same reputation as the Huns), and concentrated its main interest upon those arts which seem to be pervaded with that curious substance known as the "classical spirit."

If nevertheless the Renaissance struck a mighty blow for the liberty of conscience and for tolerance and for a better world in general, it was done in spite of the men who were considered the leaders of the new movement.

Long before the days of which we are now speaking, there had been people who had questioned the rights of a Roman bishop to dictate to Bohemian peasants and to English yeomen in what language they should say their prayers, in what spirit they should study the words of Jesus, how much they should pay for an indulgence, what books they should read and how they should bring up their children. And all of them had been crushed by the strength of that superstate, the power of which they had undertaken to defy. Even when they had acted as champions and representatives of a national cause, they had failed.

The smoldering ashes of great John Huss, thrown ignominiously into the river Rhine, were a warning to all the world that the Papal Monarchy still ruled supreme.

The corpse of Wycliffe, burned by the public executioner, told the humble peasants of Leicestershire that councils and Popes could reach beyond the grave.

Frontal attacks, evidently, were impossible.

The mighty fortress of tradition, builded slowly and carefully during fifteen centuries of unlimited power, could not be taken by assault. The scandals which had taken place within these hallowed enclosures; the wars between three rival Popes, each claiming to be the legitimate and exclusive heir to the chair of Holy Peter; the utter corruption of the courts of Rome and Avignon, where laws were made for the purpose of being broken by those who were willing to pay for such favors; the utter demoralization of monastic life; the venality of those who used the recently increased horrors of purgatory as an excuse to blackmail poor parents into paying large sums of money for the benefit of their dead children; all these things, although widely known, never really threatened the safety of the Church.

But the chance shots fired at random by certain men and women who were not at all interested in ecclesiastical matters, who had no particular grievance against either pope cr bishop, these caused the damage which finally made the old edifice collapse.

What the "thin, pale man" from Prague had failed to accomplish with his high ideals of Christian virtue was brought about by a motley crowd of private citizens who had no other ambition than to live and die (preferably at a ripe old age) as loyal patrons of all the good things of this world and faithful sons of the Mother Church.

They came from all the seven corners of Europe. They represented every sort of profession and they would have been very angry had an historian told them what they were doing.

For instance, take the case of Marco Polo.

We know him as a mighty traveler, a man who had seen such wondrous sights that his neighbors, accustomed to the smaller scale of their western cities, called him "Million Dollar Marc" and laughed uproariously when he told them of golden thrones as high as a tower and of granite walls that would stretch all the way from the Baltic to the Black Sea.

All the same, the shriveled little fellow played a most important rôle in the history of progress. He was not much of a writer. He shared the prejudice of his class and his age against the literary profession. A gentleman (even a Venetian gentleman who was supposed to be familiar with double-entry bookkeeping) handled a sword and not a goose-quill. Hence the unwillingness of Messire Marco to turn author. But the fortunes of war carried him into a Genoese prison. And there, to while away the tedious hours of his confinement, he told a poor scribbler, who happened to share his cell, the strange story of his life. In this roundabout way the people of Europe learned many things about this world which they had never known before. For although Polo was a simple-minded fellow who firmly believed that one of the mountains he had seen in Asia Minor had been moved a couple of miles by a pious saint who wanted to show the heathen "what true faith could do," and who swallowed all the stories about people without heads and chickens with three legs which were so popular in his day, his report did more to upset the geographical theories of the Church than anything that had appeared during the previous twelve hundred years.

Polo, of course, lived and died a faithful son of the Church. He would have been terribly upset if any one had compared him with his near-contemporary, the famous Roger Bacon, who was an out and out scientist and paid for his intellectual curiosity with ten years of enforced literary idleness and fourteen years of prison.

And yet of the two he was by far the more dangerous.

For whereas only one person in a hundred thousand could follow Bacon when he went chasing rainbows, and spun those fine evolutionary theories which threatened to upset all the ideas held sacred in his own time, every citizen who had been taught his ABC's could learn from Polo that the world was full of a number of things the existence of which the authors of the Old Testament had never even suspected.

I do not mean to imply that the publication of a single book caused that rebellion against Scriptural authority which was to occur before the world could gain a modicum of freedom. Popular enlightenment is ever the result of centuries of painstaking preparation. But the plain and straightforward accounts of the explorers and the navigators and the travelers, understandable to all the people, did a great deal to bring about that spirit of skepticism which characterizes the latter half of the Renaissance and which allowed people to say and write things which only a few years before would have brought them into contact with the agents of the Inquisition.

Take that strange story to which the friends of Boccaccio listened on the first day of their agreeable exile from Florence. All religious systems, so it told, were probably equally true and equally false. But if this were true, and they were all equally true and false, then how could people be condemned to the gallows for ideas which could neither be proven nor contradicted?

Read the even stranger adventures of a famous scholar like Lorenzo Valla. He died as a highly respectable member of the government of the Roman Church. Yet in the pursuit of his Latin studies he had incontrovertibly proven that the famous donation of "Rome and Italy and all the provinces of the West," which Constantine the Great was supposed to have made to Pope Sylvester (and upon which the Popes had ever since based their claims to be regarded as superlords of all Europe), was nothing but a clumsy fraud, perpetrated hundreds of years after the death of the Emperor by an obscure official of the papal chancery.

Or to return to more practical questions, what were faithful Christians, carefully reared in the ideas of Saint Augustine, who had taught that a belief in the presence of people on the other side of the earth was both blasphemous and heretical, since such poor creatures would not be able to see the second coming of Christ and therefore had no reason to exist, what indeed were the good people of the year 1499 to think of this doctrine when Vasco da Gama returned from his first voyage to the Indies and described the populous kingdoms which he had found on the other side of this planet?

What were these same simple folk, who had always been told that our world was a flat dial and that Jerusalem was the center of the universe, what were they to believe when the little "Vittoria" returned from her voyage around the globe and when the geography of the Old Testament was shown to contain some rather serious errors?

I repeat what I have said before. The Renaissance was not an era of conscious scientific endeavor. In spiritual matters it often showed a most regrettable lack of real interest. Everything during these three hundred years was dominated by a desire for beauty and entertainment. Even the Popes, who fulminated loudest against the iniquitous doctrines of some of their subjects, were only too happy to invite those self-same rebels for dinner if they happened to be good conversationalists and knew something about printing or architecture. And eager zealots for virtue, like Savonarola, ran quite as great a risk of losing their lives as the bright young agnostics who in poetry and prose attacked the fundaments of the Christian faith with a great deal more violence than good taste.

But throughout all these manifestations of a new interest in the business of living, there undoubtedly ran a severe undercurrent of discontent with the existing order of society and the restrictions put upon the development of human reason by the claims of an all-powerful Church.

Between the days of Boccaccio and those of Erasmus, there is an interval of almost two centuries. During these two centuries, the copyist and the printer never enjoyed an idle moment. And outside of the books published by the Church herself, it would be difficult to find an important piece of work which did not contain some indirect reference to the sad plight into which the world had fallen when the ancient civilizations of Greece and Rome had been superseded by the anarchy of the barbarian invaders and western society was placed under the tutelage of ignorant monks.

The contemporaries of Machiavelli and Lorenzo de' Medici were not particularly interested in ethics. They were practical men who made the best of a practical world. Outwardly they remained at peace with the Church because it was a powerful and far-reaching organization which was capable of doing them great harm and they never consciously took part in any of the several attempts at reform or questioned the institutions under which they lived.

But their insatiable curiosity concerning old facts, their continual search after new emotions, the very instability of their restless minds, caused a world which had been brought up in the conviction "We know" to ask the question "Do we really know?"

And that is a greater claim to the gratitude of all future generations than the collected sonnets of Petrarch or the assembled works of Raffael.

Chapter XII

THE REFORMATION

MODERN psychology has taught us several useful things about ourselves. One of them is the fact that we rarely do anything actuated by one single motive. Whether we give a million dollars for a new university or refuse a nickel to a hungry tramp; whether we proclaim that the true life of intellectual freedom can only be lived abroad or vow that we will never again leave the shores of America; whether we insist upon calling black white or white black, there are always a number of divergent reasons which have caused us to make our decision, and way down deep in our hearts we know this to be true. But as we would cut a sorry figure with the world in general if we should ever dare to be quite honest with ourselves or our neighbors, we instinctively choose the most respectable and deserving among our many motives, brush it up a bit for public consumption and then expose it for all the world to behold as "the reason why we did so and so."

But whereas it has been repeatedly demonstrated that it is quite possible to fool most of the people most of the time, no one has as yet discovered a method by which the average individual can fool himself for more than a few minutes.

We are all of us familiar with this most embarrassing truth and therefore ever since the beginning of civilization people have tacitly agreed with each other that this should never under any circumstances be referred to in public.

What we think in private, that is our own business. As long as we maintain an outward air of respectability, we are perfectly satisfied with ourselves and merrily act upon the principle "You believe my fibs and I will believe yours."

Nature, which has no manners, is the one great exception to this generous rule of conduct. As a result, nature is rarely allowed to enter the sacred portals of civilized society. And as history thus far has been a pastime of the few, the poor muse known as Clio has led a very dull life, especially when we compare it to the career of many of her less respectable sisters who have been allowed to dance and sing and have been invited to every party ever since the beginning of time. This of course has been a source of great annoyance to poor Clio and repeatedly in her own subtle way she has managed to get her revenge.

A perfectly human trait, this, but a very dangerous one and ofttimes very expensive in the matter of human lives and property.

For whenever the old lady undertakes to show us that systematic lying, continued during the course of centuries, will eventually play hob with the peace and happiness of the entire world, our planet is at once enveloped in the smoke of a thousand batteries. Regiments of cavalry begin to dash hither and yon and interminable rows of foot soldiers commence to crawl slowly across the landscape. And ere all these people have been safely returned to their respective homes or cemeteries, whole countries have been laid bare and innumerable exchequers have been drained down to the last kopek.

Very slowly, as I have said before, it is beginning to dawn upon the members of our guild that history is a science as well as an art and is therefore subject to certain of the immutable laws of nature which thus far have only been respected in chemical laboratories and astronomical observatories. And as a result we are now doing some very useful scientific house-cleaning which will be of inestimable benefit to all coming generations.

Which brings me at last to the subject mentioned at the head of this chapter, to wit: the Reformation.

Until not so very long ago there were only two opinions regarding this great social and spiritual upheaval. It was either wholly good or wholly bad.

According to the adherents of the former opinion it had been the result of a sudden outbreak of religious zeal on the part of a number of noble theologians who, profoundly shocked by the wickedness and the venality of the papal superstate, had established a separate church of their own where the true faith was to be henceforward taught to those who were seriously trying to be true Christians.

Those who had remained faithful to Rome were less enthusiastic.

The Reformation, according to the scholars from beyond the Alps, was the result of a damnable and most reprehensible conspiracy on the part of a number of despicable princes who wanted to get unmarried and who besides hoped to acquire the possessions which had formerly belonged to their Holy Mother the Church.

As usual, both sides were right and both sides were wrong.

The Reformation was the work of all sorts of people with all sorts of motives. And it is only within very recent times that we have begun to realize how religious discontent played only a minor rôle in this great upheaval and that it was really an unavoidable social and economic revolution with a slightly theological background.

Of course it is much easier to teach our children that good Prince Philip was a very enlightened ruler who took a profound personal interest in the reformed doctrines, than to explain to them the complicated machinations of an unscrupulous politician who willingly accepted the help of the infidel Turks in his warfare upon other Christians. In consequence whereof we Protestants have for hundreds of years made a magnanimous hero out of an ambitious young landgrave who hoped to see the house of Hesse play the rôle thus far played by the rival house of Hapsburg.

On the other hand it is so much simpler to turn Pope Clement into a loving shepherd who wasted the last remnants of his declining strength trying to prevent his flocks from following false leaders, than to depict him as a typical prince of the house of Medici who regarded the Reformation as an unseemly brawl of drunken German monks and used the power of the Church to further the interests of his own Italian fatherland, that we need feel no surprise if such a fabulous figure smiles at us from the pages of most Catholic text-books.

But while that sort of history may be necessary in Europe, we fortunate settlers in a new world are under no obligation to persist in the errors of our Continental ancestors and are at liberty to draw a few conclusions of our own.

Just because Philip of Hesse, the great friend and supporter of Luther, was a man dominated by an enormous political ambition, it does not necessarily follow that he was insincere in his religious convictions.

By no means.

When he put his name to the famous "Protest" of the year 1529, he knew as well as his fellow signers that they were about to "expose themselves to the violence of a terrible storm," and might end their lives on the scaffold. If he had not been a man of extraordinary courage, he would never have undertaken to play the rôle he actually played.

But the point I am trying to make is this: that it is exceedingly difficult, yes, almost impossible, to judge an historical character (or for that matter, any of our immediate neighbors) without a profound knowledge of all the many motives which have inspired him to do what he has done or forced him to omit doing what he has omitted to do.

The French have a proverb that "to know everything is to forgive everything." That seems too easy a solution. I would like to offer an amendment and change it as follows: "To know everything is to understand everything." We can leave the business of pardoning to the good Lord who ages ago reserved that right to himself.

Meanwhile we ourselves can humbly try to "understand" and that is more than enough for our limited human ability.

And now let me return to the Reformation, which started me upon this slight detour.

As far as I "understand" that movement, it was primarily a manifestation of a new spirit which had been born as a result of the economic and political development of the last three centuries and which came to be known as "nationalism" and which therefore was the sworn enemy of that foreign superstate into

THE PROTEST

which all European countries had been forced during the course of the last five centuries.

Without the common denominator of some such grievance, it would never have been possible to unite Germans and Finns and Danes and Swedes and Frenchmen and Englishmen and Norsemen into a single cohesive party, strong enough to batter down the walls of the prison in which they had been held for such a long time.

If all these heterogeneous and mutually envious elements had not been temporarily bound together by one great ideal, far surpassing their own private grudges and aspirations, the Reformation could never have succeeded.

It would have degenerated into a series of small local uprisings, easily suppressed by a regiment of mercenaries and half a dozen energetic inquisitors.

The leaders would have suffered the fate of Huss. Their followers would have been killed as the little groups of Waldenses and Albigenses had been slaughtered before them. And the Papal Monarchy would have scored another easy triumph, followed by an era of Schrecklichkeit among those guilty of a "breach of discipline."

Even so, the great movement for reform only succeeded by the smallest of all possible margins. And as soon as the victory had been won and the menace which had threatened the existence of all the rebels had been removed, the Protestant camp was dissolved into an infinitesimal number of small hostile groups who tried on a greatly diminished scale to repeat all the errors of which their enemies had been guilty in the heyday of their power.

A French abbé (whose name I have unfortunately forgotten, but a very wise fellow) once said that we must learn to love humanity in spite of itself.

To look back from the safe distance of almost four centuries upon this era of great hope and even greater disappointment, to think of the sublime courage of so many men and women who wasted their lives on the scaffold and on the field of battle for an ideal that was never to be realized, to contemplate the sacrifice made by millions of obscure citizens for the things they held to be holy and then to remember the utter failure of the Protestant rebellion as a movement towards a more liberal and more intelligent world, is to put one's charity to a most severe test.

For Protestantism, if the truth must be told, took away from this world many things that were good and noble and beautiful and it added a great many others that were narrow and hateful and graceless. And instead of making the history of the human race simpler and more harmonious, it made it more complicated and less orderly. All that, however, was not so much the fault of the Reformation as of certain inherent weaknesses in the mental habits of most people.

They refuse to be hurried.

They cannot possibly keep up with the pace set by their leaders.

They are not lacking in good will. Eventually they will all cross the bridge that leads into the newly discovered territory. But they will do so in their own good time and bringing with them as much of the ancestral furniture as they can possibly carry.

As a result the Great Reform, which was to establish an entirely new relationship between the individual Christian and his God, which was to do away with all the prejudices and all the corruptions of a bygone era, became so thoroughly cluttered up with the medieval baggage of its trusted followers that it could move neither forward nor backward and soon looked for all the world like a replica of that papal establishment which it held in such great abhorrence.

For that is the great tragedy of the Protestant rebellion. It could not rise above the mean average of intelligence of the majority of its adherents.

And as a result the people of western and northern Europe did not progress as much as might have been expected.

Instead of a man who was supposed to be infallible, the Reformation gave the world a book which was held to be infallible.

Instead of one potentate who ruled supreme, there arose a

thousand and one little potentates, each one of whom in his own way tried to rule supreme.

Instead of dividing all Christendom into two well defined halves, the ins and the outs, the faithful and the heretics, it created endless little groups of dissenters who had nothing in common but a most intense hatred for all those who failed to share their own opinions. Instead of establishing a reign of tolerance, it followed the example of the early Church and as

THE UNIVERSAL PRISON

soon as it had attained power and was firmly entrenched behind numberless catechisms, creeds and confessions, it declared bitter warfare upon those who dared to disagree with the officially established doctrines of the community in which they happened to live.

All this was, no doubt, most regrettable.

But it was unavoidable in view of the mental development of the sixteenth and seventeenth centuries.

To describe the courage of leaders like Luther and Calvin, there exists only one word, and rather a terrible word, "colossal."

A simple Dominican monk, a professor in a little tidewater college somewhere in the backwoods of the German hinterland, who boldly burns a Papal Bull and hammers his own rebellious opinions to the door of a church; a sickly French scholar who turns a small Swiss town into a fortress which successfully defies the whole power of the papacy; such men present us with examples of fortitude so unique that the modern world can offer no adequate comparison.

That these bold rebels soon found friends and supporters, friends with a purpose of their own and supporters who hoped to fish successfully in troubled waters, all this is neither here nor there.

When these men began to gamble with their lives for the sake of their conscience, they could not foresee that this would happen and that most of the nations of the north would eventually enlist under their banners.

But once they had been thrown into this maelstrom of their own making, they were obliged to go whither the current carried them.

Soon the mere question of keeping themselves above water took all of their strength. In far-away Rome the Pope had at last learned that this contemptible disturbance was something more serious than a personal quarrel between a few Dominican and Augustinian friars, and an intrigue on the part of a former French chaplain. To the great joy of his many creditors, he temporarily ceased building his pet cathedral and called together a council of war. The papal bulls and excommunications flew fast and furiously. Imperial armies began to move. And the leaders of the rebellion, with their backs against the wall, were forced to stand and fight.

It was not the first time in history that great men in the midst of a desperate conflict lost their sense of proportion. The same Luther who at one time proclaims that it is "against the Holy Spirit to burn heretics," a few years later goes into such a tantrum of hate when he thinks of the wickedness of those Germans and Dutchmen who have a leaning towards the ideas of the Anabaptists, that he seems to have lost his reason.

The intrepid reformer who begins his career by insisting that we must not force our own system of logic upon God, ends his days by burning an opponent whose power of reasoning was undoubtedly superior to his own.

The heretic of to-day becomes the arch-enemy of all dissenters of to-morrow.

And with all their talk of a new era in which the dawn has at last followed upon the dark, both Calvin and Luther remained faithful sons of the Middle Ages as long as they lived.

Tolerance did not and could not possibly show itself to them in the light of a virtue. As long as they themselves were outcasts, they were willing to invoke the divine right of freedom of conscience that they might use it as an argument against their enemies. Once the battle was won, this trusted weapon was carefully deposited in a corner of the Protestant junk-room, already cluttered with so many other good intentions that had been discarded as unpractical. There it lay, forgotten and neglected, until a great many years later, when it was discovered behind a trunk full of old sermons. But the people who picked it up, scraped off the rust and once more carried it into battle were of a different nature from those who had fought the good fight in the early days of the sixteenth century.

And yet, the Protestant revolution contributed greatly to the cause of tolerance. Not through what it accomplished directly. In that field the gain was small indeed. But indirectly the results of the Reformation were all on the side of progress.

In the first place, it made people familiar with the Bible. The Church had never positively forbidden people to read the Bible, but neither had it encouraged the study of the sacred book by ordinary laymen. Now at last every honest baker and candlestick maker could own a copy of the holy work; could peruse it in the privacy of his workshop and could draw his own conclusions without running the risk of being burned at the stake.

Familiarity is apt to kill those sentiments of awe and fear which we feel before the mysteries of the unknown. During the first two hundred years which followed immediately upon the Reformation, pious Protestants believed everything they read in the Old Testament from Balaam's ass to Jonah's whale. And those who dared to question a single comma (the "inspired" vowel-points of learned Abraham Colovius!) knew better than to let their skeptical tittering be heard by the community at large. Not because they were afraid any longer of the Inquisition, but Protestant pastors could upon occasion make a man's life exceedingly unpleasant and the economic consequences of a public ministerial censure were often very serious, not to say disastrous.

TWO PRISONS FOR ONE

Gradually, however, this eternally repeated study of a book which was really the national history of a small nation of shepherds and traders was to bear results which Luther and Calvin and the other reformers had never foreseen.

If they had, I am certain they would have shared the Church's dislike of Hebrew and Greek and would have kept the Scriptures carefully out of the hands of the uninitiated. For in the end, an increasing number of serious students began to appreciate the Old Testament as a singularly interesting book, but containing such dreadful and blood-curdling tales of cruelty, greed and murder that it could not possibly have been inspired and must, by the very nature of its contents, be the product of a people who had still lived in a state of semi-barbarism.

After that, of course, it was impossible for many people to regard the Bible as the only font of all true wisdom. And once this obstacle to free speculation had been removed, the current of scientific investigation, dammed up for almost a thousand years, began to flow in its natural channel and the interrupted labors of the old Greek and Roman philosophers were picked up where they had been left off twenty centuries before.

And in the second place, and this is even more important from the point of view of tolerance, the Reformation delivered northern and western Europe from the dictatorship of a power which under the guise of a religious organization had been in reality nothing but a spiritual and highly despotic continuation of the Roman Empire.

With these statements, our Catholic readers will hardly agree. But they too have reason to be grateful to a movement which was not only unavoidable, but which was to render a most salutary service to their own faith. For, thrown upon her own resources, the Church made an heroic effort to rid herself of those abuses which had made her once sacred name a byword for rapacity and tyranny.

And she succeeded most brilliantly.

After the middle of the sixteenth century, no more Borgias were tolerated in the Vatican. The Popes as ever before continued to be Italians. A deflection from this rule was practically impossible, as the Roman proletariat would have turned the city upside down if the cardinals entrusted with the election of a new pontiff had chosen a German or a Frenchman or any other foreigner.

The new pontiffs, however, were selected with great care and only candidates of the highest character could hope to be considered. And these new masters, faithfully aided by their devoted Jesuit auxiliaries, began a thorough house-cleaning.

The sale of indulgences came to an end.

Monastic orders were enjoined to study (and henceforth to obey) the rules laid down by their founders.

Mendicant friars disappeared from the streets of civilized cities.

And the general spiritual indifference of the Renaissance was replaced by an eager zeal for holy and useful lives spent in good deeds and in humble service towards those unfortunate

SPACE TO BREATHE

people who were not strong enough to carry the burden of existence by themselves.

Even so, the greater part of the territory which had been lost was never regained. Speaking with a certain geographical freedom, the northern half of Europe remained Protestant, while the southern half stayed Catholic.

But when we translate the result of the Reformation into the language of pictures, the actual changes which took place in Europe become more clearly revealed.

During the Middle Ages there had been one universal spiritual and intellectual prison-house.

The Protestant rebellion had ruined the old building and out of part of the available material it had constructed a jail of its own.

After the year 1517 there are therefore two dungeons, one reserved exclusively for the Catholics, the other for the Protestants.

At least that had been the original plan.

But the Protestants, who did not have the advantage of centuries of training along the lines of persecution and repression, failed to make their lockup dissenter-proof.

Through windows and chimneys and cellar-doors a large number of the unruly inmates escaped.

Ere long the entire building was a wreck.

At night the miscreants came and took away whole cartloads of stones and beams and iron bars which they used the next morning to build a little fortress of their own. But although this had the outward appearance of that original jail, constructed a thousand years before by Gregory the Great and Innocent III, it lacked the necessary inner strength.

No sooner was it ready for occupancy, no sooner had a new set of rules and regulations been posted upon the gates, than a wholesale walk-out occurred among the disgruntled trustees. As their keepers, now called ministers, had been deprived of the old methods of discipline (excommunication, torture, execution, confiscation and exile) they were absolutely helpless before this determined mob and were forced to stand by and look on while the rebels put up such a stockade as pleased their own theological preferences and proclaimed such new doctrines as happened to suit their temporary convictions.

This process was repeated so often that finally there developed a sort of spiritual no-man's-land between the different lockups where curious souls could roam at random and where honest people could think whatever they pleased without hindrance or molestation.

And this is the great service which Protestantism rendered to the cause of tolerance.

It reëstablished the dignity of the individual man.

Chapter XIII

ERASMUS

IN the writing of every book there occurs a crisis. Sometimes it comes during the first fifty pages. Upon other occasions it does not make itself manifest until the manuscript is almost finished. Indeed, a book without a crisis is like a child that has never had the measles. There probably is something the matter with it.

The crisis in the present volume happened a few minutes ago, for I have now reached the point where the idea of a work upon the subject of tolerance in the year of grace 1925 seems quite preposterous; where all the labor spent thus far upon a preliminary study appears in the light of so much valuable time wasted; where I would like best of all to make a bonfire of Bury and Lecky and Voltaire and Montaigne and White and use the carbon copies of my own work to light the stove.

How to explain this?

There are many reasons. In the first place, there is the inevitable feeling of boredom which overtakes an author when he has been living with his topic on a very intimate footing for too long a time. In the second place, the suspicion that books of this sort will not be of the slightest practical value. And in the third place, the fear that the present volume will be merely used as a quarry from which our less tolerant fellow citizens will dig a few easy facts with which to bolster up their own bad causes.

But apart from these arguments (which hold good for most serious books) there is in the present case the almost insurmountable difficulty of "system."

A story in order to be a success must have a beginning and an end. This book has a beginning, but can it ever have an end?

What I mean is this.

I can show the terrible crimes apparently committed in the

name of righteousness and justice, but really caused by intolerance.

I can depict the unhappy days upon which mankind fell when intolerance was elevated to the rank of one of the major virtues.

I can denounce and deride intolerance until my readers shout with one accord, "Down with this curse, and let us all be tolerant!"

But there is one thing I cannot do. I cannot tell how this highly desirable goal is to be reached. There are handbooks which undertake to give us instruction in everything from after-dinner speaking to ventriloquism. In an advertisement of a correspondence course last Sunday I read of no less than two hundred and forty-nine subjects which the institute guaranteed to teach to perfection in exchange for a very small gratuity. But no one thus far has offered to explain in forty (or in forty thousand) lessons "how to become tolerant."

And even history, which is supposed to hold the key to so many secrets, refuses to be of any use in this emergency.

Yes, it is possible to compose learned tomes devoted to slavery or free trade or capital punishment or the growth and development of Gothic architecture, for slavery and free trade and capital punishment and Gothic architecture are very definite and concrete things. For lack of all other material we could at least study the lives of the men and women who had been the champions of free trade and slavery and capital punishment and Gothic architecture or those who had opposed them. And from the manner in which those excellent people had approached their subjects, from their personal habits, their associations, their preferences in food and drink and tobacco, yea, from the very breeches they had worn, we could draw certain conclusions about the ideals which they had so energetically espoused or so bitterly denounced.

But there never were any professional protagonists of tolerance. Those who worked most zealously for the great cause did so incidentally. Their tolerance was a by-product. They were engaged in other pursuits. They were statesmen or writers or kings or physicians or modest artisans. In the midst of the king business or their medical practice or making steel engravings they found time to say a few good words for tolerance, but the struggle for tolerance was not the whole of their careers. They were interested in it as they may have been interested in playing chess or fiddling. And because they were part of a strangely assorted group (imagine Spinoza and Frederick the Great and Thomas Jefferson and Montaigne as boon companions!) it is almost impossible to discover that common trait of character which as a rule is to be found in all those who are engaged upon a common task, be it soldiering or plumbing or delivering the world from sin.

In such a case the writer is apt to have recourse to epigrams. Somewhere in this world there is an epigram for every dilemma. But upon this particular subject, the Bible and Shakespeare and Izaak Walton and even old Benham leave us in the lurch. Perhaps Jonathan Swift (I quote from memory) came nearest to the problem when he said that most men had just enough religion to hate their neighbors but not quite enough to love them. Unfortunately that bright remark does not quite cover our present difficulty. There have been people possessed of as much religion as any one individual could safely hold who have hated their neighbors as cordially as the best of them. There have been others who were totally devoid of the religious instinct who squandered their affection upon all the stray cats and dogs and human beings of Christendom.

No, I shall have to find an answer of my own. And upon due cogitation (but with a feeling of great uncertainty) I shall now state what I suspect to be the truth.

The men who have fought for tolerance, whatever their differences, had all of them one thing in common; their faith was tempered by doubt; they might honestly believe that they themselves were right, but they never reached the point where that suspicion hardened into an absolute conviction.

In this day and age of superpatriotism, with our enthusiastic clamoring for a hundred-percent this and a hundred-percent that, it may be well to point to the lesson taught by nature which seems to have a constitutional aversion to any such ideal of standardization.

Purely bred cats and dogs are proverbial idiots who are apt to die because no one is present to take them out of the rain. Hundred-percent pure iron has long since been discarded for the composite metal called steel. No jeweler ever undertook to do anything with hundred-percent pure gold or silver. Fiddles, to be any good, must be made of six or seven different varieties of wood. And as for a meal composed entirely of a hundred-percent mush, I thank you, no!

In short, all the most useful things in this world are compounds and I see no reason why faith should be an exception. Unless the base of our "certainty" contains a certain amount of the alloy of "doubt," our faith will sound as tinkly as a bell made of pure silver or as harsh as a trombone made of brass.

It was a profound appreciation of this fact which set the heroes of tolerance apart from the rest of the world.

As far as personal integrity went, honesty of conviction, unselfish devotion to duty and all the other household virtues, most of these men could have passed muster before a board of Puritan Inquisitors. I would go further than that and state that at least half of them lived and died in such a way that they would now be among the saints, if their peculiar trend of conscience had not forced them to be the open and avowed enemies of that institution which has taken upon itself the exclusive right of elevating ordinary human beings to certain celestial dignities.

But fortunately they were possessed of the divine doubt.

They knew (as the Romans and the Greeks had known before them) that the problem which faced them was so vast that no one in his right senses would ever expect it to be solved. And while they might hope and pray that the road which they had taken would evenually lead them to a safe goal, they could never convince themselves that it was the only right one, that all other roads were wrong and that the enchanting by-paths which delighted the hearts of so many simple people were evil thoroughfares leading to damnation.

All this sounds contrary to the opinions expressed in most of our catechisms and our text-books on ethics. These preach the superior virtue of a world illuminated by the pure white flame of absolute faith. Perhaps so. But during those centuries when that flame was supposed to be burning at its brightest, the average rank and file of humanity cannot be said to have been either particularly happy or extraordinarily comfortable. I don't

THOSE TERRIBLE LITTLE BOOKS

want to suggest any radical reforms, but just for a change we might try that other light, by the rays of which the brethren of the tolerant guild have been in the habit of examining the affairs of the world. If that does not prove successful, we can always go back to the system of our fathers. But if it should prove to throw an agreeable luster upon a society containing a little more kindness and forbearance, a community less beset by ugliness and greed and hatred, a good deal would have been gained and the expense, I am sure, would be quite small.

And after this bit of advice, offered for what it is worth, I must go back to my history.

When the last Roman was buried, the last citizen of the world (in the best and broadest sense of the word) perished. And it was a long time before society was once more placed upon such a footing of security that the old spirit of an all-encompassing humanity, which had been characteristic of the best minds of the ancient world, could safely return to this earth.

That, as we saw, happened during the Renaissance.

The revival of international commerce brought fresh capital to the poverty stricken countries of the west. New cities arose. A new class of men began to patronize the arts, to spend money upon books, to endow those universities which followed so closely in the wake of prosperity. And it was then that a few devoted adherents of the "humanities," of those sciences which boldly had taken all mankind as their field of experiment, arose in rebellion against the narrow limitations of the old scholasticism and strayed away from the flock of the faithful who regarded their interest in the wisdom and the grammar of the ancients as a manifestation of a wicked and impure curiosity.

Among the men who were in the front ranks of this small group of pioneers, the stories of whose lives will make up the rest of this book, few deserve greater credit than that very timid soul who came to be known as Erasmus.

For timid he was, although he took part in all the great verbal encounters of his day and successfully managed to make himself the terror of his enemies, by the precision with which he handled that most deadly of all weapons, the long-range gun of humor.

Far and wide the missiles containing the mustard-gas of his wit were shot into the enemy's country. And those Erasmian bombs were of a very dangerous variety. At a first glance they looked harmless enough. There was no sputtering of a tell-tale fuse. They had the appearance of an amusing new variety of fire-cracker, but God help those who took them home and allowed the children to play with them. The poison was sure to get into their little minds and it was of such a persistent nature that four centuries have not sufficed to make the race immune against the effects of the drug.

It is strange that such a man should have been born in one of the dullest towns of the mudbanks which are situated along the eastern coast of the North Sea. In the fifteenth century those water soaked lands had not yet attained the glories of an independent and fabulously rich commonwealth. They formed a group of little insignificant principalities, somewhere on the outskirts of civilized society. They smelled forever of herring, their chief article of export. And if ever they attracted a visitor, it was some helpless mariner whose ship had been wrecked upon their dismal shores.

But the very horror of a childhood spent among such unpleasant surroundings may have spurred this curious infant into that fury of activitiy which eventually was to set him free and make him one of the best known men of his time.

From the beginning of life, everything was against him. He was an illegitimate child. The people of the Middle Ages, being on an intimate and friendly footing both with God and with nature, were a great deal more sensible about such children than we are. They were sorry. Such things ought not to occur and of course they greatly disapproved. For the rest, however, they were too simple-minded to punish a helpless creature in a cradle for a sin which most certainly was not of its own making. The irregularity of his birth certificate inconvenienced Erasmus only in so far as both his father and his mother seem to have been exceedingly muddle-headed citizens, totally incapable of handling the situation and leaving their children to the care of relatives who were either boobs or scoundrels.

These uncles and guardians had no idea of what to do with their two little wards and after the mother had died, the children never had a home of their own. First of all they were sent to a famous school in Deventer, where several of the teachers belonged to the Society of the Brothers of the Common Life, but if we are to judge by the letters which Erasmus wrote later in life,

these young men were only "common" in a very different sense
of the word. Next the two boys were separated and the younger
was taken to Gouda, where he was placed under the immediate
supervision of the head-master of the Latin school, who was
also one of the three guardians appointed to administer his
slender inheritance. If that school in the days of Erasmus was
as bad as when I visited it four centuries later, I can only feel
sorry for the poor kid. And to make matters worse, the guardians

ROTTERDAM

by this time had wasted every penny of his money and in order
to escape prosecution (for the old Dutch courts were strict upon
such matters) they hurried the infant into a cloister, rushed
him into holy orders and bade him be happy because "now his
future was secure."

The mysterious mills of history eventually ground this terrible experience into something of great literary value. But
I hate to think of the many terrible years this sensitive youngster
was forced to spend in the exclusive company of the illiterate
boors and thick-fingered rustics who during the end of the Middle
Ages made up the population of fully half of all monasteries.

Fortunately the laxity of discipline at Steyn permitted Erasmus to spend most of his time among the Latin manuscripts which a former abbot had collected and which lay forgotten in the library. He absorbed those volumes until he finally became a walking encyclopedia of classical learning. In later years this stood him in good stead. Forever on the move, he rarely was within reach of a reference library. But that was not necessary. He could quote from memory. Those who have ever seen the

THE CLOISTER STEYN

ten gigantic folios which contain his collected works, or who have managed to read through part of them (life is so short nowadays) will appreciate what a "knowledge of the classics" meant in the fifteenth century.

Of course, eventually Erasmus was able to leave his old monastery. People like him are never influenced by circumstances. They make their own circumstances and they make them out of the most unlikely material.

And the rest of his life Erasmus was a free man, searching restlessly after a spot where he might work without being disturbed by a host of admiring friends.

But not until the fateful hour when with an appeal to the "lieve God" of his childhood he allowed his soul to slip into the slumber of death, did he enjoy a moment of that "true leisure"

which has always appeared as the highest good to those who
have followed the footsteps of Socrates and Zeno and which so
few of them have ever found.

These peregrinations have often been described and I need
not repeat them here in detail. Wherever two or more men lived
together in the name of true wisdom, there Erasmus was sooner
or later bound to make his appearance.

He studied in Paris, where as a poor scholar he almost died
of hunger and cold. He taught in Cambridge. He printed
books in Basel. He tried (quite in vain) to carry a spark of
enlightenment into that stronghold of orthodox bigotry, the far-
famed University of Louvain. He spent much of his time in
London and took the degree of Doctor of Divinity in the University of Turin. He was familiar with the Grand Canal of
Venice and cursed as familiarly about the terrible roads of Zee-
land as those of Lombardy. The sky, the parks, the walks and
the libraries of Rome made such a profound impression upon
him that even the waters of Lethe could not wash the Holy City
out of his memory. He was offered a liberal pension if he would
only move to Venice and whenever a new university was opened,
he was sure to be honored with a call to whatever chair he wished
to take or to no chair at all, provided he would grace the campus
with his occasional presence.

But he steadily refused all such invitations because they
seemed to contain a threat of permanence and dependency. Before all things he wanted to be free. He preferred a comfortable
room to a bad one, he preferred amusing companions to dull
ones, he knew the difference between the good rich wine of the
land called Burgundy and the thin red ink of the Apennines,
but he wanted to live life on his own terms and this he could
not do if he had to call any man "master."

The rôle which he had chosen for himself was really that of
an intellectual search-light. No matter what object appeared
above the horizon of contemporary events, Erasmus immediately
let the brilliant rays of his intellect play upon it, did his best
to make his neighbors see the thing as it really was, denuded

of all frills and divested of that "folly," that ignorance which he hated so thoroughly.

That he was able to do this during the most turbulent period of our history, that he managed to escape the fury of the Protestant fanatics while keeping himself aloof from the fagots of his friends of the Inquisition, this is the one point in his career upon which he has been most often condemned.

Posterity seems to have a veritable passion for martyrdom as long as it applies to the ancestors.

"Why didn't this Dutchman stand up boldly for Luther and take his chance together with the other reformers?" has been a question which seems to have puzzled at least twelve generations of otherwise intelligent citizens.

The answer is, "Why should he?"

It was not in his nature to do violent things and he never regarded himself as the leader of any movement. He utterly lacked that sense of self-righteous assurance which is so characteristic of those who undertake to tell the world how the millennium ought to be brought about. Besides he did not believe that it is necessary to demolish the old home every time we feel the necessity of rearranging our quarters. Quite true, the premises were sadly in need of repairs. The drainage was old-fashioned. The garden was all cluttered up with dirt and odds and ends left behind by people who had moved out long before. But all this could be changed if the landlord was made to live up to his promises and would only spend some money upon immediate improvements. Beyond that, Erasmus did not wish to go. And although he was what his enemies sneeringly called a "moderate," he accomplished quite as much (or more) than those out and out "radicals" who gave the world two tyrannies where only one had been before.

Like all truly great men, he was no friend of systems. He believed that the salvation of this world lies in our individual endeavors. Make over the individual man and you have made over the entire world!

Hence he made his attack upon existing abuses by way of a

direct appeal to the average citizen. And he did this in a very clever way.

In the first place, he wrote an enormous amount of letters. He wrote them to kings and to emperors and to popes and to abbots and to knights and to knaves. He wrote them (and this in the days before the stamped and self-addressed envelope) to any one who took the trouble to approach him and whenever he took his pen in hand he was good for at least eight pages.

In the second place, he edited a large number of classical texts which had been so often and so badly copied that they no longer made any sense. For this purpose he had been obliged to learn Greek. His many attempts to get hold of a grammar of that forbidden tongue was one of the reasons why so many pious Catholics insisted that at heart he must be as bad as a real heretic. This of course sounds absurd but it was the truth. In the fifteenth century, respectable Christians would never have dreamed of trying to learn this forbidden language. It was a tongue of evil repute like modern Russian. A knowledge of Greek might lead a man into all sorts of difficulties. It might tempt him to compare the original gospels with those translations that had been given to him with the assurance that they were a true reproduction of the original. And that would only be the beginning. Soon he would make a descent into the Ghetto to get hold of a Hebrew grammar. From that point to open rebellion against the authority of the Church was only a step and for a long time the possession of a book with strange and outlandish pothooks was regarded as ipso facto evidence of secret revolutionary tendencies.

Quite often rooms were raided by ecclesiastical authorities in search of this contraband, and Byzantine refugees who were trying to eke out an existence by teaching their native tongue were not infrequently forced to leave the city in which they had found an asylum.

In spite of all these many obstacles, Erasmus had learned Greek and in the asides which he added to his editions of Cyprian and Chrysostom and the other Church fathers, he hid many sly observations upon current events which could never have been printed had they been the subject of a separate pamphlet.

But this impish spirit of annotation manifested itself in an entirely different sort of literature of which he was the inventor. I mean his famous collections of Greek and Latin proverbs which he had brought together in order that the children of his time might learn to write the classics with becoming elegance. These so-called "Adagia" are filled with clever comments which in the eyes of his conservative neighbors were by no means what one had the right to expect of a man who enjoyed the friendship of the Pope.

And finally he was the author of one of those strange little books which are born of the spirit of the moment, which are really a joke conceived for the benefit of a few friends and then assume the dignity of a great literary classic before the poor author quite realizes what he has done. It was called "The Praise of Folly" and we happen to know how it came to be written.

It was in the year 1515 that the world had been startled by a pamphlet written so cleverly that no one could tell whether it was meant as an attack upon the friars or as a defense of the monastic life. No name appeared upon the title page, but those who knew what was what in the world of letters recognized the somewhat unsteady hand of one Ulrich von Hutten. And they guessed right; for that talented young man, poet laureate and town bum extraordinary, had taken no mean share in the production of this gross but useful piece of buffoonery and he was proud of it. When he heard that no one less than Thomas More, the famous champion of the New Learning in England, had spoken well of his work, he wrote to Erasmus and asked him for particulars.

Erasmus was no friend of von Hutten. His orderly mind (reflected in his orderly way of living) did not take kindly to those blowsy Teuton Ritters who spent their mornings and afternoons valiantly wielding pen and rapier for the cause of enlightenment and then retired to the nearest pot-house that they might forget the corruption of the times by drinking endless bumpers of sour beer.

But von Hutten, in his own way, was really a man of genius and Erasmus answered him civilly enough. Yea, as he wrote, he grew eloquent upon the virtues of his London friend and depicted so charming a scene of domestic contentment that the household of Sir Thomas might well serve as a model for all other families until the end of time. It was in this letter that he mentions how More, himself a humorist of no small parts, had given him the original idea for his "Praise of Folly" and very likely it was the good-natured horse-play of the More establishment (a veritable Noah's ark of sons and daughters-in-law and daughters and sons-in-law and birds and dogs and a private zoo and private theatricals and bands of amateur fiddlers) which had inspired him to write that delightful piece of nonsense with which his name is forever associated.

In some vague way the book reminds me of the Punch and Judy shows which for so many centuries were the only amusement of little Dutch children. Those Punch and Judy shows, with all the gross vulgarity of their dialogue, invariably maintained a tone of lofty moral seriousness. The hollow voiced figure of Death dominated the scene. One by one the other actors were forced to appear before this ragged hero and give an account of themselves. And one by one, to the everlasting delight of the youthful audience, they were knocked on the head with an enormous cudgel and were thrown on an imaginary scrapheap.

In the "Praise of Folly," the whole social fabric of the age is carefully taken apart while Folly, as a sort of inspired Coroner, stands by and favors the public at large with her comments. No one is spared. The whole of Medieval Main Street is ransacked for suitable characters. And of course, the go-getters of that day, the peddling friars of salvation with all their sanctimonious sales-talk, their gross ignorance and the futile pomposity of their arguments, came in for a drubbing which was never forgotten and never forgiven.

But the Pope and his cardinals and his bishops, incongruous

successors to the poverty stricken fishermen and carpenters from the land of Galilee, were also on the bill and held the stage for several chapters.

The "Folly" of Erasmus, however, was a much more substantial personage than the usual Jack-in-the-Box of humorous literature. Throughout this little book (as indeed throughout everything he wrote) Erasmus preached a gospel of his own which one might call the philosophy of tolerance.

It was this willingness to live and let live; this insistence upon the spirit of the divine law rather than upon the commas and the semicolons in the original version of that divine law; this truly human acceptance of religion as a system of ethics rather than as a form of government which made serious-minded Catholics and Protestants inveigh against Erasmus as a "godless knave" and an enemy of all true religion who "slandered Christ" but hid his real opinions behind the funny phrases of a clever little book.

This abuse (and it lasted until the day of his death) did not have any effect. The little man with the long pointed nose, who lived until the age of seventy at a time when the addition or omission of a single word from an established text might cause a man to be hanged, had no liking at all for the popular-hero business and he said so openly. He expected nothing from an appeal to swords and arquebusses and knew only too well the risk the world was running when a minor theological dispute was allowed to degenerate into an international religious war.

And so, like a gigantic beaver, he worked day and night to finish that famous dam of reason and common sense which he vaguely hoped might stem the waxing tide of ignorance and intolerance.

Of course he failed. It was impossible to stop those floods of ill will and hatred which were sweeping down from the mountains of Germany and the Alps, and a few years after his death his work had been completely washed away.

But so well had he wrought that many bits of wreckage, thrown upon the shores of posterity, proved exceedingly good material for those irrepressible optimists who believe that some day we shall have a set of dykes that will actually hold.

Erasmus departed this life in July of the year 1536.

His sense of humor never deserted him. He died in the house of his publisher.

Chapter XIV

RABELAIS

SOCIAL upheavals make strange bed-fellows.

The name of Erasmus can be printed in a respectable book intended for the entire family. But to mention Rabelais in public is considered little short of a breach of good manners. Indeed, so dangerous is this fellow that laws have been passed in our country to keep his wicked works out of the hands of our innocent children and that in many states copies of his books can only be obtained from the more intrepid among our book-leggers.

This of course is merely one of the absurdities which have been forced upon us by the reign of terror of a flivver aristocracy.

In the first place, the works of Rabelais to the average citizen of the twentieth century are about as dull reading as "Tom Jones" or "The House of the Seven Gables." Few people ever get beyond the first interminable chapter.

And in the second place, there is nothing intentionally sugges-tive in what he says. Rabelais used the common vocabulary of his time. That does not happen to be the common vernacular of our own day. But in the era of the bucolic blues, when ninety percent of the human race lived close to the soil, a spade was actually a spade and lady-dogs were not "lady-dogs."

No, the current objections to the works of this distinguished surgeon go much deeper than a mere disapproval of his rich but somewhat outspoken collection of idioms. They are caused by the horror which many excellent people experience when they come face to face with the point of view of a man who point blank refuses to be defeated by life.

The human race, as far as I can make out, is divided into two sorts of people: those who say "yes" unto life and those who say "no." The former accept it and courageously they endeavor to make the best of whatever bargain fate has handed out to them.

The latter accept it too (how could they help themselves?) but they hold the gift in great contempt and fret about it like children who have been given a new little brother when they really wanted a puppy or a railroad train.

But whereas the cheerful brethren of "yes" are willing to accept their morose neighbors at their own valuation and tolerate

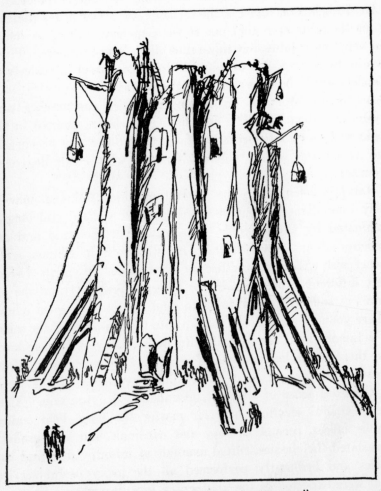

"THE OLD BUILDING WILL LAST OUR TIME"

them, and do not hinder them when they fill the landscape with
their lamentations and the hideous monuments to their own
despair, the fraternity of "no" rarely extends this same courtesy
to the parties of the first part.

Indeed if they had their own way, the "nays" would immediately purge this planet of the "yeas."

As this cannot very well be done, they satisfy the demands of
their jealous souls by the incessant persecution of those who
claim that the world belongs to the living and not to the dead.

Dr. Rabelais belonged to the former class. Few of his patients
or his thoughts ever went out to the cemetery. This, no doubt,
was very regrettable, but we cannot all be grave-diggers. There
have to be a few Poloniuses and a world composed exclusively of
Hamlets would be a terrible place of abode.

As for the story of Rabelais's life, there was nothing very
mysterious about it. The few details which are omitted in the
books written by his friends are found in the works of his enemies
and as a result we can follow his career with a fair degree of
accuracy.

Rabelais belonged to the generation which followed immediately upon Erasmus but he was born into a world still largely
dominated by monks, nuns, deacons, and a thousand and one
varieties of mendicant friars. He was born in Chinon. His
father was either an apothecary or a dealer in spirits (which
were different professions in the fifteenth century) and the old
man was sufficiently well-to-do to send his son to a good school.
There young François was thrown into the company of the scions
of a famous local family called du Bellay-Langey. These boys,
like their father, had a streak of genius. They wrote well. Upon
occasion they could fight well. They were men of the world
in the good sense of that oft misunderstood expression. They
were faithful servitors of their master the king, held endless
public offices, became bishops and cardinals and ambassadors,
translated the classics, edited manuals of infantry drill and ballistics and brilliantly performed all the many useful services
that were expected of the aristocracy in a day when a title con-

demned a man to a life of few pleasures and many duties and responsibilities.

The friendship which the du Bellays afterwards bestowed upon Rabelais shows that he must have been something more than an amusing table companion. During the many ups and downs of his life he could always count upon the assistance and the support of his former classmates. Whenever he was in trouble with his clerical superiors he found the door of their castle wide open and if perchance the soil of France became a little too hot for this blunt young moralist, there was always a du Bellay conveniently going upon a foreign mission and greatly in need of a secretary who should be somewhat of a physician besides being a polished Latin scholar.

This was no small detail. More than once when it seemed that the career of our learned doctor was about to come to an abrupt and painful end, the influence of his old friends saved him from the fury of the Sorbonne or from the anger of those much disappointed Calvinists who had counted upon him as one of their own and who were greatly incensed when he pilloried the jaundiced zeal of their Genevan master as mercilessly as he had derided the three-bottled sanctity of his erstwhile colleagues in Fontenay and Maillezais.

Of these two enemies, the former was of course by far the more dangerous. Calvin could fulminate to his heart's content, but outside of the narrow boundaries of a small Swiss canton, his lightning was as harmless as a fire-cracker.

The Sorbonne, on the other hand, which together with the University of Oxford stood firmly for orthodoxy and the Old Learning, knew of no mercy when her authority was questioned and could always count upon the hearty coöperation of the king of France and his hangman.

And alas! Rabelais, as soon as he left school, was a marked man. Not because he liked to drink good wine and told funny stories about his fellow monks. He had done much worse, he had succumbed to the lure of the wicked Greek tongue.

When rumor thereof had first reached the abbot of his cloister, it was decided to search his cell. It was found to be full of literary contraband, a copy of Homer, one of the New Testament, one of Herodotus.

This was a terrible discovery and it had taken a great deal of wire-pulling on the part of his influential friends to get him out of this scrape.

It was a curious period in the development of the Church.

Originally, as I told you before, the monasteries had been advance posts of civilization and both friars and nuns had rendered inestimable service in promoting the interest of the Church. More than one Pope, however, had foreseen the danger that might come from a too powerful development of the monastic institutions. But as so often happens, just because every one knew that something ought to be done about these cloisters, nothing was ever done.

Among the Protestants there seems to be a notion that the Catholic Church is a placid institution which is run silently and almost automatically by a small body of haughty autocrats and which never suffers from those inner upheavals which are an integral part of every other organization composed of ordinary mortals.

Nothing is further from the truth.

Perhaps, as is so often the case, this opinion has been caused by the misinterpretation of a single word.

A world addicted to democratic ideals is easily horrified at the idea of an "infallible" human being.

"It must be easy," so the popular argument runs, "to administer this big institution when it is enough for one man to say that a thing is so to have all the others fall upon their knees and shout amen and obey him."

It is extremely difficult for one brought up in Protestant countries to get a correct and fair view of this rather intricate subject. But if I am not mistaken, the "infallible" utterances of the supreme pontiff are as rare as constitutional amendments in the United States.

Furthermore, such important decisions are never reached until the subject has been thoroughly discussed and the debates which precede the final verdict often rock the very body of the Church.

Such pronunciamentos are therefore "infallible" in the sense that our own constitutional amendments are infallible, because they are "final" and because all further argument is supposed to come to an end as soon as they have been definitely incorporated into the highest law of the land.

If any one were to proclaim that it is an easy job to govern these United States because in case of an emergency all the people are found to stand firmly behind the Constitution, he would be just as much in error as if he were to state that all Catholics who in supreme matters of faith recognize the absolute authority of their pope are docile sheep and have surrendered every right to an opinion of their own.

If this were true, the occupants of the Lateran and the Vatican palaces would have had an easy life. But even the most superficial study of the last fifteen hundred years will show the exact opposite. And those champions of the reformed faith who sometimes write as if the Roman authorities had been ignorant of the many evils which Luther and Calvin and Zwingli denounced with such great vehemence are either ignorant of the facts or are not quite fair in their zeal for the good cause.

Such men as Adrian VI and Clement VII knew perfectly well that something very serious was wrong with their Church. But it is one thing to express the opinion that there is something rotten in the state of Denmark. It is quite a different matter to correct the evil, as even poor Hamlet was to learn.

Nor was that unfortunate prince the last victim of the pleasant delusion that hundreds of years of misgovernment can be undone overnight by the unselfish efforts of an honest man.

Many intelligent Russians knew that the old official structure which dominated their empire was corrupt, inefficient and a menace to the safety of the nation.

They made Herculean efforts to bring about reforms and they failed.

How many of our citizens who have ever given the matter an hour's thought fail to see that a democratic instead of a representative form of government (as intended by the founders of the Republic) must eventually lead to systematized anarchy?

WHOLESALE METHODS OF PERSUASION

And yet, what can they do about it?

Such problems, by the time they have begun to attract public attention, have become so hopelessly complicated that they are rarely solved except by a social cataclysm. And social cataclysms are terrible things from which most men shy away. Rather than run to such extremes, they try to patch up the old, decrepit machinery and meanwhile they pray that some miracle will occur which will make it work.

An insolent religious and social dictatorship, set up and maintained by a number of religious orders, was one of the most flagrant evils of the out-going Middle Ages.

For the so-many-eth time in history, the army was about to run away with the commander-in-chief. In plain words, the situation had grown entirely beyond the control of the Popes. All they could do was to sit still, improve their own party organization, and meanwhile try to mitigate the fate of those who had incurred the displeasure of their common enemies, the friars.

Erasmus was one of the many scholars who had frequently enjoyed the protection of the Pope. Let Louvain storm and the Dominicans rave, Rome would stand firm and woe unto him who disregarded her command, "Leave the old man alone!"

And after these few introductory remarks, it will be no matter of surprise that Rabelais, a mutinous soul but a brilliant mind withal, could often count upon the support of the Holy See when the superiors of his own order wished to punish him and that he readily obtained permission to leave his cloister when constant interference with his studies began to make his life unbearable.

And so with a sigh of relief, he shook the dust of Maillezais off his feet and went to Montpellier and to Lyons to follow a course in medicine.

Surely here was a man of extraordinary talents! Within less than two years the former Benedictine monk had become chief physician of the city hospital of Lyons. But as soon as he had achieved these new honors, his restless soul began to look for pastures new. He did not give up his powders and pills but in addition to his anatomical studies (a novelty almost as dangerous as the study of Greek) he took up literature.

Lyons, situated in the center of the valley of the Rhone, was an ideal city for a man who cared for belles lettres. Italy was nearby. A few days' easy travel carried the traveler to the Provence and although the ancient paradise of the Troubadours had suffered dreadfully at the hands of the Inquisition, the grand old literary tradition had not yet been entirely lost. Furthermore, the printing-presses of Lyons were famous for the excellence of their product and her book stores were well stocked with all the latest publications.

When one of the master printers, Sebastian Gryphius by name, looked for some one to edit his collection of medieval classics, it was natural that he should bethink himself of the new doctor who was also known as a scholar. He hired Rabelais and set him to work. In rapid succession almanachs and chap-books followed upon the learned treatises of Galen and Hippocrates. And out of these inconspicuous beginnings grew that strange tome which was to make its author one of the most popular writers of his time.

The same talent for novelty which had turned Rabelais into a successful medical practitioner brought him his success as a novelist. He did what few people had dared to do before him. He began to write in the language of his own people. He broke with a thousand-year-old tradition which insisted that the books of a learned man must be in a tongue unknown to the vulgar multitude. He used French and, furthermore, he used the unadorned vernacular of the year 1532.

I gladly leave it to the professors of literature to decide where and how and when Rabelais discovered his two pet heroes, Gargantua and Pantagruel. Maybe they were old heathenish Gods who, after the nature of their species, had managed to live through fifteen hundred years of Christian persecution and neglect.

Then again, he may have invented them in an outburst of gigantic hilarity.

However that be, Rabelais contributed enormously to the gayety of nations and greater praise no author can gain than that he has added something to the sum total of human laughter. But at the same time, his works were not funny books in the terrible modern sense of the word. They had their serious side and struck a bold blow for the cause of tolerance by their caricature of the people who were responsible for that clerical reign of terror which caused such untold misery during the first fifty years of the sixteenth century.

Rabelais, a skillfully trained theologian, was able to avoid all such direct statements as might have got him into trouble, and acting upon the principle that one cheerful humorist out of jail is better than a dozen gloomy reformers behind the bars, refrained from a too brazen exposition of his highly unorthodox opinions.

But his enemies knew perfectly well what he was trying to do. The Sorbonne condemned his books in unmistakable terms and the Parliament of Paris put him on their index and confiscated and burned all such copies of his works as could be found within their jurisdiction. But notwithstanding the activities of the hangman (who in those days was also the official book destroyer) the "Lives and Heroic Deeds and Sayings of Gargantua and his Sonne Pantagruel" remained a popular classic. For almost four centuries it has continued to edify those who can derive pleasure from a clever mixture of good-natured laughter and bantering wisdom and it will never cease to irritate those others who firmly believe that the Goddess of Truth, caught with a smile on her lips, cannot possibly be a good woman.

As for the author himself, he was and is a "man of one book." His friends, the du Bellays, remained faithful to him until the end, but most of his life Rabelais practiced the virtue of discretion and kept himself at a polite distance from the residence of that Majesty by whose supposed "privilege" he published his nefarious works.

He ventured, however, upon a visit to Rome and met with no difficulties, but on the contrary was received with every manifestation of a cordial welcome. In the year 1550 he returned to France and went to live in Meudon. Three years later he died.

It is of course quite impossible to measure the exact and positive influence exercised by such a man. After all, he was a human being and not an electric current or a barrel of gasoline.

It has been said that he was merely destructive.

Perhaps so.

But he was destructive in an age when there was a great and crying need for a social wrecking crew, headed by just such people as Erasmus and Rabelais.

That many of the new buildings were going to be just as uncomfortable and ugly as the old ones which they were supposed to replace was something which no one was able to foresee.

And, anyway, that was the fault of the next generation.

They are the people we ought to blame.

They were given a chance such as few people ever enjoyed to make a fresh start.

May the Lord have mercy upon their souls for the way in which they neglected their opportunities.

Chapter XV

NEW SIGNBOARDS FOR OLD

THE greatest of modern poets saw the world as a large ocean upon which sailed many ships. Whenever these little vessels bumped against each other, they made a "wonderful music" which people call history.

I would like to borrow Heine's ocean, but for a purpose and a simile of my own. When we were children it was fun to drop pebbles into a pond. They made a nice splash and then the pretty little ripples caused a series of ever widening circles and that was very nice. If bricks were handy (which sometimes was the case) one could make an Armada of nutshells and matches and submit this flimsy fleet to a nice artificial storm, provided the heavy projectile did not create that fatal loss of equilibrium which sometimes overtakes small children who play too near the water's edge and sends them to bed without their supper.

THE WORLD-WIDE OCEAN
214

In that special universe reserved for grown-ups, the same pastime is not entirely unknown, but the results are apt to be far more disastrous.

Everything is placid and the sun is shining and the water-wigglers are skating merrily, and then suddenly a bold, bad boy comes along with a piece of mill-stone (Heaven only knows where he found it!) and before any one can stop him he has heaved it right into the middle of the old duck pond and then there is a great ado about who did it and how he ought to be spanked and some say, "Oh, let him go," and others, out of sheer envy of the kid who is attracting all the attention, pick up any old thing that happens to lie around and they dump it into the water and everybody gets splashed and one thing leading to another, the usual result is a free-for-all fight and a few million broken heads.

Alexander was such a bold, bad boy.

And Helen of Troy, in her own charming way, was such a bad, bold girl, and history is just full of them.

But by far the worst offenders are those wicked citizens who play this game with ideas and use the stagnant pool of man's spiritual indifference as their playground. And I for one don't wonder that they are hated by all right-thinking citizens and are punished with great severity if ever they are unfortunate enough to let themselves be caught.

Think of the damage they have done these last four hundred years.

They were the leaders of the rebirth of the ancient world. The stately moats of the Middle Ages reflected the image of a society that was harmonious in both color and texture. It was not perfect. But people liked it. They loved to see the blending of the brick-red walls of their little homes with the somber gray of those high cathedral towers that watched over their souls.

Came the terrible splash of the Renaissance and overnight everything was changed. But it was only a beginning. For just when the poor burghers had almost recovered from the shock, that dreadful German monk appeared with a whole cart-load of specially prepared bricks and dumped them right into

GENEVA

the heart of the pontifical lagoon. Really, that was too much. And no wonder that it took the world three centuries to recover from the shock.

The older historians who studied this period often fell into a slight error. They saw the commotion and decided that the ripples had been started by a common cause, which they alternately called the Renaissance and the Reformation.

To-day we know better.

The Renaissance and the Reformation were movements which professed to be striving after a common purpose. But the means by which they hoped to accomplish their ultimate object were so utterly different that Humanist and Protestant not infrequently came to regard each other with bitter hostility.

They both believed in the supreme rights of man. During the Middle Ages the individual had been completely merged in the community. He did not exist as John Doe, a bright citizen who came and went at will, who sold and bought as he liked, who went to any one of a dozen churches (or to none at all, as suited his tastes and his prejudices). His life from the time of his birth to the hour of his death was lived according to a rigid handbook of economic and spiritual etiquette. This taught him that his body was a shoddy garment, casually borrowed from Mother Nature and of no value except as a temporary receptacle for his immortal soul.

It trained him to believe that this world was a half-way house to future glory and should be regarded with that profound contempt which travelers destined for New York bestow upon Queenstown and Halifax.

And now unto the excellent John, living happily in the best of all possible worlds (since it was the only world he knew), came the two fairy godmothers, Renaissance and Reformation, and said: "Arise, noble citizen, from now on thou art to be free."

But when John asked, "Free to do what?" the answers greatly differed.

"Free to go forth in quest of Beauty," the Renaissance replied.

"Free to go in quest of Truth," the Reformation admonished him.

"Free to search the records of the past when the world was truly the realm of men. Free to realize those ideals which once filled the hearts of poets and painters and sculptors and architects. Free to turn the universe into thine eternal laboratory, that thou mayest know all her secrets," was the promise of the Renaissance.

"Free to study the word of God, that thou mayest find salvation for thy soul and forgiveness for thy sins," was the warning of the Reformation.

And they turned on their heels and left poor John Doe in the possession of a new freedom which was infinitely more embarrassing than the thralldom of his former days.

Fortunately or unfortunately, the Renaissance soon made her peace with the established order of things. The successors of Phidias and Horace discovered that a belief in the established Deity and outward conformity to the rules of the Church were two very different things and that one could paint pagan pictures and compose heathenish sonnets with complete impunity if one took the precaution to call Hercules, John the Baptist, and Hera, the Virgin Mary.

They were like tourists who go to India and who obey certain laws which mean nothing to them at all in order that they may gain entrance to the temples and travel freely without disturbing the peace of the land.

But in the eyes of an honest follower of Luther, the most trifling of details at once assumed enormous importance. An erroneous comma in Deuteronomy might mean exile. As for a misplaced full stop in the Apocalypse, it called for instant death.

LOYOLA

To people like these, who took what they considered their religious convictions with bitter seriousness, the merry compromise of the Renaissance seemed a dastardly act of cowardice.

As a result, Renaissance and Reformation parted company, never to meet again.

Whereupon the Reformation, alone against all the world, buckled on the armor of righteousness and made ready to defend her holiest possessions.

In the beginning, the army of revolt was composed almost exclusively of Germans. They fought and suffered with extreme bravery, but that mutual jealousy which is the bane and the curse of all northern nations soon lamed their efforts and forced them to accept a truce. The strategy which led to the ultimate victory was provided by a very different sort of genius. Luther stepped aside to make room for Calvin.

It was high time.

In that same French college where Erasmus had spent so

many of his unhappy Parisian days, a black-bearded young
Spaniard with a limp (the result of a Gallic gun-shot) was
dreaming of the day when he should march at the head of a new
army of the Lord to rid the world of the last of the heretics.

It takes a fanatic to fight a fanatic.

And only a man of granite, like Calvin, would have been able
to defeat the plans of Loyola.

Personally, I am glad that I was not obliged to live in Geneva
in the sixteenth century. At the same time I am profoundly
grateful that the Geneva of the sixteenth century existed.

Without it, the world of the twentieth century would have
been a great deal more uncomfortable and I for one would probably be in jail.

The hero of this glorious fight, the famous Magister Joannes
Calvinus (or Jean Calvini or John Calvin) was a few years
younger than Luther. Date of birth: July 10, 1509. Place
of birth: the city of Noyon in northern France. Background:
French middle class. Father: a small clerical official. Mother:
the daughter of an inn-keeper. Family: five sons and two daughters. Characteristic qualities of early education: thrift, simplicity, and a tendency to do all things in an orderly manner,
not stingily, but with minute and efficient care.

John, the second son, was meant for the priesthood. The
father had influential friends, and could eventually get him into
a good parish. Before he was thirteen years old, he already
held a small office in the cathedral of his home city. This gave
him a small but steady income. It was used to send him to a
good school in Paris. A remarkable boy. Every one who came
in contact with him said, "Watch out for that youngster!"

The French educational system of the sixteenth century was
well able to take care of such a child and make the best of his
many gifts. At the age of nineteen, John was allowed to preach.
His future as a duly established deacon seemed assured.

But there were five sons and two daughters. Advancement
in the Church was slow. The law offered better opportunities.
Besides, it was a time of great religious excitement and the
future was uncertain. A distant relative, a certain Pierre

Olivétan, had just translated the Bible into French. John, while in Paris, had spent much time with his cousin. It would never do to have two heretics in one family. John was packed off to Orleans and was apprenticed to an old lawyer that he might learn the business of pleading and arguing and drawing up briefs.

Here the same thing happened as in Paris. Before the end of the year, the pupil had turned teacher and was coaching his less industrious fellow students in the principles of jurisprudence. And soon he knew all there was to know and was ready to start upon that course which, so his father fondly hoped, would some day make him the rival of those famous avocats who got a hundred gold pieces for a single opinion and who drove in a coach and four when they were called upon to see the king in distant Compiègne.

But nothing came of these dreams. John Calvin never practiced law.

Instead, he returned to his first love, sold his digests and his pandects, devoted the proceeds to a collection of theological works and started in all seriousness upon that task which was to make him one of the most important historical figures of the last twenty centuries.

The years, however, which he had spent studying the principles of Roman law put their stamp upon all his further activities. It was impossible for him to approach a problem by way of his emotions. He felt things and he felt them deeply. Read his letters to those of his followers who had fallen into the hands of Catholics and who had been condemned to be roasted to death over slow burning coal fires. In their helpless agony they are as fine a bit of writing as anything of which we have a record. And they show such a delicate understanding of human psychology that the poor victims went to their death blessing the name of the man whose teaching had brought them into their predicament.

No, Calvin was not, as so many of his enemies have said, a man without a heart. But life to him was a sacred duty.

And he tried so desperately hard to be honest with himself and with his God that he must first reduce every question to certain fundamental principles of faith and doctrine before he dared to expose it to the touchstone of human sentiment.

When Pope Pius IV heard of his death, he remarked, "The power of that heretic lay in the fact that he was indifferent to money." If His Holiness meant to pay his enemy the compliment of absolute personal disinterestedness, he was right. Calvin lived and died a poor man and refused to accept his last quarterly salary because "illness had made it impossible for him to earn that money as he should have done."

But his strength lay elsewhere.

He was a man of one idea, his life centered around one all-overpowering impulse; the desire to find the truth of God as revealed in the Scriptures. When he finally had reached a conclusion that seemed proof against every possible form of argument and objection, then at last he incorporated it into his own code of life. And thereafter he went his way with such utter disregard for the consequences of his decision that he became both invincible and irresistible.

This quality, however, was not to make itself manifest until many years later. During the first decade after his conversion he was obliged to direct all his energies toward the very commonplace problem of keeping alive.

A short triumph of the "new learning" in the University of Paris, an orgy of Greek declensions, Hebrew irregular verbs and other forbidden intellectual fruit had been followed by the usual reaction. When it appeared that even the rector of that famous seat of learning had been contaminated with the pernicious new German doctrines, steps were taken to purge the institution of all those who in terms of our modern medical science might be considered "idea carriers." Calvin, who, 'twas said, had given the rector the material for several of his most objectionable speeches, was among those whose names appeared at the top of the list of suspects. His rooms were searched. His papers were confiscated and an order was issued for his arrest.

He heard of it and hid himself in the house of a friend.

But storms in an academic tea-pot never last very long. All

the same, a career in the Church of Rome had become an impossibility. The moment had arrived for a definite choice.

In the year 1534 Calvin broke away from the old faith. Almost at the same moment, on the hills of Montmartre, high above the French capital, Loyola and a handful of his fellow students were taking that solemn vow which shortly afterwards was to be incorporated into the constitution of the Society of Jesus.

Thereupon they both left Paris.

Ignatius set his face towards the east, but remembering the unfortunate outcome of his first assault upon the Holy Land, he retraced his steps, went to Rome and there began those activities which were to carry his fame (or otherwise) to every nook and corner of our planet.

John was of a different caliber. His Kingdom of God was bound to neither time nor place and he wandered forth that he might find a quiet spot and devote the rest of his days to reading, to contemplation and to the peaceful expounding of his ideas.

He happened to be on his way to Strassburg when the outbreak of a war between Charles V and Francis I forced him to make a detour through western Switzerland. In Geneva he was welcomed by Guillaume Farel, one of the stormy petrels of the French Reformation, fugitive extraordinary from all ecclesiastical and inquisitorial dungeons. Farel welcomed him with open arms, spoke to him of the wondrous things that might be accomplished in this little Swiss principality and bade him stay. Calvin asked time to consider. Then he stayed.

In this way did the chances of war decree that the New Zion should be built at the foot of the Alps.

It is a strange world.

Columbus sets forth to discover the Indies and stumbles upon a new continent.

Calvin, in search of a quiet spot where he may spend the rest of his days in study and holy meditation, wanders into a third-rate Swiss town and makes it the spiritual capital of those who soon afterwards turn the domains of their most Catholic Majesties into a gigantic Protestant empire.

Why should any one ever read fiction when history serves all purposes?

I do not know whether the family Bible of Calvin has been preserved. But if it still exists, the volume will show considerable wear on that particular page which contains the sixth chapter of the book of Daniel. The French reformer was a modest man, but often he must have found consolation in the story of that other steadfast servant of the living God who also had been cast into a den of lions and whose innocence had saved him from a gruesome and untimely death.

Geneva was no Babylon. It was a respectable little city inhabited by respectable Swiss cloth makers. They took life seriously, but not quite so seriously as that new master who was now holding forth in the pulpit of their Saint Peter.

And furthermore, there was a Nebuchadnezzar in the form of a Duke of Savoy. It was during one of their interminable quarrels with the house of Savoy that the descendants of Cæsar's Allobroges had decided to make common cause with the other Swiss cantons and join the Reformation. The alliance therefore between Geneva and Wittenberg was a marriage of convenience, an engagement based upon common interests rather than common affection.

But no sooner had the news spread abroad that "Geneva had gone Protestant," than all the eager apostles of half a hundred new and crazy creeds flocked to the shores of Lake Leman. With tremendous energy they began to preach some of the queerest doctrines ever conceived by mortal man.

Calvin detested these amateur prophets with all his heart. He fully appreciated what a menace they would prove to the cause of which they were such ardent but ill-guided champions. And the first thing he did as soon as he had enjoyed a few months leisure was to write down as precisely and briefly as he could what he expected his new parishioners to hold true and what he expected them to hold false. And that no man might claim the ancient and time-worn excuse, "I did not know the law," he, together with his friend Farel, personally examined all Genevans in batches of ten and allowed only those to the full rights of citizenship who swore the oath of allegiance to this strange religious constitution.

Next he composed a formidable catechism for the benefit of the younger generation.

Next he prevailed upon the Town Council to expel all those who still clung to their old erroneous opinions.

Then, having cleared the ground for further action, he set about to found him a state along the lines laid down by the political economists of the books of Exodus and Deuteronomy. For Calvin, like so many other of the great reformers, was really much more of an ancient Jew than a modern Christian. His lips did homage to the God of Jesus, but his heart went out to the Jehovah of Moses.

This, of course, is a phenomenon often observed during periods of great emotional stress. The opinions of the humble Nazarene carpenter upon the subject of hatred and strife are so definite and so clear cut that no compromise has ever been found possible between them and those violent methods by which nations and individuals have, during the last two thousand years, tried to accomplish their ends.

Hence, as soon as war breaks out, by silent consent of all concerned, we temporarily close the pages of the Gospels and cheerfully wallow in the blood and thunder and the eye-for-an-eye philosophy of the Old Testament.

And as the Reformation was really a war and a very atrocious one, in which no quarter was asked and very little quarter was given, it need not surprise us that the state of Calvin was in reality an armed camp in which all semblance of personal liberty was gradually suppressed.

Of course, all this was not accomplished without tremendous opposition, and in the year 1538 the attitude of the more liberal elements in the community became so threatening that Calvin was forced to leave the city. But in 1541 his adherents returned to power. Amidst the ringing of many bells and the loud hosannas of the deacons, Magister Joannes returned to his citadel on the river Rhone. Thereafter he was the uncrowned King of Geneva and the next twenty-three years he devoted to the estab-

THE NEW TYRANNY

lishment and the perfection of a theocratic form of government, the like of which the world had not seen since the days of Ezekiel and Ezra.

The word "discipline," according to the Oxford Concise Dictionary, means "to bring under control, to train to obedience and order, to drill." It expresses best the spirit which permeated the entire political-clerical structure of Calvin's dreams.

Luther, after the nature of most Germans, had been a good deal of a sentimentalist. The Word of God alone, so it seemed to him, would show a man the way to the life everlasting.

This was much too indefinite to suit the taste of the great French reformer. The Word of God might be a beacon light of hope, but the road was long and dark and many were the temptations that made people forget their true destination.

The minister, however, could not go astray. He was a man set apart. He knew all pitfalls. He was incorruptible. And if perchance he felt inclined to wander from the straight path, the weekly meetings of the clergy, at which these worthy gentlemen were invited to criticize each other freely, would speedily bring him back to a realization of his duties. Hence he was the ideal held before all those who truly aspired after salvation.

Those of us who have ever climbed mountains know that professional guides can upon occasion be veritable tyrants. They know the perils of a pile of rocks, the hidden dangers of an innocent-looking snowfield. Wherefore they assume complete command of the party that has entrusted itself to their care and profanity raineth richly upon the head of the foolish tourist who dares to disobey their orders.

The ministers of Calvin's ideal state had a similar conception of their duties. They were ever delighted to extend a helping hand to those who stumbled and asked that they be supported. But when willful people purposely left the beaten track and wandered away from the flock, then that hand was withdrawn and became a fist which meted out punishment that was both quick and terrible.

In many other communities the dominies would have been delighted to exercise a similar power. But the civil authorities, jealous of their own prerogatives, rarely allowed the clergy to compete with the courts and the executioners. Calvin knew this and within his own bailiwick he established a form of church discipline which practically superseded the laws of the land.

Among the curious historical misconceptions which have gained such popularity since the days of the Great War, none is more surprising than the belief that the French people (in contrast to their Teuton neighbors) are a liberty-loving race and detest all regimentation. The French have for centuries submitted to the rule of a bureaucracy quite as complicated and infinitely less efficient than the one which existed in Prussia in the pre-war days. The officials are a little less punctual about their office hours and the spotlessness of their collars and they are given to sucking a particularly vile sort of cigarette. Otherwise they are quite as meddlesome and as obnoxious as those in the eastern republic, and the public accepts their rudeness with a meekness that is astonishing in a race so addicted to rebellion.

Calvin was the ideal Frenchman in his love for centralization. In some details he almost approached the perfection for detail which was the secret of Napoleon's success. But unlike the great emperor, he was utterly devoid of all personal ambition. He was just a dreadfully serious man with a weak stomach and no sense of humor.

He ransacked the Old Testament to discover what would be agreeable to his particular Jehovah. And then the people of Geneva were asked to accept this interpretation of the Jewish chronicles as a direct revelation of the divine will. Almost overnight the merry city on the Rhone became a community of rueful sinners. A civic inquisition composed of six ministers and twelve elders watched night and day over the private opinions of all citizens. Whosoever was suspected of an inclination towards "forbidden heresies" was cited to appear before an ecclesiastic tribunal that he might be examined upon all points of doctrine and explain where, how and in what way he had obtained the books which had given him the pernicious ideas which had led him astray. If the culprit showed a repentant spirit, he might escape with a sentence of enforced attendance at Sunday School.

But in case he showed himself obstinate, he must leave the city within twenty-four hours and never again show himself within the jurisdiction of the Genevan commonwealth.

But a proper lack of orthodox sentiment was not the only thing that could get a man into trouble with the so-called Consistorium. An afternoon spent at a bowling-alley in a nearby village, if properly reported (as such things invariably are), could be reason enough for a severe admonition. Jokes, both practical and otherwise, were considered the height of bad form. An attempt at wit during a wedding ceremony was sufficient cause for a jail sentence.

Gradually the New Zion was so encumbered with laws, edicts, regulations, rescripts and decrees that life became a highly complicated affair and lost a great deal of its old flavor.

Dancing was not allowed. Singing was not allowed. Card playing was not allowed. Gambling, of course, was not allowed. Birthday parties were not allowed. County fairs were not allowed. Silks and satins and all manifestations of external splendor were not allowed. What was allowed was going to church and going to school. For Calvin was a man of positive ideas.

The verboten sign could keep out sin, but it could not force a man to love virtue. That had to come through an inner persuasion. Hence the establishment of excellent schools and a first-rate university and the encouragement of all learning. And the establishment of a rather interesting form of communal life which absorbed a good deal of the surplus energy of the community and which made the average man forget the many hardships and restrictions to which he was submitted. If it had been entirely lacking in human qualities, the system of Calvin could never have survived and it certainly would not have played such a very decisive rôle in the history of the last three hundred years. All of which however belongs in a book devoted to the development of political ideas. This time we are interested in the question of what Geneva did for tolerance and we come to the conclusion that the Protestant Rome was not a whit better than its Catholic namesake.

The extenuating circumstances I have enumerated a few pages back. In a world which was forced to stand by and witness such bestial occurrences as the massacre of St. Bartholomew and the wholesale extermination of scores of Dutch cities, it was unreasonable to expect that one side (the weaker one at that) should practice a virtue which was equivalent to a self-imposed sentence of death.

This, however, does not absolve Calvin from the crime of having aided and abetted in the legal murder of Gruet and Servetus.

In the case of the former, Calvin might have put up the excuse that Jacques Gruet was seriously suspected of having incited his fellow citizens to riot and that he belonged to a political party which was trying to bring about the downfall of the Calvinists. But Servetus could hardly be called a menace to the safety of the community, as far as Geneva was concerned.

He was what the modern passport regulations call a "transient." Another twenty-four hours and he would have been gone. But he missed his boat. And so he came to lose his life, and it is a pretty terrible story.

Miguel Serveto, better known as Michael Servetus, was a Spaniard. His father was a respectable notary public (a semi-legal position in Europe and not just a young man with a stamping machine who charges you a quarter for witnessing your signature) and Miguel was also destined for the law. He was sent to the University of Toulouse, for in those happy days when all lecturing was done in Latin learning was international and the wisdom of the entire world was open to those who had mastered five declensions and a few dozen irregular verbs.

At the French university Servetus made the acquaintance of one Juan de Quintana who shortly afterwards became the confessor of the Emperor Charles V.

During the Middle Ages, an imperial coronation was a good deal like a modern international exhibition. When Charles was crowned in Bologna in the year 1530, Quintana took his friend Michael with him as his secretary, and the bright young Spaniard saw all there was to be seen. Like so many men of his time, he was of an insatiable curiosity and he spent the next ten years dabbling in an infinite variety of subjects, medicine, astronomy, astrology, Hebrew, Greek, and, most fatal of all, theology. He was a very competent doctor and in the pursuit of his theological studies he hit upon the idea of the circulation of the blood. It is to be found in the fifteenth chapter of the first one of his books against the doctrine of the Trinity. It shows the one-sidedness of the theological mind of the sixteenth century that none of those who examined the works of Servetus ever discovered that this man had made one of the greatest discoveries of all ages.

If only Servetus had stuck to his medical practice! He might have died peacefully in his bed at a ripe old age.

But he simply could not keep away from the burning questions of his day, and having access to the printing shops of Lyons, he began to give vent to his opinions upon sundry subjects.

Nowadays a generous millionaire can persuade a college to change its name from Trinity College to that of a popular brand of tobacco and nothing happens. The press says, "Isn't it good of Mr. Dingus to be so generous with his money!" and the public at large shouts "Amen!"

In a world which seems to have lost all capacity for being shocked by such a thing as blasphemy, it is not easy to write of a time when the mere suspicion that one of its fellow citizens had spoken disrespectfully of the Trinity would throw an entire community into a state of panic. But unless we fully appreciate this fact, we shall never be able to understand the horror in which Servetus was held by all good Christians of the first half of the sixteenth century.

And yet he was by no means a radical.

He was what to-day we would call a liberal.

He rejected the old belief in the Trinity as held by both the Protestants and the Catholics, but he believed so sincerely (one feels inclined to say, so naïvely) in the correctness of his own views, that he committed the grave error of writing letters to Calvin suggesting that he be allowed to visit Geneva for a personal interview and a thorough discussion of the entire problem.

He was not invited.

And, anyway, it would have been impossible for him to accept. The Inquisitor General of Lyons had already taken a hand in the affair and Servetus was in jail. This inquisitor (curious readers will find a description of him in the works of Rabelais who refers to him as Doribus, a pun upon his name, which was Ory) had got wind of the Spaniard's blasphemies through a letter which a private citizen of Geneva, with the connivance of Calvin, had sent to his cousin in Lyons.

Soon the case against him was further strengthened by several samples of Servetus' handwriting, also surreptitiously supplied by Calvin. It really looked as if Calvin did not care who hanged the poor fellow as long as he got hung, but the inquisitors were negligent in their sacred duties and Servetus was able to escape.

First he seems to have tried to reach the Spanish frontier. But the long journey through southern France would have been very dangerous to a man who was so well known and so he decided to follow the rather roundabout route via Geneva, Milan, Naples and the Mediterranean Sea.

Late one Saturday afternoon in August of the year 1553 he reached Geneva. He tried to find a boat to cross to the other side of the lake, but boats were not supposed to sail so shortly before the Sabbath day and he was told to wait until Monday.

The next day was Sunday. As it was a misdemeanor for both natives and strangers to stay away from divine service, Servetus went to church. He was recognized and arrested. By what right he was put into jail was never explained. Servetus was a Spanish subject and was not accused of any crime against the laws of Geneva. But he was a liberal in the matter of doctrine, a blasphemous and profane person who dared to have opinions of his own upon the subject of the Trinity. It was absurd that such a person should invoke the protection of the law. A common criminal might do so. A heretic, never! And without further ado he was locked up in a filthy and damp hole, his money and his personal belongings were confiscated and two days later he was taken to court and was asked to answer a questionnaire containing thirty-eight different points.

The trial lasted two months and twelve days.

In the end he was found guilty of "heresies against the foundations of the Christian religion." The answers which he had given during the discussions of his opinions had exasperated his judges. The usual punishment for cases of his sort, especially if the accused were a foreigner, was perpetual banishment from the territory of the city of Geneva. In the case of Servetus an exception was made. He was condemned to be burned alive.

In the meantime the French tribunal had reopened the case of the fugitive and the officials of the Inquisition had come to the same conclusion as their Protestant colleagues. They too had condemned Servetus to death and had dispatched their sheriff to Geneva with the request that the culprit be surrendered to him and be brought back to France.

This request was refused.

Calvin was able to do his own burning.

As for that terrible walk to the place of execution, with a delegation of arguing ministers surrounding the heretic upon his last journey, the agony which lasted for more than half an hour and did not really come to an end until the crowd, in their pity for the poor martyr, had thrown a fresh supply of fagots upon the flames, all this makes interesting reading for those who care for that sort of thing, but it had better be omitted. One execution more or less, what difference did it make during a period of unbridled religious fanaticism?

But the case of Servetus really stands by itself. Its consequences were terrible. For now it was shown, and shown with brutal clearness, that those Protestants who had clamored so loudly and persistently for "the right to their own opinions" were merely Catholics in disguise, that they were just as narrow-minded and cruel to those who did not share their own views as their enemies and that they were only waiting for the opportunity to establish a reign of terror of their own.

This accusation is a very serious one. It cannot be dismissed by a mere shrug of the shoulders and a "Well, what would you expect?"

We possess a great deal of information upon the trial and know in detail what the rest of the world thought of this execution. It makes ghastly reading. It is true that Calvin, in an outburst of generosity, suggested that Servetus be decapitated instead of burned. Servetus thanked him for his kindness, but offered still another solution. He wanted to be set free. Yea, he insisted (and the logic was all on his side) that the court had no jurisdiction over him, that he was merely an honest man in search for the truth and that therefore he had the right to be heard in open debate with his opponent, Dr. Calvin.

But of this Calvin would not hear.

He had sworn that this heretic, once he fell into his hands, should never be allowed to escape with his life, and he was going to be as good as his word. That he could not get a conviction without the coöperation of his arch-enemy, the Inquisition, made no difference to him. He would have made common cause with the Pope if His Holiness had been in the possession of some documents that would further incriminate the unfortunate Spaniard.

But worse was to follow.

On the morning of his death, Servetus asked to see Calvin and the latter came to the dark and filthy dungeon that had served his enemy as a prison.

Upon this occasion at least he might have been generous; more, he might have been human.

He was neither.

He stood in the presence of a man who within another hour would be able to plead his case before the throne of God and he argued. He debated and sputtered, grew green and lost his temper. But not a word of pity, of charity, or kindliness. Not a word. Only bitterness and hatred, the feeling of "Serve you right, you obstinate scoundrel. Burn and be damned!"

* * * * * * * *

All this happened many, many years ago.

Servetus is dead.

All our statues and memorial tablets will not bring him back to life again.

Calvin is dead.

A thousand volumes of abuse will not disturb the ashes of his unknown grave.

They are all of them dead, those ardent reformers who during the trial had shuddered with fear lest the blasphemous scoundrel be allowed to escape, those staunch pillars of the Church who after the execution broke forth into pæans of praise and wrote each other, "All hail to Geneva! The deed is done."

They are all of them dead, and perhaps it were best they were forgotten too.

Only let us have a care.

Tolerance is like liberty.

No one ever gets it merely by asking for it. No one keeps it except by the exercise of eternal care and vigilance.

For the sake of some future Servetus among our own children, we shall do well to remember this.

Chapter XVI

THE ANABAPTISTS

EVERY generation has a bogey-man all its own.

We have our "Reds."

Our fathers had their Socialists.

Our grandfathers had their Molly Maguires.

Our great-great-grandfathers had their Jacobins.

And our ancestors of three hundred years ago were not a bit better off.

They had their Anabaptists.

The most popular "Outline of History" of the sixteenth cen-

THE ANABAPTISTS
235

tury was a certain "World Book" or chronicle, which Sebastian Frank, soap-boiler, prohibitionist and author, living in the good city of Ulm, published in the year 1534.

Sebastian knew the Anabaptists. He had married into an Anabaptist family. He did not share their views, for he was a confirmed free thinker. But this is what he wrote about them: "that they taught nothing but love and faith and the crucifixion of the flesh, that they manifested patience and humility under all suffering, assisted one another with true helpfulness, called each other brother and believed in having all things in common."

It is surely a curious thing that people of whom all those nice things could be truthfully said should for almost a hundred years have been hunted down like wild animals, and should have been exposed to all the most cruel punishments of the most bloodthirsty of centuries.

But there was a reason and in order to appreciate it you must remember certain facts about the Reformation.

The Reformation really settled nothing.

It gave the world two prisons instead of one, made a book infallible in the place of a man and established (or rather, tried to establish) a rule by black garbed ministers instead of white garbed priests.

Such meager results after half a century of struggle and sacrifice had filled the hearts of millions of people with desperate disappointment. They had expected a millennium of social and religious righteousness and they were not at all prepared for a new Gehenna of persecution and economic slavery.

They had been ready for a great adventure. Then something had happened. They had slipped between the wall and the ship. And they had been obliged to strike out for themselves and keep above water as best they could.

They were in a terrible position. They had left the old church. Their conscience did not allow them to join the new faith. Officially they had, therefore, ceased to exist. And yet they lived. They breathed. They were sure that they were God's beloved children. As such it was their duty to keep on living and breathing, that they might save a wicked world from its own folly.

Eventually they survived, but do not ask how!

Deprived of their old associations, they were forced to form groups of their own, to look for a new leadership.

But what man in his senses would take up with these poor fanatics?

As a result, shoemakers with second sight and hysterical midwives with visions and hallucinations assumed the rôle of prophets and prophetesses and they prayed and preached and raved until the rafters of their dingy meeting places shook with the hosannas of the faithful and the tip-staffs of the village were forced to take notice of the unseemly disturbance.

Then half a dozen men and women were sent to jail and their High and Mightinesses, the town councilors, began what was good-naturedly called "an investigation."

These people did not go to the Catholic church. They did not worship in the Protestant kirk. Then would they please explain who they were and what they believed?

To give the poor councilors their due, they were in a difficult predicament. For their prisoners were the most uncomfortable of all heretics, people who took their religious convictions absolutely seriously. Many of the most respectable reformers were of this earth earthy and willingly made such small compromises as were absolutely necessary, if one hoped to lead an agreeable and respectable existence.

Your true Anabaptist was of a different caliber. He frowned upon all half-way measures. Jesus had told his followers to turn the other cheek when smitten by an enemy, and had taught that all those who take the sword shall perish by the sword. To the Anabaptists this meant a positive ordinance to use no violence. They did not care to dilly-dally with words and murmur that circumstances alter cases, that, of course, they were against war, but that this was a different kind of a war and that therefore they felt that for this once God would not mind if they threw a few bombs or fired an occasional torpedo.

A divine ordinance was a divine ordinance, and that was all there was to it.

And so they refused to enlist and refused to carry arms and

in case they were arrested for their pacifism (for that is what their enemies called this sort of applied Christianity) they went willingly forth to meet their fate and recited Matthew xxvi: 52 until death made an end to their suffering.

But anti-militarism was only a small detail in their program of queerness. Jesus had preached that the Kingdom of God and the Kingdom of Cæsar were two entirely different entities and could not and should not be reconciled. Very well. These words were clear. Henceforth all good Anabaptists carefully abstained from taking part in their country's government, refused to hold public office and spent the time which other people wasted upon politics, reading and studying the Holy Scriptures.

Jesus had cautioned his disciples against unseemly quarrels and the Anabaptists would rather lose their rightful possessions than submit a difference of opinion to a law court. There were several other points which set these peculiar people apart from the rest of the world, but these few examples of their odd behavior will explain the suspicion and detestation in which they were held by their fat and happy neighbors who invariably mixed their piety with a dose of that comfortable doctrine which bids us live and let live.

Even so, the Anabaptists, like the Baptists and many other dissenters, might in the end have discovered a way to placate the authorities, if only they had been able to protect themselves from their own friends.

Undoubtedly there are many honest Bolshevists who dearly love their fellow proletarians and who spend their waking hours trying to make this world a better and happier place. But when the average person hears the word "Bolshevik," he thinks of Moscow and of a reign of terror established by a handful of scholarly cutthroats, of jails full of innocent people and firing squads jeering at the victims they are about to shoot. This picture may be slightly unfair, but it is no more than natural that it should be part of the popular myth after the unspeakable things which have happened in Russia during the last seven years.

The really good and peaceful Anabaptists of the sixteenth century suffered from a similar disadvantage. As a sect they were suspected of many strange crimes, and with good reason. In the first place, they were inveterate Bible readers. This, of course, is not a crime at all, but let me finish my sentence. The Anabaptists studied the Scriptures without any discrimination and that is a very dangerous thing when one has a strong predilection for the Book of Revelation.

This strange work which even as late as the fifth century was rejected as a bit of "spurious writing" was just the sort of thing to appeal to people who lived during a period of intense emotional passions. The exile of Patmos spoke a language which these poor, hunted creatures understood. When his impotent rage drove him into hysterical prophecies anent the modern Babylon, all the Anabaptists shouted "Amen" and prayed for the speedy coming of the New Heaven and the New Earth.

It was not the first time that weak minds gave way under the stress of a great excitement. And almost every persecution of the Anabaptists was followed by violent outbursts of religious insanity. Men and women would rush naked through the streets, announcing the end of the world, trying to indulge in weird sacrifices that the fury of God might be appeased. Old hags would enter the divine services of some other sect and break up the meeting, stridently shrieking nonsense about the coming of the Dragon.

Of course, this sort of affliction (in a mild degree) is always with us. Read the daily papers and you will see how in some remote hamlet of Ohio or Iowa or Florida a woman has butchered her husband with a meat cleaver because "she was told to do so" by the voice of an angel; or how an otherwise reasonable father has just killed his wife and eight children in anticipation of the sounding of the Seven Trumpets. Such cases, however, are rare exceptions. They can be easily handled by the local police and they really do not have great influence upon the life or the safety of the Republic.

But what had happened in the year 1534 in the good town of Münster was something very different. There the New Zion, upon strictly Anabaptist principles, had actually been proclaimed.

And people all over northern Europe shuddered when they thought of that terrible winter and spring.

The villain in the case was a good-looking young tailor by the name of Jan Beukelszoon. History knows him as John of Leiden, for Jan was a native of that industrious little city and had spent his childhood along the banks of the sluggish old Rhine. Like all other apprentices of that day, he had traveled extensively and had wandered far and wide to learn the secrets of his trade.

He could read and write just enough to produce an occasional play, but he had no real education. Neither was he possessed of that humility of spirit which we so often find in people who are conscious of their social disadvantages and their lack of knowledge. But he was a very good-looking young man, endowed with unlimited cheek and as vain as a peacock.

After a long absence in England and Germany, he went back to his native land and set up in the cloak and suit business. At the same time he went in for religion and that was the beginning of his extraordinary career. For he became a disciple of Thomas Münzer.

This man Münzer, a baker by profession, was a famous character. He was one of the three Anabaptist prophets who, in the year 1521, had suddenly made their appearance in Wittenberg that they might show Luther how to find the true road to salvation. Although they had acted with the best of intentions, their efforts had not been appreciated and they had been chased out of the Protestant stronghold with the request that never again they show their unwelcome selves within the jurisdiction of the Dukes of Saxony.

Came the year 1534 and the Anabaptists had suffered so many defeats that they decided to risk everything on one big, bold stroke.

That they selected the town of Münster in Westphalia as the spot for their final experiment surprised no one. Franz von

Waldeck, the prince-bishop of that city, was a drunken bounder who for years had lived openly with a score of women and who ever since his sixteenth year had offended all decent people by the outrageous bad taste of his private conduct. When the town went Protestant, he compromised. But being known far and wide for a liar and a cheat, his treaty of peace did not give his Protestant subjects that feeling of personal security without which life is indeed a very uncomfortable experience. In consequence whereof the inhabitants of Münster remained in a state of high agitation until the next elections. These brought a surprise. The city government fell into the hands of the Anabaptists. The chairman became one Bernard Knipper-dollinck, a cloth merchant by day and a prophet after dark.

The bishop took one look at his new councilors and fled.

It was then that John of Leiden appeared upon the scene. He had come to Münster as the apostle of a certain Jan Matthysz, a Haarlem baker who had started a new sect of his own and was regarded as a very holy man. And when he heard of the great blow that had been struck for the good cause, he remained to help celebrate the victory and purge the bishopric of all popish contamination. The Anabaptists were nothing if not thorough. They turned the churches into stone quarries. They confiscated the convents for the benefit of the homeless. All books except the Bible were publicly burned. And as a fitting climax, those who refused to be rebaptized after the Anabaptist fashion were driven into the camp of the Bishop, who decapitated them or drowned them on the general principle that they were heretics and small loss to the community.

That was the prologue.

The play itself was no less terrible.

From far and wide the high priests of half a hundred new creeds hastened to the New Jerusalem. There they were joined by all those who believed themselves possessed of a call for the great uplift, honest and sincere citizens, but as innocent as babes when it came to politics or statecraft.

The siege of Münster lasted five months, and during that time every scheme, system and program of social and spiritual regeneration was tried out; every new-fangled prophet had his day in court.

But, of course, a little town chuck full of fugitives, pestilence and hunger, was not a fit place for a sociological laboratory and the dissensions and quarrels between the different factions lamed all the efforts of the military leaders. During that crisis John the tailor stepped forward.

The short hour of his glory had come.

In that community of starving men and suffering children, all things were possible. John began his régime by introducing an exact replica of that old theocratic form of government of which he had read in his Old Testament. The burghers of Münster were divided into the twelve tribes of Israel and John himself was chosen to be their king. He had already married the daughter of one prophet, Knipperdollinck. Now he married the widow of another, the wife of his former master, John Matthysz. Next he remembered Solomon and added a couple of concubines. And then the ghastly farce began.

All day long John sat on the throne of David in the market place and all day long the people stood by while the royal court chaplain read the latest batch of ordinances. These came fast and furiously, for the fate of the city was daily growing more desperate and the people were in dire need.

John, however, was an optimist and thoroughly believed in the omnipotence of paper decrees.

The people complained that they were hungry. John promised that he would tend to it. And forthwith a royal ukase, duly signed by His Majesty, ordained that all wealth in the city be divided equally among the rich and the poor, that the streets be broken up and used as vegetable gardens, that all meals be eaten in common.

So far so good. But there were those who said that some of the rich people had hidden part of their treasures. John bade his subjects not to worry. A second decree proclaimed that all those who broke a single law of the community would be immediately decapitated. And, mind you, such a warning was no idle threat. For this royal tailor was as handy with his sword as with his scissors and frequently undertook to be his own executioner.

Then came the period of hallucinations when the populace suffered from a diversity of religious manias; when the market place was crowded day and night with thousands of men and women, awaiting the trumpet blasts of the angel Gabriel.

Then came the period of terror, when the prophet kept up the courage of his flock by a constant orgy of blood and cut the throat of one of his own queens.

And then came the terrible day of retribution when two citizens in their despair opened the gates to the soldiers of the bishop and when the prophet, locked in an iron cage, was shown at all the Westphalian country fairs and was finally tortured to death.

A weird episode, but of terrible consequence to many a God-fearing and simple soul.

From that moment on, all Anabaptists were outlawed. Such leaders as had escaped the carnage of Münster were hunted down like rabbits and were killed wherever found. From every pulpit, ministers and priests fulminated against the Anabaptists and with many curses and anathemas they denounced them as communists and traitors and rebels, who wanted to upset the existing order of things and deserved less mercy than wolves or mad dogs.

Rarely has a heresy hunt been so successful. As a sect, the Anabaptists ceased to exist. But a strange thing happened. Many of their ideas continued to live, were picked up by other denominations, were incorporated into all sorts of religious and philosophic systems, became respectable, and are to-day part and parcel of everybody's spiritual and intellectual inheritance.

It is a simple thing to state such a fact. To explain how it actually came about, that is quite a different story.

Almost without exception the Anabaptists belonged to that class of society which regards an inkstand as an unnecessary luxury.

Anabaptist history, therefore, was writ by those who regarded the sect as a particularly venomous kind of denominational radicalism. Only now, after a century of study, are we beginning

245

to understand the great rôle the ideas of these humble peasants and artisans have played in the further development of a more rational and more tolerant form of Christianity.

But ideas are like lightning. One never knows where they will strike next. And what is the use of lightning rods in Münster, when the storm breaks loose over Sienna?

Chapter XVII

THE SOZZINI FAMILY

In Italy the Reformation had never been successful. It could not be. In the first place, the people of the south did not take their religion seriously enough to fight about it, and in the second place, the close proximity of Rome, the center of a particularly well equipped office of the Inquisition, made indulgence in private opinions a dangerous and costly pastime.

But, of course, among all the thousands of humanists who populated the peninsula, there were bound to be a few black sheep who cared a great deal more for the good opinion of Aristotle than for that of Saint Chrysostom. Those good people, however, were given many opportunities to get rid of their surplus spiritual energy. There were clubs and coffee-houses and discreet salons where men and women could give vent to their intellectual enthusiasm without

THE SOZZINIS

upsetting empires. All of which was very pleasant and restful. And besides, wasn't all life a compromise? Hadn't it always been a compromise? Would it not in all likelihood be a compromise until the end of time?

Why get excited about such a small detail as one's faith?

After these few introductory remarks, the reader will surely not expect to hear a loud fanfaronade or the firing of guns when our next two heroes make their appearance. For they are soft-spoken gentlemen, and go about their business in a dignified and pleasant way.

In the end, they are to do more to upset the dogmatic tyranny under which the world had suffered for such a long time than a whole army of noisy reformers. But that is one of those curious things which no one can foresee. They happen. We are grateful. But how it comes about, that, alas, is something which we do not fully understand.

The name of these two quiet workmen in the vineyard of reason was Sozzini.

They were uncle and nephew.

For some unknown reason, the older man, Lelio Francesco, spelled his name with one "z" and the younger, Fausto Paolo, spelled his with two "z's." But as they are both of them much better known by the Latinized form of their name, Socinius, than by the Italian Sozzini, we can leave that detail to the grammarians and etymologists.

As far as their influence was concerned, the uncle was much less important than the nephew. We shall, therefore, deal with him first and speak of the nephew afterwards.

Lelio Sozini was a Siennese, the descendant of a race of bankers and judges and himself destined for a career at the bar, via the University of Bologna. But like so many of his contemporaries, he allowed himself to slip into theology, stopped reading law, played with Greek and Hebrew and Arabic and ended (as so often happens with people of his type) as a rationalistic mystic—a man who was at once very much of this world and yet never quite of it. This sounds complicated. But those who understand what I mean will understand without any further explanation, and the others would not understand, no matter what I said.

His father, however, seems to have had a suspicion that the son might amount to something in the world of letters. He gave his boy a check and bade him go forth and see whatever there was to be seen. And so Lelio left Sienna and during the next ten years he traveled from Venice to Geneva and from Geneva to Zurich and from Zurich to Wittenberg and then to London and then to Prague and then to Vienna and then to Cracow, spending a few months or years in every town and hamlet where he hoped to find interesting company and might be able to learn something new and interesting. It was an age when people talked religion just as incessantly as to-day they talk business. Lelio must have collected a strange assortment of ideas and by keeping his ears open he was soon familiar with every heresy between the Mediterranean and the Baltic.

When, however, he carried himself and his intellectual luggage to Geneva, he was received politely but none too cordially. The pale eyes of Calvin looked upon this Italian visitor with grave suspicion. He was a distinguished young man of excellent family and not a poor, friendless wanderer like Servetus. It was said, however, that he had Servetian inclinations. And that was most disturbing. The case for or against the Trinity, so Calvin thought, had been definitely settled when the Spanish heretic was burned. On the contrary! The fate of Servetus had become a subject of conversation from Madrid to Stockholm, and serious-minded people all over the world were beginning to take the side of the anti-trinitarian. But that was not all. They were using Gutenberg's devilish invention to spread their views broadcast and being at a safe distance from Geneva they were often far from complimentary in their remarks.

Only a short while before had appeared a very learned tract which contained everything the fathers of the Church had ever said or written upon the subject of persecuting and punishing heretics. It had an instantaneous and enormous sale among those who "hated God," as Calvin said, or who "hated Calvin," as they themselves protested. Calvin had let it be known that he would like to have a personal interview with the author of this precious booklet. But the author, anticipating such a request, had wisely omitted his name from the title-page.

It was said that he was called Sebastian Castellio, that he had been a teacher in one of the Geneva high schools and that his moderate views upon diverse theological enormities had gained him the hatred of Calvin and the approbation of Montaigne. No one, however, could prove this. It was mere hearsay. But where one had gone before, others might follow.

Calvin, therefore, was distantly polite to Sozzini, but suggested that the mild air of Basel would suit his Siennese friend much better than the damp climate of Savoy and heartily bade him Godspeed when he started on his way to the famous old Erasmian stronghold.

Fortunately for Calvin, the Sozzini family soon afterwards fell under the suspicion of the Inquisition, Lelio was deprived of his funds and, falling ill of a fever, he died in Zürich at the age of only thirty-seven.

Whatever joy his untimely demise may have caused in Geneva, it was short-lived.

For Lelio, besides a widow and several trunks of notes, left a nephew, who not only fell heir to his uncle's unpublished manuscripts but soon gained for himself the reputation of being even more of a Servetus enthusiast than his uncle had been.

During his younger years, Faustus Socinius had traveled almost as extensively as the older Lelio. His grandfather had left him a small estate and, as he did not marry until he was nearly fifty, he was able to devote all his time to his favorite subject, theology.

For a short while he seems to have been in business in Lyons.

What sort of a salesman he made, I do not know, but his experience in buying and selling and dealing in concrete commodities rather than spiritual values seems to have strengthened him in his conviction that very little is ever gained by killing a competitor or losing one's temper if the other man has the better of a deal. And as long as he lived, he showed himself possessed of that sober common sense which is often found in a counting-house but is very rarely part of the curriculum of a religious seminary.

In the year 1563 Faustus returned to Italy. On his way home he visited Geneva. It does not appear that he ever paid his respects to the local patriarch. Besides, Calvin was a very sick man at that time. The visit from a member of the Sozzini family would only have disturbed him.

The next dozen years, young Socinius spent in the service of Isabella de' Medici. But in the year 1576 this lady, after a few days of matrimonial bliss, was murdered by her husband, Paolo Orsini. Thereupon Socinius resigned, left Italy for good and went to Basel to translate the Psalms into colloquial Italian and write a book on Jesus.

Faustus, so it appeared from his writings, was a careful man. In the first place, he was very deaf and such people are by nature cautious.

In the second place, he derived his income from certain estates situated on the other side of the Alps and the Tuscan authorities had given him a hint that it might be just as well for one suspected of "Lutheran leanings" not to be too bold while dealing with subjects which were held in disfavor by the Inquisition. Hence he used a number of pseudonyms and never printed a book unless it had been passed upon by a number of friends and had been declared to be fairly safe.

Thus it happened that his books were not placed on the Index. It also happened that a copy of his life of Jesus was carried all the way to Transylvania and there fell into the hands of another liberal-minded Italian, the private physician of a number of Milanese and Florentine ladies who had married into the Polish and Transylvanian nobility.

Transylvania in those days was the "far east" of Europe. A wilderness until the early part of the twelfth century, it had been used as a convenient home for the surplus population of Germany. The hard-working Saxon peasants had turned this fertile land into a prosperous and well regulated little country with cities and schools and an occasional university. But it remained a country far removed from the main roads of travel and trade. Hence it had always been a favorite place of residence for those who for one reason or another preferred to keep a few miles of marsh and mountain between themselves and the henchmen of the Inquisition.

As for Poland, this unfortunate country has for so many centuries been associated with the general idea of reaction and jingoism that it will come as an agreeable surprise to many of my readers when I tell them that during the first half of the sixteenth century, it was a veritable asylum for all those who in other parts of Europe suffered on account of their religious convictions.

This unexpected state of affairs had been brought about in a typically Polish fashion.

That the Republic for quite a long time had been the most scandalously mismanaged country of the entire continent was even then a generally known fact. The extent, however, to which the higher clergy had neglected their duties was not appreciated quite so clearly in those days when dissolute bishops and drunken village priests were the common affliction of all western nations.

But during the latter half of the fifteenth century it was noticed that the number of Polish students in the different German universities was beginning to increase at a rate of speed which caused great concern among the authorities of Wittenberg and Leipzig. They began to ask questions. And then it developed that the ancient Polish academy of Cracow, administered by the Polish church, had been allowed to fall into such a state of utter decay that the poor Polanders were forced to go abroad for their education or do without. A little later, when the Teuton universities fell under the spell of the new doctrines, the bright young men from Warsaw and Radom and Czenstochowa quite naturally followed suit.

And when they returned to their home towns, they did so as full-fledged Lutherans.

At that early stage of the Reformation it would have been quite easy for the king and the nobility and the clergy to stamp out this epidemic of erroneous opinions. But such a step would have obliged the rulers of the republic to unite upon a definite and common policy and that of course was directly in contradiction to the most hallowed traditions of this strange country where a single dissenting vote could upset a law which had the support of all the other members of the diet.

And when (as happened shortly afterwards) it appeared that the religion of the famous Wittenberg professor carried with it a by-product of an economic nature. consisting of the confiscation of all Church property, the Boleslauses and Wladislauses and the other knights, counts, barons, princes and dukes who populated the fertile plains between the Baltic and the Black Sea began to show a decided leaning towards a faith which meant money in their pockets.

The unholy scramble for monastic real estate which followed upon the discovery caused one of those famous "interims" with which the Poles, since time immemorial, have tried to stave off the day of reckoning. During such periods all authority came to a standstill and the Protestants made such a good use of their opportunity that in less than a year they had established churches of their own in every part of the kingdom.

Eventually of course the incessant theological haggling of the new ministers drove the peasants back into the arms of the Church and Poland once more became one of the strongholds of a most uncompromising form of Catholicism. But during the latter half of the sixteenth century, the country enjoyed complete religious license. When the Catholics and Protestants of western Europe began their war of extermination upon the Anabaptists, it was a foregone conclusion that the survivors should flee eastward and should eventually settle down along the banks of the Vistula, and it was then that Doctor Blandrata got hold of Socinius' book on Jesus and expressed a wish to make the author's acquaintance.

Giorgio Blandrata was an Italian, a physician and a man of parts. He had graduated at the University of Montpellier and had been remarkably successful as a woman's specialist. First and last he was a good deal of a scoundrel, but a clever one. Like so many doctors of his time (think of Rabelais and Servetus) he was as much of a theologian as a neurologist and frequently played one rôle out against the other. For example, he cured the Queen Dowager of Poland, Bona Sforza (widow of King Sigismund), so successfully of the obsession that those who doubted the Trinity were wrong, that she repented of her errors and thereafter only executed those who held the doctrine of the Trinity to be true.

The good queen, alas, was gone (murdered by one of her

lovers) but two of her daughters had married local noblemen and as their medical adviser, Blandrata exercised a great deal of influence upon the politics of his adopted land. He knew that the country was ripe for civil war and that it would happen very soon unless something be done to make an end to the ever-lasting religious quarrels. Wherefore he set to work to bring about a truce between the different opposing sects. But for this purpose he needed some one more skilled in the intricacies of a religious debate than he was himself. Then he had an inspira-tion. The author of the life of Jesus was his man.

He sent Socinius a letter and asked him to come east.

Unfortunately when Socinius reached Transylvania the pri-vate life of Blandrata had just led to so grave a public scandal that the Italian had been forced to resign and leave for parts unknown. Socinius, however, remained in this far-away land, married a Polish girl and died in his adopted country in the year 1604.

These last two decades of his life proved to be the most inter-esting period of his career. For it was then that he gave a con-crete expression to his ideas upon the subject of tolerance.

They are to be found in the so-called "Catechism of Rakow," a document which Socinius composed as a sort of common con-stitution for all those who meant well by this world and wished to make an end to future sectarian strife.

The latter half of the sixteenth century was an era of cate-chisms, confessions of faith, credos and creeds. People were writ-ing them in Germany and in Switzerland and in France and in Holland and in Denmark. But everywhere these carelessly printed little booklets gave expression to the ghastly belief that they (and they alone) contained the real Truth with a great big capital T and that it was the duty of all authorities who had solemnly pledged themselves to uphold this one particular form of Truth with a great big capital T to punish with the sword and the gallows and the stake those who willfully remained faith-ful to a different sort of truth (which was only written with a small t and therefore was of an inferior quality).

The Socinian confession of faith breathed an entirely different spirit. It began by the flat statement that it was not the intention of those who had signed this document to quarrel with anybody else.

"With good reason," it continued, "many pious people complain that the various confessions and catechisms which have hitherto been published and which the different churches are now publishing are apples of discord among the Christians because they all try to impose certain principles upon people's conscience and to consider those who disagree with them as heretics."

Thereupon it denied in the most formal way that it was the intention of the Socinians to proscribe or oppress any one else on account of his religious convictions, and turning to humanity in general, it made the following appeal:

"Let each one be free to judge of his own religion, for this is the rule set forth by the New Testament and by the example of the earliest church. Who are we, miserable people, that we would smother and extinguish in others the fire of divine spirit which God has kindled in them? Have any of us a monopoly of the knowledge of the Holy Scriptures? Why do we not remember that our only master is Jesus Christ and that we are all brothers and that to no one has been given power over the souls of others? It may be that one of our brothers is more learned than the others, yet in regard to liberty and the relationship with Christ we are all equal."

All this was very fine and very wonderful, but it was said three hundred years ahead of the times. Neither the Socinians nor any of the other Protestant sects could in the long run hope to hold their own in this turbulent part of the world. The counterreformation had begun in all seriousness. Veritable hordes of Jesuit fathers were beginning to be turned loose upon the lost provinces. While they worked, the Protestants quarreled. Soon the people of the eastern frontier were back within the fold of Rome. To-day the traveler who visits these distant parts of civilized Europe would hardly guess that, once upon a time, they were a stronghold of the most advanced and liberal thought of the age. Nor would he suspect that somewhere among those dreary Lithuanian hills there lies a village where the world was for the first time presented with a definite program for a practical system of tolerance.

Driven by idle curiosity, I took a morning off recently and went to the library and read through the index of all our most popular text-books out of which the youth of our country learns the story of the past. Not a single one mentioned Socinianism or the Sozzinis. They all jumped from Social Democrats to Sophia of Hanover and from Saracens to Sobieski. The usual leaders of the great religious revolution were there, including Œcolampadius and the lesser lights.

One volume only contained a reference to the two great Siennese humanists but they appeared as a vague appendix to something Luther or Calvin had said or done.

It is dangerous to make predictions, but I have a suspicion that in the popular histories of three hundred years hence, all this will have been changed and that the Sozzinis shall enjoy the luxury of a little chapter of their own and that the traditional heroes of the Reformation shall be relegated to the bottom of the page.

They have the sort of names that look terribly imposing in footnotes.

Chapter XVIII

MONTAIGNE

In the Middle Ages it used to be said that city air made for freedom.

That was true.

A man behind a high stone wall could thumb his nose safely at baron and priest.

A little later, when conditions upon the European continent had improved so much that international commerce was once more becoming a possibility, another historical phenomenon began to make itself manifest.

Done into words of three syllables it read: "Business makes for tolerance."

You can verify this statement any day of the week and most of all on Sunday in any part of our country.

Winesburg, Ohio, can afford to support the Ku Klux Klan, but New York cannot. If the people of New York should ever start a movement for the exclusion of all Jews and all Catholics and all foreigners in general, there would be such a panic in Wall Street and such an upheaval in the labor movement that the town would be ruined beyond the hope of repair.

The same held true during the latter half of the Middle Ages. Moscow, the seat of a small grand ducal count, might rage against the pagans, but Novgorod, the international trading post, must be careful lest she offend the Swedes and Norwegians and the Germans and the Flemish merchants who visited her market place and drive them to Wisby.

A purely agricultural state could with impunity regale its peasantry with a series of festive autos da fé. But if the Venetians or the Genoese or the people of Bruges had started a pogrom among the heathen within their walls, there would have been an immediate exodus of all those who represented foreign business houses and the subsequent withdrawal of capital would have driven the city into bankruptcy.

A few countries which were constitutionally unable to learn from experience (like Spain and the papal dominions and certain possessions of the Hapsburgs), actuated by a sentiment, which they proudly called "loyalty to their convictions," ruthlessly expelled the enemies of the true faith. As a result they either ceased to exist altogether or dwindled down to the rank of seventh rate Ritter states.

"OUR LORD OF THE ATTICK"

Commercial nations and cities, however, are as a rule governed by men who have a profound respect for established facts, who know on which side their bread is buttered, and who therefore maintain such a state of spiritual neutrality that their Catholic and Protestant and Jewish and Chinese customers can do business as usual and yet remain faithful to their own particular religion.

For the sake of outward respectability Venice might pass a law against the Calvinists, but the Council of Ten was careful to explain to their gendarmes that this decree must not be taken too seriously and that unless the heretics actually tried to get hold of San Marco and convert it into a meeting house of their own, they must be left alone and must be allowed to worship as they saw fit.

Their good friends in Amsterdam did likewise. Every Sunday their ministers fulminated against the sins of the "Scarlet Woman." But in the next block the terrible papists were quietly saying mass in some inconspicuous looking house, and outside the Protestant chief-of-police stood watch lest an overzealous admirer of the Geneva catechism try to break up this forbidden meeting and frighten the profitable French and Italian visitors away.

This did not in the least mean that the mass of the people in Venice or Amsterdam ceased to be faithful sons of their respective churches. They were as good Catholics or Protestants as they had ever been. But they remembered that the good will of a dozen profitable heretics from Hamburg or Lübeck or Lisbon was worth more than the approbation of a dozen shabby clerics from Geneva or Rome and they acted accordingly.

It may seem a little far-fetched to connect the enlightened and liberal opinions (they are not always the same) of Montaigne with the fact that his father and grandfather had been in the herring business and that his mother was of Spanish-Jewish descent. But it seems to me that these commercial antecedents had a great deal to do with the man's general point of view, and that the intense dislike of fanaticism and bigotry which characterized his entire career as a soldier and statesman had originated in a little fish-shop somewhere off the main quai of Bordeaux.

Montaigne himself would not have thanked me if I had been able to make this statement to his face. For when he was born, all vestiges of mere "trade" had been carefully wiped off the resplendent family escutcheon.

His father had acquired a bit of property called Montaigne and had spent money lavishly that his son might be brought up as a gentleman. Before he was fairly able to walk private tutors had stuffed his poor little head full of Latin and Greek. At the age of six he had been sent to high-school. At thirteen he had begun to study law. And before he was twenty he was a full-fledged member of the Bordeaux town council.

Then followed a career in the army and a period at court, until at the age of thirty-eight, after the death of his father, he retired from all active business and spent the last twenty-one years of his life (with the exception of a few unwilling excursions into politics) among his horses and his dogs and his books and learned as much from the one as he did from the other.

Montaigne was very much a man of his time and suffered from several weaknesses. He was never quite free from certain affectations and mannerisms which he, the fish-monger's grandson, believed to be a part of true gentility. Until the end of his days he protested that he was not really a writer at all, only a country gentleman who occasionally whiled away the tedious hours of winter by jotting down a few random ideas upon subjects of a slightly philosophic nature. All this was pure buncombe. If ever a man put his heart and his soul and his virtues and his vices and everything he had into his books, it was this cheerful neighbor of the immortal d'Artagnan.

And as this heart and this soul and these virtues and these vices were the heart and the soul and the virtues and the vices of an essentially generous, well-bred and agreeable person, the sum total of Montaigne's works has become something more than literature. It has developed into a definite philosophy of life, based upon common sense and an ordinary practical variety of decency.

Montaigne was born a Catholic. He died a Catholic, and in his younger years he was an active member of that League of Catholic Noblemen which was formed among the French nobility to drive Calvinism out of France.

But after that fateful day in August of the year 1572 when news reached him of the joy with which Pope Gregory XIII had celebrated the murder of thirty thousand French Protestants, he turned away from the Church for good. He never went so far as to join the other side. He continued to go through certain formalities that he might keep his neighbors' tongues from wagging, but those of his chapters written after the night of Saint Bartholomew might just as well have been the work of Marcus Aurelius or Epictetus or any of a dozen other Greek or Roman philosophers. And in one memorable essay, entitled "On the Freedom of Conscience," he spoke as if he had been a contemporary of Pericles rather than a servant of Her Majesty Catherine de' Medici and he used the career of Julian the Apos-

MONTAIGNE

tate as an example of what a truly tolerant statesman might hope to accomplish.

It is a very short chapter. It is only five pages long and you will find it in part nineteen of the second book.

Montaigne had seen too much of the incorrigible obstinacy of both Protestants and Catholics to advocate a system of absolute freedom, which (under the existing circumstances) could only provoke a new outbreak of civil war. But when circumstances allowed it, when Protestants and Catholics no longer slept with a couple of daggers and pistols underneath their pillows, then an intelligent government should keep away as much as possible from interfering with other people's consciences and should permit all of its subjects to love God as best suited the happiness of their own particular souls.

Montaigne was neither the only nor the first Frenchman who had hit upon this idea or had dared to express it in public. As early as the year 1560, Michel de l'Hôpital, a former chancellor of Catherine de' Medici and a graduate of half a dozen Italian universities (and incidentally suspected of being tarred with the Anabaptist brush) had suggested that heretics be attacked exclusively with verbal arguments. He had based his somewhat startling opinion upon the ground that conscience being what it was, it could not possibly be changed by force, and two years later he had been instrumental in bringing about the royal Edict of Toleration which had given the Huguenots the right to hold meetings of their own, to call synods to discuss the affairs of their church and in general to behave as if they were a free and independent denomination and not merely a tolerated little sect.

Jean Bodin, a Parisian lawyer, a most respectable citizen (the man who had defended the rights of private property against the communistic tendencies expressed in Thomas More's "Utopia"), had spoken in a similar vein when he denied the right of sovereigns to use violence in driving their subjects to this or that church.

But the speeches of chancellors and the Latin treatises of political philosophers very rarely make best sellers. Whereas Montaigne was read and translated and discussed wherever civilized people came together in the name of intelligent company and good conversation, and continued to be read and translated and discussed for more than three hundred years.

His very amateurishness, his insistence that he just wrote for the fun of it and had no axes to grind, made him popular with large numbers of people who otherwise would never dream of buying (or borrowing) a book that was officially classified under "philosophy."

Chapter XIX

ARMINIUS

The struggle for tolerance is part of the age-old conflict between "organized society" which places the continued safety of the "group" ahead of all other considerations and those private citizens of unusual intelligence or energy who hold that such improvement as the world has thus far experienced was invariably due to the efforts of the individual and not due to the efforts of the mass (which by its very nature is distrustful of all innovations) and that therefore the rights of the individual are far more important than those of the mass.

If we agree to accept these premises as true, it follows that the amount of tolerance in any given country must be in direct proportion to the degree of individual liberty enjoyed by the majority of its inhabitants.

Now in the olden days it sometimes happened that an exceptionally enlightened ruler spake unto his children and said, "I firmly believe in the principle of live and let live. I expect all my beloved subjects to practice tolerance towards their neighbors or bear the consequences."

In that case, of course, eager citizens hastened to lay in a supply of the official buttons bearing the proud inscription, "Tolerance first."

But these sudden conversions, due to a fear of His Majesty's hangman, were rarely of a lasting nature and only bore fruit if the sovereign accompanied his threat by an intelligent system of gradual education along the lines of practical everyday politics.

Such a fortunate combination of circumstances occurred in the Dutch Republic during the latter half of the sixteenth century.

In the first place, the country consisted of several thousand semi-independent towns and villages and these for the greater part were inhabited by fishermen, sailors and traders, three classes of people who are accustomed to a certain amount of independence of action and who are forced by the nature of their trade to make quick decisions and to judge the casual occurrences of the day's work upon their own merits.

I would not for a moment claim that, man for man, they were a whit more intelligent or broad-minded than their neighbors in other parts of the world. But hard work and tenacity of purpose had made them the grain and fish carriers of all northern and western Europe. They knew that the money of a Catholic was just as good as that of a Protestant and they preferred a Turk who paid cash to a Presbyterian who asked for six months' credit. An ideal country therefore to start a little experiment in tolerance and furthermore the right man was in the right place and what is infinitely more important the right man was in the right place at the right moment.

William the Silent was a shining example of the old maxim that "those who wish to rule the world must know the world." He began life as a very fashionable and rich young man, enjoying a most enviable social position as the confidential secretary of the greatest monarch of his time. He wasted scandalous sums of money upon dinners and dances, married several of the better known heiresses of his day and lived gayly without a care for the day of to-morrow. He was not a particularly studious person and racing charts interested him infinitely more than religious tracts.

The social unrest which followed in the wake of the Reformation did not at first impress him as anything more serious than still another quarrel between capital and labor, the sort of thing that could be settled by the use of a little tact and the display of a few brawny police constables.

But once he had grasped the true nature of the issue that had arisen between the sovereign and his subjects, this amiable grand seigneur was suddenly transformed into the exceedingly able leader of what, to all intents and purposes, was the prime lost cause of the age. The palaces and horses, the gold plate and the country estates were sold at short notice (or confiscated at no notice at all) and the sporting young man from Brussels became the most tenacious and successful enemy of the house of Hapsburg.

This change of fortune, however, did not affect his private character. William had been a philosopher in the days of plenty. He remained a philosopher when he lived in a couple of furnished rooms and did not know how to pay for Saturday's clean wash. And just as in the olden days he had worked hard to frustrate the plans of a cardinal who had expressed the intention of building a sufficient number of gallows to accommodate all Protestants, he now made it a point to bridle the energy of those ardent Calvinists who wished to hang all Catholics.

His task was wellnigh hopeless.

Between twenty and thirty thousand people had already been killed, the prisons of the Inquisition were full of new candidates for martyrdom and in far-off Spain new armies were being recruited to smash the rebellion before it should spread to other parts of the Empire.

To tell people who were fighting for their lives that they must love those who had just hanged their sons and brothers and uncles and grandfathers was out of the question. But by his personal example, by his conciliatory attitude towards those who opposed him, William was able to show his followers how a man of character can invariably rise superior to the old Mosaic law of an eye for an eye and a tooth for a tooth.

In this campaign for public decency he enjoyed the support of a very remarkable man. In the church of Gouda you may this very day read a curious monosyllabic epitaph which enumerates the virtues of one Dirck Coornhert, who lies buried there. This Coornhert was an interesting fellow. He was the son of well-to-do people and had spent many years of his youth traveling in foreign lands and getting some first hand information about Germany, Spain and France. As soon as he had returned home from this trip he fell in love with a girl who did not have a cent. His careful Dutch father had forbidden the marriage. When his son married the girl just the same, he did what those ancestral patriarchs were supposed to do under the circumstances: he talked about filial ingratitude and disinherited the boy.

This was inconvenient, in so far as young Coornhert was now obliged to go to work for a living. But he was a young man of parts, learned a trade and set up as a copper-engraver.

Alas! once a Dutchman, always a dominie. When evening came, he hastily dropped the burin, picked up the goose-quill and wrote articles upon the events of the day. His style was not exactly what one would nowadays call "amusing." But his books contained a great deal of that amiable common sense which had distinguished the work of Erasmus and they made him many friends and brought him into contact with William the Silent who thought so highly of his abilities that he employed him as one of his confidential advisers.

Now William was engaged in a strange sort of debate. King Philip, aided and abetted by the Pope, was trying to rid the world of the enemy of the human race (to wit, his own enemy, William) by a standing offer of twenty-five thousand golden ducats and a patent of nobility and forgiveness of all sins to whosoever would go to Holland and murder the arch-heretic. William, who had already lived through five attempts upon his life, felt it his duty to refute the arguments of good King Philip in a series of pamphlets and Coornhert assisted him.

That the house of Hapsburg, for whom these arguments were intended, should thereby be converted to tolerance was of course an idle hope. But as all the world was watching the duel between William and Philip, those little pamphlets were translated and read everywhere and they caused a healthy discussion of many subjects that people had never before dared to mention above a whisper.

Unfortunately the debates did not last very long. On the ninth of July of the year 1584 a young French Catholic gained that reward of twenty-five thousand ducats and six years later Coornhert died before he had been able to finish the translation of the works of Erasmus into the Dutch vernacular.

As for the next twenty years, they were so full of the noise of battle that even the fulminations of the different theologians went unheard. And when finally the enemy had been driven from the territory of the new republic, there was no William to take hold of internal affairs and three score sects and denominations, who had been forced into temporary but unnatural friendship by the presence of a large number of Spanish mercenaries, flew at each other's throats.

Of course, they had to have a pretext for their quarrel, but who ever heard of a theologian without a grievance?

In the University of Leiden there were two professors who disagreed. That was nothing either new or unusual But these

THE QUARRELING PROFESSORS

two professors disagreed upon the question of the freedom of the will and that was a very serious matter. At once the delighted populace took a hand in the discussion and within less than a month the entire country was divided into two hostile camps.

On the one side, the friends of Arminius.

On the other, the followers of Gomarus.

The latter, although born of Dutch parents, had lived all his life in Germany and was a brilliant product of the Teuton system of pedagogy. He possessed immense learning combined with a total absence of ordinary horse-sense. His mind was versed in the mysteries of Hebrew prosody but his heart beat according to the rules of the Aramaic syntax.

His opponent, Arminius, was a very different sort of man. He was born in Oudewater, a little city not far away from that cloister Steyn where Erasmus had spent the unhappy years of his early manhood. As a child he had won the friendship of a neighbor, a famous mathematician and professor of astronomy in the University of Marburg. This man, Rudolf Snellius, had

taken Arminius back with him to Germany that he might be properly educated. But when the boy went home for his first vacation he found that his native town had been sacked by the Spaniards and that all his relatives had been murdered.

That seemed to end his career, but fortunately some rich people with kind hearts heard of the sad plight of the young orphan and they put up a purse and sent him to Leiden to study theology. He worked hard and after half a dozen

ARMINIUS

years he had learned all there was to be learned and looked for fresh intellectual grazing grounds.

In those days, brilliant students could always find a patron willing to invest a few dollars in their future. Soon Arminius, provided with a letter of credit issued by certain guilds of Amsterdam, was merrily trotting southward in search of future educational opportunities.

As behooved a respectable candidate of theology, he went first of all to Geneva. Calvin was dead, but his man Friday, the learned Theodore Beza, had succeeded him as shepherd of the seraphic flock. The fine nose of this old heresy hunter at once detected a slight odor of Ramism in the doctrines of the young Dutchman and the visit of Arminius was cut short.

The word Ramism means nothing to modern readers. But three hundred years ago it was considered a most dangerous religious novelty, as those who are familiar with the assembled works of Milton will know. It had been invented or originated (or what you please) by a Frenchman, a certain Pierre de la Ramée. As a student, de la Ramée had been so utterly exasperated by the antiquated methods of his professors that he had chosen as subject for his doctor's dissertation the somewhat startling text, "Everything ever taught by Aristotle is absolutely wrong."

Needless to say this subject did not gain him the good will of his teachers. When a few years afterwards he elaborated his idea in a number of learned volumes, his death was a foregone conclusion. He fell as one of the first victims of the massacre of Saint Bartholomew.

But his books, those pesky books which refuse to be assassinated together with their authors, had survived and Ramée's curious system of logic had gained great popularity throughout northern and western Europe. Truly pious people, however, believed that Ramism was the password to Hades, and Arminius was advised to go to Basel where "libertines" (a sixteenth century colloquialism meaning "liberals") had been considered good form ever since that unfortunate city had fallen under the spell of the quizzical Erasmus.

Arminius, thus forewarned, traveled northward and then decided upon something quite unusual. He boldly invaded the enemy's territory, studied for a few semesters in the University of Padua and paid a visit to Rome. This made him a dangerous person in the eyes of his fellow countrymen when he returned to his native country in the year 1587. But as he seemed to develop neither horns nor a tail, he was gradually taken back into their good favor and was allowed to accept a call as minister to Amsterdam.

There he made himself not only useful but he gained quite a reputation as a hero during one of the many outbreaks of the plague. Soon he was held in such genuine esteem that he was entrusted with the task of reorganizing the public school system of that big city and when in the year 1603 he was called to Leiden as a full-fledged professor of theology, he left the capital amidst the sincere regrets of the entire population.

If he had known beforehand what was awaiting him in Leiden, I am sure he would never have gone. He arrived just when the battle between the Infralapsarians and the Supralapsarians was at its height.

Arminius was by both nature and education an Infralapsarian. He tried to be fair to his colleague, the Supralapsarian Gomarus. But alas, the differences between the Supralapsarians and the Infralapsarians were such as allowed of no compromise. And Arminius was forced to declare himself an out and out Infralapsarian.

Of course, you will ask me what Supra- and Infralapsarians were. I don't know, and I seem unable to learn such things. But as far as I can make out, it was the age-old quarrel between those who believed (as did Arminius) that man is to a certain extent possessed of a free will and able to shape his own destinies and those who like Sophocles and Calvin and Gomarus taught that everything in our lives has been pre-ordained ages before we were born and that our fate therefore depends upon a throw of the divine dice at the hour of creation.

In the year 1600 by far the greater number of the people of northern Europe were Supralapsarians. They loved to listen to sermons which doomed the majority of their neighbors to eternal perdition, and those few ministers who dared to preach a gospel of good will and charity were at once suspected of criminal weakness, fit rivals of those tender-hearted doctors who fail to prescribe malodorous medicines and kill their patients by their kindness.

As soon as the gossiping old women of Leiden had discovered that Arminius was an Infralapsarian, his usefulness had come to an end. The poor man died under the torrent of abuse that was let loose upon him by his former friends and supporters. And then, as seemed unavoidable during the seventeenth century, Infralapsarianism and Supralapsarianism made their entrance into the field of politics, and the Supralapsarians won at the polls and the Infralapsarians were declared enemies of the public order and traitors to their country.

Before this absurd quarrel had come to end, Oldenbarnevelt, the man who next to William the Silent had been responsible for the foundation of the Republic, lay dead with his head between his feet; Grotius, whose moderation had made him the first great advocate of an equitable system of international law, was eating the bread of charity at the court of the Queen of Sweden; and the work of William the Silent seemed entirely undone.

But Calvinism did not gain the triumph it had hoped.

The Dutch Republic was a republic only in name. It was really a sort of merchants' and bankers' club, ruled by a few hundred influential families. These gentlemen were not at all interested in equality and fraternity, but they did believe in law and order. They recognized and supported the established church. On Sundays with a great display of unction they proceeded to the large whitewashed sepulchers which in former days had been Catholic Cathedrals and which now were Protestant lecture halls. But on Monday, when the clergy paid its respects to the Honorable Burgomaster and Town Councilors, with a long list of grievances against this and that and the other person, their lordships were "in conference" and unable to receive the reverend gentlemen. If the reverend gentlemen insisted, and induced (as frequently happened) a few thousand of their loyal parishioners to "demonstrate" in front of the town hall, then their lordships would graciously deign to accept a neatly written copy of the reverend gentlemen's complaints and suggestions. But as soon as the door had been closed upon the last of the darkly garbed petitioners, their lordships would use the document to light their pipes.

For they had adopted the useful and practical maxim of "once is enough and too many" and they were so horrified by what had happened during the terrible years of the great Supralapsarian civil war that they uncompromisingly suppressed all further forms of religious frenzy.

Posterity has not always been kind to those aristocrats of

the ledger. Undoubtedly they regarded the country as their private property and did not always differentiate with sufficient nicety between the interests of their fatherland and those of their own firm. They lacked that broad vision which goes with empire and almost invariably they were penny-wise and pound-foolish. But they did something which deserves our hearty commendation. They turned their country into an international clearing-house where all sorts of people with all sorts of ideas were given the widest degree of liberty to say, think, write and print whatever pleased them.

I do not want to paint too rosy a picture. Here and there, under a threat of ministerial disapprobation, the Town Councilors were sometimes obliged to suppress a secret society of Catholics or to confiscate the pamphlets printed by a particularly noisy heretic. But generally speaking, as long as one did not climb on a soap-box in the middle of the market place to denounce the doctrine of predestination or carry a big rosary into a public dining-hall or deny the existence of God in the South Side Methodist Church of Haarlem, one enjoyed a degree of personal immunity which for almost two centuries made the Dutch Republic a veritable haven of rest for all those who in other parts of the world were persecuted for the sake of their opinions.

Soon the rumor of this Paradise Regained spread abroad. And during the next two hundred years, the print shops and the coffee-houses of Holland were filled with a motley crew of enthusiasts, the advance guard of a strange new army of spiritual liberation.

Chapter XX

BRUNO

It has been said (and with a good deal of reason) that the Great War was a war of non-commissioned officers. While the generals and the colonels and the three-star strategists sat in solitary splendor in the halls of some deserted château and contemplated miles of maps until they could evolve a new bit of tactics that was to give them half a square mile of territory (and lose some thirty thousand men), the junior officers, the sergeants and the corporals, aided and abetted by a number of intelligent privates, did the so-called "dirty work" and eventually brought about the collapse of the German line of defense.

The great crusade for spiritual independence was fought along similar lines.

There were no frontal attacks which drew into action half a million soldiers.

There were no desperate charges to provide the enemy's gunners with an easy and agreeable target.

I might go even further and say that the vast majority of the people never knew that there was any fighting at all. Now and then, curiosity may have compelled them to ask who was being burned that morning or who was going to be hanged the next afternoon. Then perhaps they discovered that a few desperate individuals continued to fight for certain principles of freedom of which both Catholics and Protestants disapproved most heartily. But I doubt whether such information affected them beyond the point of mild regret and the comment that it must be very sad for their poor relatives to bear, that uncle had come to such a terrible end.

It could hardly have been otherwise. What martyrs actually accomplish for the cause for which they give their lives cannot possibly be reduced to mathematical formulas or be expressed in terms of amperes or horsepower.

Any industrious young man in search of a Ph.D. may read carefully through the assembled works of Giordano Bruno and by the patient collection of all sentences containing such sentiments as "the state has no right to tell people what to think" or "society may not punish with the sword those who dissent from the generally approved dogmas," he may be able to write an acceptable dissertation upon "Giordano Bruno (1549-1600) and the principles of religious freedom."

But those of us no longer in search of those fatal letters must approach the subject from a different angle.

There were, so we say in our final analysis, a number of devout men who were so profoundly shocked by the fanaticism of their day, by the yoke under which the people of all countries were forced to exist, that they rose in revolt. They were poor devils. They rarely owned more than the cloak upon their back and they were not always certain of a place to sleep. But they burned with a divine fire. Up and down the land they traveled, talking and writing, drawing the learned professors of learned academies into learned disputes, arguing humbly with the humble country folk in humble rustic inns, eternally preaching a gospel of good will, of understanding, of charity towards others. Up and down the land they traveled in their shabby clothes with their little bundles of books and pamphlets until they died of pneumonia in some miserable village in the hinterland of Pomerania or were lynched by drunken peasants in a Scotch hamlet or were broken on the wheel in a provincial borough of France.

And if I mention the name of Giordano Bruno, I do not mean to imply that he was the only one of his kind. But his life, his ideas, his restless zeal for what he held to be true and desirable, were so typical of that entire group of pioneers that he will serve very well as an example.

The parents of Bruno were poor people. Their son, an average Italian boy of no particular promise, followed the usual course and went into a monastery. Later he became a Dominican monk. He had no business in that order for the Dominicans were the

BRUNO GOES TO GENEVA

most ardent supporters of all forms of persecution, the "police-dogs of the true faith," as their contemporaries called them. And they were clever. It was not necessary for a heretic to have his ideas put into print to be nosed out by one of those eager detectives. A single glance, a gesture of the hand, a shrug of the shoulders, were often sufficient to give a man away and bring him into contact with the Inquisition.

How Bruno, brought up in an atmosphere of unquestioning obedience, turned rebel and deserted the Holy Scriptures for the works of Zeno and Anaxagoras, I do not know. But before this strange novice had finished his course of prescribed studies, he was expelled from the Dominican order and henceforth he was a wanderer upon the face of the earth.

He crossed the Alps. How many other young men before him had braved the dangers of those ancient mountain passes that they might find freedom in the mighty fortress which the new faith had erected at the junction of the Rhone and the Arve!

And how many of them had turned away, broken hearted when they discovered that here as there it was the inner spirit which guided the hearts of men and that a change of creed did not necessarily mean a change of heart and mind.

Bruno's residence in Geneva lasted less than three months. The town was full of Italian refugees. These brought their fellow countryman a new suit of clothes and found him a job as proof-reader. In the evenings he read and wrote. He got hold of a copy of de la Ramée's works. There at last was a man after his own heart. De la Ramée believed too that the world could not progress until the tyranny of the medieval text-books was broken. Bruno did not go as far as his famous French teacher and did not believe that everything the Greeks had ever taught was wrong. But why should the people of the sixteenth century be bound by words and sentences that were written in the fourth century before the birth of Christ? Why, indeed?

"Because it has always been that way," the upholders of the orthodox faith answered him.

"What have we to do with our grandfathers and what have they to do with us? Let the dead bury the dead," the young iconoclast answered.

And very soon afterwards the police paid him a visit and suggested that he had better pack his satchels and try his luck elsewhere.

Bruno's life thereafter was one endless peregrination in search of a place where he might live and work in some degree of liberty and security. He never found it. From Geneva he went to Lyons and then to Toulouse. By that time he had taken up the study of astronomy and had become an ardent supporter of the ideas of Copernicus, a dangerous step in an age when all the contemporary Bryans brayed, "The world turning around the sun! The world a commonplace little planet turning around the sun! Ho-ho and hee-hee! Who ever heard such nonsense?"

Toulouse became uncomfortable. He crossed France, walking to Paris. And next to England as private secretary to a French ambassador. But there another disappointment awaited him. The English theologians were no better than the Continental ones. A little more practical, perhaps. In Oxford, for example, they did not punish a student when he committed an error against the teachings of Aristotle. They fined him ten shillings.

Bruno became sarcastic. He began to write brilliantly dangerous bits of prose, dialogues of a religious-philosophic-political nature in which the entire existing order of things was turned topsy-turvy and submitted to a minute but none too flattering examination.

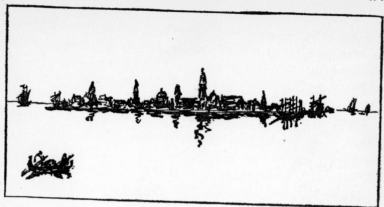

BRUNO GOES TO VENICE

And he did some lecturing upon his favorite subject, astronomy.

But college authorities rarely smile upon professors who please the hearts of their students. Bruno once more found himself invited to leave. And so back again to France and then to Marburg, where not so long before Luther and Zwingli had debated upon the true nature of the transubstantiation in the castle of pious Elisabeth of Hungary.

Alas! his reputation as a "Libertine" had preceded him. He was not even allowed to lecture. Wittenberg proved more hospitable. That old stronghold of the Lutheran faith, however, was beginning to be overrun by the disciples of Dr. Calvin. After that there was no further room for a man of Bruno's liberal tendencies.

Southward he wended his way to try his luck in the land of John Huss. Further disappointment awaited him. Prague had become a Hapsburg capital and where the Hapsburg entered, freedom went out by the city gates. Back to the road and a long, long walk to Zürich.

There he received a letter from an Italian youth, Giovanni Mocenigo, who asked him to come to Venice. What made Bruno accept, I do not know. Perhaps the Italian peasant in him was impressed by the luster of an old patrician name and felt flattered by the invitation.

Giovanni Mocenigo, however, was not made of the stuff which had enabled his ancestors to defy both Sultan and Pope. He was a weakling and a coward and did not move a finger when officers of the Inquisition appeared at his house and took his guest to Rome.

As a rule, the government of Venice was terribly jealous of its rights. If Bruno had been a German merchant or a Dutch skipper, they would have protested violently and they might even have gone to war when a foreign power dared to arrest some one within their own jurisdiction. But why incur the hostility of the Pope on account of a vagabond who had brought nothing to their city but his ideas?

It was true he called himself a scholar. The Republic was highly flattered, but she had scholars enough of her own.

And so farewell to Bruno and may San Marco have mercy upon his soul.

Seven long years Bruno was kept in the prison of the Inquisition.

On the seventeenth of February of the year 1600 he was burned at the stake and his ashes were blown to the winds.

He was executed on the Campo dei Fiori. Those who know Italian may therein find inspiration for a pretty little allegory.

Chapter XXI

SPINOZA

THERE are certain things in history which I have never been able to understand and one of these is the amount of work done by some of the artists and literary men of bygone ages.

The modern members of our writing guild, with typewriters and dictaphones and secretaries and fountain pens, can turn out between three and four thousand words a day. How did Shakespeare, with half a dozen other jobs to distract his mind, with a scolding wife and a clumsy goose-quill, manage to write thirty-seven plays?

Where did Lope de Vega, veteran of the Invincible Armada and a busy man all his life, find the necessary ink and paper for eighteen hundred comedies and five hundred essays?

What manner of man was this strange Hofkonzertmeister, Johann Sebastian Bach, who in a little house filled with the noise of twenty children found time to compose five oratorios, one hundred and ninety church cantatas, three wedding cantatas, and a dozen motets, six solemn masses, three fiddle concertos, a concerto for two violins which alone would have made his name immortal, seven concertos for piano and orchestra, three concertos for two pianos, two concertos for three pianos, thirty orchestral scores, and enough pieces for the flute, the harpsichord, the organ, the bull-fiddle and the French horn to keep the average student of music busy for the rest of his days?

Or again, by what process of industry and application could painters like Rembrandt and Rubens produce a picture or an etching at the rate of almost four a month during more than thirty years? How could a humble citizen like Antonio Stradivarius turn out five hundred and forty fiddles, fifty violoncellos and twelve violas in a single lifetime?

I am not now discussing the brains capable of devising all these plots, hearing all these melodies, seeing all these diversified com-

277

binations of color and line, choosing all this wood. I am just wondering at the physical part of it. How did they do it? Didn't they ever go to bed? Didn't they sometimes take a few hours off for a game of billiards? Were they never tired? Had they ever heard of nerves?

Both the seventeenth and eighteenth centuries were full of that sort of people. They defied all the laws of hygiene, ate and drank everything that was bad for them, were totally unconscious of their high destinies as members of the glorious human race, but they had an awfully good time and their artistic and intellectual output was something terrific.

And what was true of the arts and the sciences held equally true of such finicky subjects as theology.

Go to any of the libraries that date back two hundred years and you will find their cellars and attics filled with tracts and homilies and discussions and refutations and digests and commentaries in duodecimo and octodecimo and octavo, bound in leather and in parchment and in paper, all of them covered with dust and oblivion, but without exception containing an enormous if useless amount of learning.

The subjects of which they treated and many of the words they used have lost all meaning to our modern ears. But somehow or other these moldy compilations served a very useful purpose. If they accomplished nothing else, they at least cleared the air. For they either settled the questions they discussed to the general satisfaction of all concerned, or they convinced their readers that those particular problems could not possibly be decided with an appeal to logic and argument and might therefore just as well be dropped right then and there.

This may sound like a back-handed compliment. But I hope that critics of the thirtieth century shall be just as charitable when they wade through the remains of our own literary and scientific achievements.

*   *   *   *   *   *   *   *

Baruch de Spinoza, the hero of this chapter, did not follow the fashion of his time in the matter of quantity. His assembled works consist of three or four small volumes and a few bundles of letters.

But the amount of study necessary for the correct mathematical solution of his abstract problems in ethics and philosophy would have staggered any normally healthy man. It killed the poor consumptive who had undertaken to reach God by way of the table of multiplication.

Spinoza was a Jew. His people, however, had never suffered the indignities of the Ghetto. Their ancestors had settled down in the Spanish peninsula when that part of the world was a Moorish province. After the reconquest and the introduction of that policy of "Spain for the Spaniard" which eventually forced that country into bankruptcy, the Spinozas had been forced to leave their old home. They had sailed for the Netherlands, had bought a small house in Amsterdam, had worked hard, had saved their money and soon were known as one of the most respectable families of the "Portuguese colony."

If nevertheless their son Baruch was conscious of his Jew-

SPINOZA

ish origin, this was due more to the training he received in his Talmud school than to the gibes of his little neighbors. For the Dutch Republic was so chock full of class prejudice that there was little room left for mere race prejudice and therefore lived in perfect peace and harmony with all the alien races that had found a refuge along the banks of the North and Zuider Seas. And this was one of the most characteristic bits of Dutch life which contemporary travelers never failed to omit from their "Souvenirs de Voyage" and with good reason.

In most other parts of Europe, even at that late age, the relation between the Jew and the non-Jew was far from satisfactory. What made the quarrel between the two races so hopeless was the fact that both sides were equally right and equally wrong and that both sides could justly claim to be the victim of their opponent's intolerance and prejudice. In the light of the theory put forward in this book that intolerance is merely a form of self-protection of the mob, it becomes clear that as long as they were faithful to their own respective religions, the Christian and the Jew must have conceded each other as enemies. In the first place, they both of them maintained that their God was the only true God and that all the other Gods of all the other nations were false. In the second place, they were each other's most dangerous commercial rivals. The Jews had come to western Europe as they had originally come to Palestine, as immigrants in search of a new home. The labor unions of that day, the Guilds, had made it impossible for them to take up a trade. They had therefore been obliged to content themselves with such economic makeshifts as pawnbroking and banking. In the Middle Ages these two professions, which closely resembled each other, were not thought fit occupations for decent citizens. Why the Church, until the days of Calvin, should have felt such a repugnance towards money (except in the form of taxes) and should have regarded the taking of interest as a crime, is hard to understand. Usury, of course, was something no government could tolerate and already the Babylonians, some forty centuries before, had passed drastic laws against the money changers who tried to make a profit out of other people's money. In several chapters of the Old Testament, written two thousand years later, we read how Moses too had expressly forbidden his followers to lend money at exorbitant rates of interest to any one except foreigners. Still later, the great Greek philosophers, including Aristotle and Plato, had given expression to their great disapproval of money that was born of other money. The Church fathers had been even more explicit upon this subject. All during the Middle Ages the money lenders were held in profound contempt. Dante even provided a special little alcove in his Hell for the exclusive benefit of his banker friends.

Theoretically perhaps it could be proved that the pawnbroker and his colleague, the man behind the "banco," were undesirable citizens and that the world would be better off without them. At the same time, as soon as the world had ceased to be entirely agricultural, it was found to be quite impossible to transact even the simplest business operations without the use of credit. The money lender therefore had become a necessary evil and the Jew, who (according to the views of the Christians) was doomed to eternal damnation anyway, was urged to occupy himself with a trade which was necessary but which no respectable man would touch.

In this way these unfortunate exiles were forced into certain unpleasant trades which made them the natural enemy of both the rich and the poor, and then, as soon as they had established themselves, these same enemies turned against them, called them names, locked them up in the dirtiest part of the city and in moments of great emotional stress hanged them as wicked unbelievers or burned them as renegade Christians.

It was all so terribly silly. And besides it was so stupid. These endless annoyances and persecutions did not make the Jews any fonder of their Christian neighbors. And as a direct result, a large volume of first-rate intelligence was withdrawn from public circulation, thousands of bright young fellows, who might have advanced the cause of commerce and science and the arts, wasted their brains and energy upon the useless study of certain old books filled with abstruse conundrums and hairsplitting syllogisms and millions of helpless boys and girls were doomed to lead stunted lives in stinking tenements, listening on the one hand to their elders who told them that they were God's chosen people who would surely inherit the earth and all the wealth thereof, and on the other hand being frightened to death by the curses of their neighbors who never ceased to inform them that they were pigs and only fit for the gallows or the wheel.

To ask that people (any people) doomed to live under such adverse circumstances shall retain a normal outlook upon life is to demand the impossible.

Again and again the Jews were goaded into some desperate act by their Christian compatriots and then, when white with rage, they turned upon their oppressors, they were called "traitors" and "ungrateful villains" and were subjected to further humiliations and restrictions. But these restrictions had only one result. They increased the number of Jews who had a grievance, turned the others into nervous wrecks and generally made the Ghetto a ghastly abode of frustrated ambitions and pent-up hatreds.

Spinoza, because he was born in Amsterdam, escaped the misery which was the birthright of most of his relatives. He went first of all to the school maintained by his synagogue (appropriately called "the Tree of Life") and as soon as he could conjugate his Hebrew verbs was sent to the learned Dr. Franciscus Appinius van den Ende, who was to drill him in Latin and in the sciences.

Dr. Franciscus, as his name indicates, was of Catholic origin. Rumor had it that he was a graduate of the University of Louvain and if one were to believe the best informed deacons of the town, he was really a Jesuit in disguise and a very dangerous person. This, however, was nonsense. Van den Ende in his youth had actually spent a few years at a Catholic seminary. But his heart was not in his work and he had left his native city of Antwerp, had gone to Amsterdam and there had opened a private school of his own.

He had such a tremendous flair for choosing the methods that would make his pupils like their classical lessons, that heedless of the man's popish past, the Calvinistic burghers of Amsterdam willingly entrusted their children to his care and were very proud of the fact that the pupils of his school invariably out-hexametered and out-declined the little boys of all other local academies.

Van den Ende taught little Baruch his Latin, but being an enthusiastic follower of all the latest discoveries in the field of science and a great admirer of Giordano Bruno, he undoubtedly taught the boy several things which as a rule were not mentioned in an orthodox Jewish household.

For young Spinoza, contrary to the customs of the times, did not board with the other boys, but lived at home. And he so impressed his family by his profound learning that all the relations proudly pointed to him as the little professor and liberally supplied him with pocket money. He did not waste it upon tobacco. He used it to buy books on philosophy.

One author especially fascinated him.

That was Descartes.

René Descartes was a French nobleman born in that region between Tours and Poitiers where a thousand years before the grandfather of Charlemagne had stopped the Mahometan conquest of Europe. Before he was ten years old he had been sent to the Jesuits to be educated and he spent the next decade making a nuisance of himself. For this boy had a mind of his own and accepted nothing without "being shown." The Jesuits are probably the only people in the world who know how to handle such difficult children and who can train them successfully without breaking their spirit. The proof of the educational pudding is in the eating. If our modern pedagogues would study the methods of Brother Loyola, we might have a few Descartes of our own.

When he was twenty years old, René entered military service and went to the Netherlands where Maurice of Nassau had so thoroughly perfected his military system that his armies were the post-graduate school for all ambitious young men who hoped to become generals. Descartes's visit to the headquarters of the Nassau prince was perhaps a little irregular. A faithful Cath-

olic taking service with a Protestant chieftain! It sounds like
high treason. But Descartes was interested in problems of
mathematics and artillery but not of religion or politics. Therefore as soon as Holland had concluded a truce with Spain, he
resigned his commission, went to Munich and fought for a while
under the banner of the Catholic Duke of Bavaria.

But that campaign did not last very long. The only fighting
of any consequence then still going on was near La Rochelle,
the city which the Huguenots were defending against Richelieu.
And so Descartes went back to France that he might learn the
noble art of siege-craft. But camp life was beginning to pall
upon him. He decided to give up a military career and devote
himself to philosophy and science.

He had a small income of his own. He had no desire to marry.
His wishes were few. He anticipated a quiet and happy life
and he had it.

Why he chose Holland as a place of residence, I do not know.
But it was a country full of printers and publishers and book-
shops and as long as one did not openly attack the established
form of government or religion, the existing law on censorship
remained a dead letter. Furthermore, as he never learned a
single word of the language of his adopted country (a trick
not difficult to a true Frenchman), Descartes was able to avoid
undesirable company and futile conversations and could give
all his time (some twenty hours per day) to his own work.

This may seem a dull existence for a man who had been a
soldier. But Descartes had a purpose in life and it seems that
he was perfectly contented with his self-inflicted exile. He had
during the course of years become convinced that the world was
still plunged in a profound gloom of abysmal ignorance; that
what was then being called science had not even the remotest
resemblance to true science, and that no general progress would
be possible until the whole ancient fabric of error and false-
hood had first of all been razed to the ground. No small order,
this. Descartes, however, was possessed of endless patience and
at the age of thirty he set to work to give us an entirely new
system of philosophy. Warming up to his task he added geom-

etry and astronomy and physics to his original program and he performed his task with such noble impartiality of mind that the Catholics denounced him as a Calvinist and the Calvinists cursed him for an atheist.

This clamor, if ever it reached him, did not disturb him in the least. He quietly continued his researches and died peacefully in the city of Stockholm, whither he had gone to talk philosophy with the Queen of Sweden.

Among the people of the seventeenth century, Cartesianism (the name under which his philosophies became known) made quite as much of a stir as Darwinism was to make among the contemporaries of Queen Victoria. To be a Cartesian in the year 1680 meant something terrible, something almost indecent. It proclaimed one an enemy of the established order of society, a Socinian, a low fellow who by his own confession had set himself apart from the companionship of his respectable neighbors. This did not prevent the majority of the intelligent classes from accepting Cartesianism as readily and as eagerly as our grandfathers accepted Darwinism. But among the orthodox Jews of Amsterdam, such subjects were never even mentioned. Cartesianism was not mentioned in either Talmud or Torah. Hence it did not exist. And when it became apparent that it existed just the same in the mind of one Baruch de Spinoza, it was a foregone conclusion that said Baruch de Spinoza would himself cease to exist as soon as the authorities of the synagogue had been able to investigate the case and take official action.

The Amsterdam synagogue had at that moment passed through a severe crisis. When little Baruch was fifteen years old, another Portuguese exile by the name of Uriel Acosta had arrived in Amsterdam, had forsworn Catholicism, which he had accepted under a threat of death, and had returned to the faith of his fathers. But this fellow Acosta had not been an ordinary Jew. He was a gentleman accustomed to carry a feather in his hat and a sword at his side. To him the arrogance of the Dutch rabbis, trained in the German and Polish schools of learning, had come as a most unpleasant surprise, and he had been too proud and too indifferent to hide his opinions.

In a small community like that, such open defiance could not possibly be tolerated. A bitter struggle had followed. On the one side a solitary dreamer, half prophet, half hidalgo. On the other side the merciless guardians of the law.

It had ended in tragedy.

First of all Acosta had been denounced to the local police as the author of certain blasphemous pamphlets which denied the immortality of the soul. This had got him into trouble with the Calvinist ministers. But the matter had been straightened out and the charge had been dropped. Thereupon the synagogue had excommunicated the stiff-necked rebel and had deprived him of his livelihood.

For months thereafter the poor man had wandered through the streets of Amsterdam until destitution and loneliness had driven him back to his own flock. But he was not readmitted until he had first of all publicly apologized for his evil conduct and had then suffered himself to be whipped and kicked by all the members of the congregation. These indignities had unbalanced his mind. He had bought a pistol and had blown his brains out.

This suicide had caused a tremendous lot of talk among the principal citizens of Amsterdam. The Jewish community felt that it could not risk the chance of another public scandal. When it became evident that the most promising pupil of the "Tree of Life" had been contaminated by the new heresies of Descartes, a direct attempt was made to hush things up. Baruch was approached and was offered a fixed annual sum if he would give his word that he would be good, would continue to show himself in the synagogue and would not publish or say anything against the law.

Now Spinoza was the last man to consider such a compromise. He curtly refused to do anything of the sort. In consequence whereof he was duly read out of his own church according to that famous ancient Formula of Damnation which leaves very little to the imagination and goes back all the way to the days of Jericho to find the appropriate number of curses and execrations.

As for the victim of these manifold maledictions, he remained quietly in his room and read about the occurrence in next day's paper. Even when an attempt was made upon his life by an overzealous follower of the law, he refused to leave town.

This came as a great blow to the prestige of the Rabbis who apparently had invoked the names of Joshua and Elisha in vain and who saw themselves publicly defied for the second time in less than half a dozen years. In their anxiety they went so far as to make an appeal to the town hall. They asked for an interview with the Burgomasters and explained that this Baruch de Spinoza whom they had just expelled from their own church was really a most dangerous person, an agnostic who refused to believe in God and who therefore ought not to be tolerated in a respectable Christian community like the city of Amsterdam.

Their lordships, after their pleasant habit, washed their hands of the whole affair and referred the matter to a sub-committee of clergymen. The sub-committee studied the question, discovered that Baruch de Spinoza had done nothing that could be construed as an offense against the ordinances of the town, and so reported to their lordships. At the same time they considered it to be good policy for members of the cloth to stand together and therefore they suggested that the Burgomasters ask this young man, who seemed to be so very independent, to leave Amsterdam for a couple of months and not to return until the thing had blown over.

From that moment on the life of Spinoza was as quiet and uneventful as the landscape upon which he looked from his bedroom windows. He left Amsterdam and hired a small house in the village of Rijnsberg near Leiden. He spent his days polishing lenses for optical instruments and at night he smoked his pipe and read or wrote as the spirit moved him. He never married. There was rumor of a love affair between him and a daughter of his former Latin teacher, van den Ende. But as the child was ten years old when Spinoza left Amsterdam, this does not seem very likely.

He had several very loyal friends and at least twice a year

they offered to give him a pension that he might devote all his time to his studies. He answered that he appreciated their good intentions but that he preferred to remain independent and with the exception of an allowance of eighty dollars a year from a rich young Cartesian, he never touched a penny and spent his days in the respectable poverty of the true philosopher.

He had a chance to become a professor in Germany, but he declined. He received word that the illustrious King of Prussia would be happy to become his patron and protector, but he answered nay and remained faithful to the quiet routine of his pleasant exile.

After a number of years in Rijnsberg he moved to the Hague. He had never been very strong and the particles of glass from his half-finished lenses had affected his lungs.

He died quite suddenly and alone in the year 1677.

To the intense disgust of the local clergy, not less than six private carriages belonging to prominent members of the court followed the "atheist" to his grave. And when two hundred years later a statue was unveiled to his memory, the police reserves had to be called out to protect the participants in this solemn celebration against the fury of a rowdy crowd of ardent Calvinists.

So much for the man. What about his influence? Was he merely another of those industrious philosophers who fill endless books with endless theories and speak a language which drove even Omar Khayyám to an expression of exasperated annoyance?

No, he was not.

Neither did he accomplish his results by the brilliancy of his wit or the plausible truth of his theories. Spinoza was great mainly by force of his courage. He belonged to a race that knew only one law, a set of hard and fast rules laid down for all times in the dim ages of a long forgotten past, a system of spiritual tyranny created for the benefit of a class of professional priests who had taken it upon themselves to interpret this sacred code.

He lived in a world in which the idea of intellectual freedom was almost synonymous with political anarchy.

He knew that his system of logic must offend both Jews and Gentiles.

But he never wavered.

He approached all problems as universal problems. He regarded them without exception as the manifestation of an omnipresent will and believed them to be the expression of an ultimate reality which would hold good on Doomsday as it had held good at the hour of creation.

And in this way he greatly contributed to the cause of human tolerance.

Like Descartes before him, Spinoza discarded the narrow boundaries laid down by the older forms of religion and boldly built himself a new system of thought based upon the rocks of a million stars.

By so doing he made man what man had not been since the days of the ancient Greeks and Romans, a true citizen of the universe.

Chapter XXII

THE NEW ZION

THERE was little reason to fear that the works of Spinoza would ever be popular. They were as amusing as a text-book on trigonometry and few people ever get beyond the first two or three sentences of any given chapter.

It took a different sort of man to spread the new ideas among the mass of the people.

In France the enthusiasm for private speculation and investigation had come to an end as soon as the country had been turned into an absolute monarchy.

In Germany the poverty and the horror which had followed in the wake of the Thirty Years' War had killed all personal initiative for at least two hundred years.

During the second half of the seventeenth century, therefore, England was the only one among the larger countries of Europe where further progress along the lines of independent thought was still possible and the prolonged quarrel between the Crown and Parliament was adding an element of instability which proved to be of great help to the cause of personal freedom.

First of all we must consider the English sovereigns. For years these unfortunate monarchs had been between the devil of Catholicism and the deep sea of Puritanism.

Their Catholic subjects (which included a great many faithful Episcopalians with a secret leaning towards Rome) were forever clamoring for a return to that happy era when the British kings had been vassals of the Pope.

Their Puritan subjects on the other hand, with one eye firmly glued upon the example of Geneva, dreamed of the day when there should be no king at all and England should be a replica of the happy commonwealth tucked away in a little corner of the Swiss mountains.

But that was not all.

The men who ruled England were also kings of Scotland and their Scottish subjects, when it came to religion, knew exactly what they wanted. And so thoroughly were they convinced that they themselves were right that they were firmly opposed to the idea of liberty of conscience. They thought it wicked that other denominations should be suffered to exist and to worship freely within the confines of their own Protestant land. And they insisted not only that all Catholics and Anabaptists be exiled from the British Isles but furthermore that Socinians, Arminians, Cartesians, in short, all those who did not share their own views upon the existence of a living God, be hanged.

This triangle of conflicts, however, produced an unexpected result. It forced the men who were obliged to keep peace between those mutually hostile parties to be much more tolerant than they would have been otherwise.

If both the Stuarts and Cromwell at different times of their careers insisted upon equal rights for all denominations, and history tells us they did, they were most certainly not animated by a love for Presbyterians or High Churchmen, or vice versa. They were merely making the best of a very difficult bargain. The terrible things which happened in the colonies along the Bay of Massachusetts, where one sect finally became all powerful, show us what would have been the fate of England if any one of the many contending factions had been able to establish an absolute dictatorship over the entire country.

Cromwell of course reached the point where he was able to do as he liked. But the Lord Protector was a very wise man. He knew that he ruled by the grace of his iron brigade and carefully avoided such extremes of conduct or of legislation as would have forced his opponents to make common cause. Beyond that, however, his ideas concerning tolerance did not go.

As for the abominable "atheists"—the aforementioned Socinians and Arminians and Cartesians and other apostles of the divine right of the individual human being—their lives were just as difficult as before.

Of course, the English "Libertines" enjoyed one enormous

advantage. They lived close to the sea. Only thirty-six hours of sickness separated them from the safe asylum of the Dutch cities. As the printing shops of these cities were turning out most of the contraband literature of southern and western Europe, a trip across the North Sea really meant a voyage to one's publisher and gave the enterprising traveler a chance to gather in his royalties and see what were the latest additions to the literature of intellectual protest.

Among those who at one time or another availed themselves of this convenient opportunity for quiet study and peaceful reflection, no one has gained a more deserving fame than John Locke.

He was born in the same year as Spinoza. And like Spinoza (indeed like most independent thinkers) he was the product of an essentially pious household. The parents of Baruch were orthodox Jews. The parents of John were orthodox Christians. Undoubtedly they both meant well by their children when they trained them in the strict doctrines of their own respective creeds. But such an education either breaks a boy's spirit or it turns him into a rebel. Baruch and John, not being the sort that ever surrenders, gritted their teeth, left home and struck out for themselves.

At the age of twenty Locke went to Oxford and there for the first time heard of Descartes. But among the dusty bookstalls of St. Catherine Street he found certain other volumes that were much to his taste. For example, there were the works of Thomas Hobbes.

An interesting figure, this former student of Magdalen College, a restless person who had visited Italy and had held converse with Galileo, who had exchanged letters with the great Descartes himself and who had spent the greater part of his life on the Continent, an exile from the fury of the Puritans. Between times he had composed an enormous book which contained all his ideas upon every conceivable subject and which bore the inviting title of "Leviathan, or the Matter, Form and Power of a Commonwealth, Ecclesiastical and Civil."

This learned tome made its appearance when Locke was in

his sophomore year. It was so outspoken upon the nature of princes, their rights and most especially their duties, that even the most thoroughgoing Cromwellian must approve of it, and that many of Cromwell's partisans felt inclined to pardon this doubting Thomas who was a full-fledged royalist yet exposed the royalist pretensions in a volume that weighed not less than five pounds. Of course Hobbes was the sort of person whom it has never been easy to classify. His contemporaries called him a Latitudinarian. That meant that he was more interested in the ethics of the Christian religion than in the discipline and the dogmas of the Christian church and believed in allowing people a fair degree of "latitude" in their attitude upon those questions which they regarded as non-essential.

Locke had the same temperament as Hobbes. He too remained within the Church until the end of his life but he was heartily in favor of a most generous interpretation both of life and of faith. What was the use, Locke and his friends argued, of ridding the country of one tyrant (who wore a golden crown) if it only led up to a fresh abuse of power by another tyrant (who wore a black slouch hat)? Why renounce allegiance to one set of priests and then the next day accept the rule of another set of priests who were fully as overbearing and arrogant as their predecessors? Logic undoubtedly was on their side but such a point of view could not possibly be popular among those who would have lost their livelihood if the "latitude men" had been successful and had changed a rigid social system into an ethical debating society?

And although Locke, who seems to have been a man of great personal charm, had influential friends who could protect him against the curiosity of the sheriffs, the day was soon to come when he would no longer be able to escape the suspicion of being an atheist.

That happened in the fall of the year 1683, and Locke there-upon went to Amsterdam. Spinoza had been dead for half a dozen years, but the intellectual atmosphere of the Dutch capital continued to be decidedly liberal and Locke was given a chance to study and write without the slightest interference on the part of the authorities. He was an industrious fellow and during the four years of his exile he composed that famous "Letter on Tolerance" which makes him one of the heroes of our little history. In this letter (which under the criticism of his opponents grew into three letters) he flatly denied that the state had the right to interfere with religion. The state, as Locke saw it (and in this he was borne out by a fellow exile, a Frenchman by the name of Pierre Bayle, who was living in Rotterdam at that time composing his incredibly learned one-man encyclopedia), the state was merely a sort of protective organization which a certain number of people had created and continued to maintain for their mutual benefit and safety. Why such an organization should presume to dictate what the individual citizens should believe and what not—that was something which Locke and his disciples failed to understand. The state did not undertake to tell them what to eat or drink. Why should it force them to visit one church and keep away from another?

The seventeenth century, as a result of the half-hearted victory of Protestantism, was an era of strange religious compromises.

The peace of Westphalia which was supposed to make an end to all religious warfare had laid down the principle that "all subjects shall follow the religion of their ruler." Hence in one six-by-nine principality all citizens were Lutherans (because the local grand duke was a Lutheran) and in the next they were all Catholics (because the local baron happened to be a Catholic).

"If," so Locke reasoned, "the State has the right to dictate to the people concerning the future weal of their souls, then one-half of the people are foreordained to perdition, for since both religions cannot possibly be true (according to article I of their own catechisms) it follows that those who are born on one side of a boundary line are bound for Heaven and those who are born on the other side are bound for Hell and in this way the geographical accident of birth decides one's future salvation."

That Locke did not include Catholics in his scheme of tolerance is regrettable, but understandable. To the average Britisher of the seventeenth century Catholicism was not a form of religious conviction but a political party which had never ceased to plot against the safety of the English state, which had built Armadas and had bought barrels of gunpowder with which to destroy the parliament of a supposedly friendly nation.

Hence Locke refused to his Catholic opponents those rights which he was willing to grant to the heathen in his colonies and asked that they continue to be excluded from His Majesty's domains, but solely on the ground of their dangerous political activities and not because they professed a different faith.

One had to go back almost sixteen centuries to hear such sentiments. Then a Roman emperor had laid down the famous principle that religion was an affair between the individual man and his God and that God was quite capable of taking care of himself whenever he felt that his dignity had been injured.

The English people who had lived and prospered through four changes of government within less than sixty years were inclined to see the fundamental truth of such an ideal of tolerance based upon common sense.

When William of Orange crossed the North Sea in the year 1688, Locke followed him on the next ship, which carried the new Queen of England. Henceforth he lived a quiet and uneventful existence and when he died at the ripe old age of seventy-two he was known as a respectable author and no longer feared as a heretic.

Civil war is a terrible thing but it has one great advantage. It clears the atmosphere.

The political dissensions of the seventeenth century had completely consumed the superfluous energy of the English nation and while the citizens of other countries continued to kill each other for the sake of the Trinity and prenatal damnation, religious persecution in Great Britain came to an end. Now and then a too presumptuous critic of the established church, like Daniel Defoe, might come into unpleasant contact with the law, but the author of "Robinson Crusoe" was pilloried because he was a humorist rather than an amateur theologian and because the Anglo-Saxon race, since time immemorial, has felt an inborn suspicion of irony. Had Defoe written a serious defense of tolerance, he would have escaped with a reprimand. When he turned his attack upon the tyranny of the church into a semi-humorous pamphlet entitled "The Shortest Way with Dissenters," he showed that he was a vulgar person without a decent sense of the proprieties and one who deserved no better than the companionship of the pickpockets of Newgate Prison.

Even then Defoe was fortunate that he had never extended his travels beyond the confines of the British Isles. For intolerance, having been driven from the mother country, had found a most welcome refuge in certain of the colonies on the other side of the ocean. And this was due not so much to the character of the people who had moved into these recently discovered regions as to the fact that the new world offered infinitely greater economic advantages than the old one.

In England itself, a small island so densely populated that it offered standing room only to the majority of her people, all business would soon have come to an end if the people had not been willing to practice the ancient and honorable rule of "give and take." But in America, a country of unknown extent and unbelievable riches, a continent inhabited by a mere handful of farmers and workmen, no such compromise was necessary.

And so it happened that a small communist settlement on the shores of Massachusetts Bay could develop into such a stronghold of self-righteous orthodoxy that the like of it had not been seen since the happy days when Calvin exercised the functions of Chief of Police and Lord High Executioner in western Switzerland.

The credit for the first permanent settlement in the chilly regions of the Charles River usually goes to a small group of people who are referred to as the Pilgrim Fathers. A Pilgrim, in the usual sense of the word, is one who "journeys to a sacred place as an act of religious devotion." The passengers of the *Mayflower* were not pilgrims in that sense of the word. They were English bricklayers and tailors and cord-wainers and blacksmiths and wheelwrights who had left their country to escape certain of those hated "poperies" which continued to cling to the worship in most of the churches around them.

First they had crossed the North Sea and had gone to Holland where they arrived at a moment of great economic depression. Our school-books continue to ascribe their desire for further travel to their unwillingness to let their children learn the Dutch language and otherwise to see them absorbed by the country of their adoption. It seems very unlikely, however, that those simple folk were guilty of such shocking ingratitude and purposely followed a most reprehensible course of hyphenation. The truth is that most of the time they were forced to live in the slums, that they found it very difficult to make a living in an already over-populated country, and that they expected a better revenue from tobacco planting in America than from wool-carding in Leiden. Hence to Virginia they sailed, but having been thrown by adverse currents and bad seamanship upon the shores of Massachusetts, they decided to stay where they were rather

THE NEW ZION

than risk the horrors of another voyage in their leaky tub.

But although they had now escaped the dangers of drowning and seasickness, they were still in a highly perilous position. Most of them came from small cities in the heart of England and had little aptitude for a life of pioneering. Their communistic ideas were shattered by the cold, their civic enthusiasm was chilled by the endless gales and their wives and children were killed by an absence of decent food. And, finally, the few who survived the first three winters, good-natured people accustomed to the rough and ready tolerance of the home country, were entirely swamped by the arrival of thousands of new colonists who without exception belonged to a sterner and less compromising variety of Puritan faith and who made Massachusetts what it was to remain for several centuries, the Geneva on the Charles River.

Hanging on for dear life to their small stretch of land, forever on the verge of disaster, they felt more than ever inclined to find an excuse for everything they thought and did within the pages of the Old Testament. Cut off from polite human society and books, they began to develop a strange religious psyche of their own. In their own eyes they had fallen heir to the tradi-

THE WINTER OF A NEW WORLD

tions of Moses and Gideon and soon became veritable Maccabees to their Indian neighbors of the west. They had nothing to reconcile them to their lives of hardship and drudgery except the conviction that they were suffering for the sake of the only true faith. Hence their conclusion (easily arrived at) that all other people must be wrong. Hence the brutal treatment of those who failed to share their own views, who suggested by implication that the Puritan way of doing and thinking was not the only right way. Hence the exclusion from their country of all harmless dissenters who were either unmercifully flogged and then driven into the wilderness or suffered the loss of their ears and tongues unless they were fortunate enough to find a refuge in one of the neighboring colonies which belonged to the Swedes and the Dutch.

No, for the cause of religious freedom or tolerance, this colony achieved nothing except in that roundabout and involuntary fashion which is so common in the history of human progress. The very violence of their religious despotism brought about a reaction in favor of a more liberal policy. After almost two centuries of ministerial tyranny, there arose a new generation which was the open and avowed enemy of all forms of priest-rule, which believed profoundly in the desirability of the separation of state and church and which looked askance upon the ancestral admixture of religion and politics.

By a stroke of good luck this development came about very slowly and the crisis did not occur until the period immediately before the outbreak of hostilities between Great Britain and her American colonies. As a result, the Constitution of the United States was written by men who were either freethinkers or secret enemies of the old-fashioned Calvinism and who incorporated into this document certain highly modern principles which have proved of the greatest value in maintaining the peaceful balance of our republic.

But ere this happened, the new world had experienced a most unexpected development in the field of tolerance and curiously enough it took place in a Catholic community, in that part of America now covered by the free state of Maryland.

The Calverts, who were responsible for this interesting experiment, were of Flemish origin, but the father had moved to England and had rendered very distinguished services to the house of Stuart. Originally they had been Protestants, but George Calvert, private secretary and general utility man to King James I, had become so utterly disgusted with the futile theological haggling of his contemporaries that he returned to the old faith. Good, bad or indifferent, it called black, black and white, white and did not leave the final settlement of every point of doctrine to the discretion of a board of semi-literate deacons.

This George Calvert, so it seems, was a man of parts. His back-sliding (a very serious offense in those days!) did not lose him the favor of his royal master. On the contrary, he was made Baron Baltimore of Baltimore and was promised every sort of assistance when he planned to establish a little colony of his own for the benefit of persecuted Catholics. First, he tried his luck in Newfoundland. But his settlers were frozen out of house and home and his Lordship then asked for a few thousand square miles in Virginia. The Virginians, however, staunchly Episcopalian, would have naught of such dangerous neighbors and Baltimore then asked for a slice of that wilderness which lay between Virginia and the Dutch and Swedish possessions of the north. Ere he received his charter he died. His son Cecil, however, continued the good work, and in the winter of 1633-1634 the little ships, the *Ark* and the *Dove*, under command of Leonard Calvert, brother to George, crossed the ocean, and in March of 1634 they safely landed their passengers on the shores of the Chesapeake Bay. The new country was called Maryland. This was done in honor of Mary, daughter of that French king, Henri IV, whose plans for a European League of Nations had been cut short by the dagger of a crazy monk, and wife to that English monarch who soon afterwards was to lose his head at the hands of his Puritan subjects.

THE FOUNDATION OF MARYLAND

This extraordinary colony which did not exterminate its Indian neighbors and offered equal opportunities to both Catholics and Protestants passed through many difficult years. First of all it was overrun by Episcopalians who tried to escape the fierce intolerance of the Puritans in Massachusetts. Next it was invaded by Puritans who tried to escape the fierce intolerance of the Episcopalians in Virginia. And the two groups of fugitives, with the usual arrogance of that sort of people, tried hard to introduce their own "correct form of worship" into the commonwealth that had just offered them refuge. As "all disputes which might give rise to religious passions" were expressly forbidden on Maryland territory, the older colonists were entirely within their right when they bade both Episcopalians and Puritans to keep the peace. But soon afterwards war broke out in the home country between the Cavaliers and the Roundheads and the Marylanders feared that, no matter who should win, they would lose their old freedom. Hence, in April of the year 1649 and shortly after news of the execution of Charles I had reached them, and at the direct suggestion of Cecil Calvert, they passed their famous Act of Tolerance which, among other things, contained this excellent passage:

"That since the coercion of conscience in the matter of religion has often produced very harmful results in those communities in which it was exercised, for the more tranquil and pacific government in this province and for the better preservation of mutual love and unity among its inhabitants, it is hereby decided that nobody in this province who professes faith in Jesus Christ shall be disturbed, molested or persecuted in any way for reasons respecting his religion or the free exercise thereof."

That such an act could be passed in a country in which the Jesuits occupied a favorite position shows that the Baltimore family was possessed of remarkable political ability and of more than ordinary courage. How profoundly this generous spirit was appreciated by some of their guests was shown in the same year when a number of Puritan exiles overthrew the government of Maryland, abolished the Act of Tolerance and replaced it by an "Act Concerning Religion" of their own which granted full religious liberty to all those who declared themselves Christians "with the exception of Catholics and Episcopalians."

This period of reaction fortunately did not last long. In the year 1660 the Stuarts returned to power and once more the Baltimores reigned in Maryland.

The next attack upon their policy came from the other side. The Episcopalians gained a complete victory in the mother country and they insisted that henceforth their church should be the official church of all the colonies. The Calverts continued to fight but they found it impossible to attract new colonists. And so, after a struggle which lasted another generation, the experiment came to an end.

Protestantism triumphed.

So did intolerance.

Chapter XXIII

THE SUN KING

THE eighteenth century is usually referred to as an era of despotism. And in an age which believes in the dogma of democracy, despotism, however enlightened, is not apt to be regarded as a desirable form of government.

Historians who mean well by the human race are very apt to point the finger of scorn at that great monarch Louis XIV and ask us to draw our own conclusions. When this brilliant sovereign came to the throne, he inherited a country in which the forces of Catholicism and Protestantism were so evenly balanced that the two parties, after a century of mutual assassination (with the odds heavily in favor of the Catholics), had at last concluded a definite peace and had promised to accept each other as unwelcome but unavoidable neighbors and fellow citizens. The "perpetual and irrevocable" Edict of Nantes of the year 1598, which contained the terms of agreement, stated that the Catholic religion was the official religion of the state but that the Protestants should enjoy complete liberty of conscience and should not suffer any persecution on account of their belief. They were furthermore allowed to build churches of their own and to hold public office. And as a token of good faith, the Protestants were allowed to hold two hundred fortified cities and villages within the realm of France.

This, of course, was an impossible arrangement. The Huguenots were no angels. To leave two hundred of the most prosperous cities and villages of France in the hands of a political party which was the sworn enemy of the government was quite as absurd as if we should surrender Chicago and San Francisco and Philadelphia to the Democrats to make them accept a Republican administration, or vice versa.

Richelieu, as intelligent a man as ever ruled a country, recog-

303

nized this. After a long struggle he deprived the Protestants of their political power, but although a cardinal by profession, he scrupulously refrained from any interference with their religious freedom. The Huguenots could no longer conduct independent diplomatic negotiations with the enemies of their own country, but otherwise they enjoyed the same privileges as before and could sing psalms and listen to sermons or not as pleased them.

Mazarin, the next man to rule France in the real sense of the word, had followed a similar policy. But he died in the year 1661. Then young Louis XIV personally undertook to rule his domains, and there was an end to the era of good will.

It seems most unfortunate that when this brilliant if disreputable Majesty was forced for once in his life into the companionship of decent people he should have fallen into the clutches of a good woman who was also a religious fanatic. Françoise d'Aubigné, the widow of a literary hack by the name of Scarron, had begun her career at the French court as governess to the seven illegitimate children of Louis XIV and the Marquise de Montespan. When that lady's love philters ceased to have the desired effect and the King began to show occasional signs of boredom, it was the governess who stepped into her shoes. Only she was different from all her predecessors. Before she agreed to move into His Majesty's apartments, the Archbishop of Paris had duly solemnized her marriage to the descendant of Saint Louis.

During the next twenty years the power behind the throne was therefore in the hands of a woman who was completely dominated by her confessor. The clergy of France had never forgiven either Richelieu or Mazarin for their conciliatory attitude towards the Protestants. Now at last they had a chance to undo the work of these shrewd statesmen and they went to it with a will. For not only were they the official advisers of the Queen, but they also became the bankers of the King.

That again is a curious story.

During the last eight centuries the monasteries had accumulated the greater part of the wealth of France and as they paid no taxes in a country which suffered perpetually from a depleted treasury, their surplus wealth was of great importance. And His Majesty, whose glory was greater than his credit, made a grateful use of this opportunity to replenish his own coffers and in exchange for certain favors extended to his clerical supporters he was allowed to borrow as much money as he wanted.

In this way the different stipulations of the "irrevocable" Edict of Nantes were one by one revoked. At first the Protestant religion was not actually forbidden, but life for those who remained faithful to the Huguenot cause was made exasperatingly uncomfortable. Whole regiments of dragoons were turned loose upon those provinces where the false doctrines were supposed to be most strongly entrenched. The soldiers were billeted among the inhabitants with instructions to make themselves thoroughly detestable. They ate the food and drank the wine and stole the forks and spoons and broke

THE ROYAL "SCRAP OF PAPER"

the furniture and insulted the wives and daughters of perfectly harmless citizens and generally behaved as if they were in a conquered territory. When their poor hosts, in their despair, rushed to the courts for some form of redress and protection, they were laughed at for their trouble and were told that they had brought their misfortunes upon their own heads and knew perfectly well how they could get rid of their unwelcome guests and at the same time regain the good will of the government.

A few, a very few, followed this suggestion and allowed themselves to be baptized by the nearest village priest. But the vast majority of these simple people remained faithful to the ideals of their childhood. At last, however, when one after another their churches were closed and their clergy were sent to 'the galleys, they began to understand that they were doomed. Rather than surrender, they decided to go into exile. But when they reached the frontier, they were told that no one was allowed to leave the country, that those who were caught in the act were to be hanged, and that those who aided and abetted such fugitives were liable to be sent to the galleys for life.

There are apparently certain things which this world will never learn.

From the days of the Pharaohs to those of Lenin, all governments at one time or another have tried the policy of "closing the frontier" and none of them has ever been able to score a success.

People who want to get out so badly that they are willing to take all sorts of risks can invariably find a way. Hundreds of thousands of French Protestants took to the "underground route" and soon afterwards appeared in London or Amsterdam or Berlin or Basel. Of course, such fugitives were not able to carry much ready cash. But they were known everywhere as honest and hard working merchants and artisans. Their credit was good and their energy undiminished. After a few years they usually regained that prosperity which had been their share in the old country and the home government was deprived of a living economic asset of incalculable value.

Indeed, it is no exaggeration to say that the revocation of the Edict of Nantes was the prelude to the French Revolution.

France had been and still was a very rich country. But commerce and clericalism have never been able to coöperate.

From the moment that the French government surrendered to petticoats and cassocks, her fate was sealed. The same pen that decreed the expulsion of the Huguenots signed the death-warrant of Louis XVI.

Chapter XXIV

FREDERICK THE GREAT

THE house of Hohenzollern has never been famous for its love of popular forms of government. But ere the crazy strain of the Bavarian Wittelsbachs had tainted this sober-minded family of bookkeepers and overseers, they rendered some very useful service to the cause of tolerance.

In part this was the result of a practical necessity. The Hohenzollerns had fallen heir to the poorest part of Europe, a half-populated wilderness of sand and forests. The Thirty Years' War had left them bankrupt. They needed both men and money to start in business once more and they set out to get them, regardless of race, creed or previous condition of servitude.

The father of Frederick the Great, a vulgarian with the manners of a coal-heaver and the personal tastes of a bartender, could grow quite tender when he was called upon to meet a delegation of foreign fugitives. "The more the merrier," was his motto in all matters pertaining to the vital statistics of his kingdom and he collected the disinherited of all nations as carefully as he collected the six-foot-three grenadiers of his lifeguard.

His son was of a very different caliber, a highly civilized human being who, having been forbidden by his father to study Latin and French, had made a specialty of both languages and greatly preferred the prose of Montaigne to the poetry of Luther and the wisdom of Epictetus to that of the Minor Prophets. The Old Testament severity of his father (who ordered the boy's best friend to be decapitated in front of his window so as to teach him a lesson in obedience) had not inclined his heart toward those Judæan ideals of rectitude of which the Lutheran and Calvinist ministers of his day were apt to speak with such great praise. He came to regard all religion as a survival of prehistoric fear and ignorance, a mood of subservience carefully encouraged by a small class of clever and unscrupulous fellows who knew how to make good use of their own preëminent position by living pleasantly at the expense of their neighbors. He was interested in Christianity and even more so in the person of Christ himself, but he approached the subject by way of Locke and Socinius and as a result he was, in religious matters at least, a very broad-minded person, and could truly boast that in his country "every one could find salvation after his own fashion."

This clever saying he made the basis for all his further experiments along the line of Tolerance. For example, he decreed that all religions were good as long as those who professed them were upright people who led decent, law-abiding lives; that therefore all creeds must enjoy equal rights and the state must never interfere in religious questions, but must content herself with playing policeman and keeping the peace between the different denominations. And because he truly believed this, he asked nothing of his subjects except that they be obedient and faithful and leave the final judgment of their thoughts and deeds "to Him alone who knew the conscience of men" and of whom he (the King) did not venture to form so small an opinion as to believe him to be in need of that human assistance which imagines that it can further the divine purpose by the exercise of violence and cruelty.

In all these ideas, Frederick was a couple of centuries ahead of his day. His contemporaries shook their heads when the king gave his Catholic subjects a piece of land that they might build themselves a church right in the heart of his capital. They began to murmur ominous words of warning when he made himself the protector of the Jesuit order, which had just been driven out of most Catholic countries, and they definitely ceased to regard him as a Christian when he claimed that ethics and religion had nothing to do with each other and that each man could believe whatever he pleased as long as he paid his taxes and served his time in the army.

Because at that time they happened to live within the boundaries of Prussia, these critics held their peace, for His Majesty was a master of epigram and a witty remark on the margin of a royal rescript could do strange things to the career of those who in some way or another had failed to please him.

The fact, however, remains that it was the head of an unlimited monarchy, an autocrat of thirty years' standing, who gave Europe a first taste of almost complete religious liberty.

In this distant corner of Europe, Protestant and Catholic and Jew and Turk and Agnostic enjoyed for the first time in their lives equal rights and equal prerogatives. Those who preferred to wear red coats could not lord it over their neighbors who preferred to wear green coats, and vice versa. And the people who went back for their spiritual consolation to Nicæa were forced to live in peace and amity with others who would as soon have supped with the Devil as with the Bishop of Rome.

That Frederick was entirely pleased with the outcome of his labors, I rather doubt. When he felt his last hour approaching, he sent for his faithful dogs. They seemed better company in this supreme hour than the members of "the so-called human race." (His Majesty was a columnist of no mean ability.)

And so he died, another Marcus Aurelius who had strayed into the wrong century and who, like his great predecessor, left an heritage which was entirely too good for his successors.

Chapter XXV

VOLTAIRE

In this day and age we hear a great deal of talk about the nefarious labors of the press agent and many good people denounce "publicity" as an invention of the modern devil of success, a new-fangled and disreputable method of attracting attention to a person or to a cause. But this complaint is as old as the hills. Events of the past, when examined without prejudice, completely contradict the popular notion that publicity is something of recent origin.

The prophets of the Old Testament, both major and minor, were past-masters in the art of attracting a crowd. Greek history and Roman history are one long succession of what we people of the journalistic profession call "publicity stunts." Some of that publicity was dignified. A great deal of it was of so patent and blatant a nature that to-day even Broadway would refuse to fall for it.

Reformers like Luther and Calvin fully understood the tremendous value of carefully prearranged publicity. And we cannot blame them. They were not the sort of men who could be happy growing humbly by the side of the road like the blushing daisies. They were very much in earnest. They wanted their ideas to live. How could they hope to succeed without attracting a crowd of followers?

A Thomas à Kempis can become a great moral influence by spending eighty years in a quiet corner of a monastery, for such long voluntary exile, if duly advertised (as it was), becomes an excellent selling point and makes people curious to see the little book which was born of a lifetime of prayer and meditation. But a Francis of Assisi or a Loyola, who hope to see some tangible results of their work while they are still on this planet, must willy-nilly resort to methods now usually associated with a circus or a new movie star.

Christianity lays great stress upon modesty and praises those who are humble of spirit. But the sermon which extols these virtues was delivered under circumstances which have made it a subject of conversation to this very day.

No wonder that those men and women who were denounced as the arch-enemies of the Church took a leaf out of the Holy Book and resorted to certain rather obvious methods of publicity when they began their great fight upon the spiritual tyranny which held the western world in bondage.

VOLTAIRE GOES TO SCHOOL IN FRANCE

I offer this slight explanation because Voltaire, the greatest of all virtuosos in the field of free advertisement, has very often been blamed for the way in which he sometimes played upon the tom-tom of public consciousness. Perhaps he did not always show the best of good taste. But those whose lives he saved may have felt differently about it.

And furthermore, just as the proof of the pudding is in the eating, the success or failure of a man like Voltaire should be measured by the services he actually rendered to his fellow men and not by his predilection for certain sorts of dressing-gowns, jokes and wall-paper.

In an outburst of justifiable pride this strange creature once said, "What of it if I have no scepter? I have got a pen." And right he was. He had a pen. Any number of pens. He was the born enemy of the goose and used more quills than two dozen ordinary writers. He belonged to that class of literary giants who all alone and under the most adverse circumstances can turn out as much copy as an entire syndicate of modern sport writers. He scribbled on the tables of dirty country inns. He composed endless hexameters in the chilly guest-rooms of lonely country-houses. His scrawls littered the floors of dingy boarding-houses in Greenwich. He spattered ink upon the carpets of the royal Prussian residence and used reams of the private stationery which bore the monogram of the governor of the Bastille. Before he had ceased to play with a hoop and marbles, Ninon de Lenclos had presented him with a considerable sum of pocket-money that he might "buy some books," and eighty years later, in the self-same town of Paris, we hear him ask for a pad of foolscap and unlimited coffee that he may finish yet one more volume before the inevitable hour of darkness and rest.

His tragedies, however, and his stories, his poetry and his treatises upon philosophy and physics, do not entitle him to an entire chapter of this book. He wrote no better verses than half a hundred other sonneteers of that era. As a historian he was both unreliable and dull, while his ventures in the realm of science were no better than the sort of stuff we find in the Sunday papers.

But as the brave and unyielding enemy of all that was stupid and narrow and bigoted and cruel, he wielded an influence which has endured until the beginning of the Great Civil War of the year 1914.

The age in which he lived was a period of extremes. On the one hand, the utter selfishness and corruption of a religious, social and economic system which had long since outlived its usefulness. On the other side, a large number of eager but over-zealous young men and young women ready to bring about a millennium which was based upon nothing more substantial than their good intentions. A humorous fate dropped this pale and sickly son of an inconspicuous notary public into this maelstrom of sharks and pollywogs, and bade him sink or swim. He preferred to swim and struck out for shore. The methods he employed during his long struggle with adverse circumstances were often of a questionable nature. He begged and flattered and played the clown. But this was in the days before royalties and literary agents. And let the author who never wrote a potboiler throw the first stone!

Not that Voltaire would have been greatly worried by a few additional bricks. During a long and busy life devoted to warfare upon stupidity, he had experienced too many defeats to worry about such trifles as a public beating or a couple of well aimed banana peels. But he was a man of indomitable good cheer. If to-day he must spend his leisure hours in His Majesty's prison, to-morrow he may find himself honored with a high titulary position at the same court from which he has just been banished. And if all his life he is obliged to listen to angry village priests denouncing him as the enemy of the Christian religion, isn't there somewhere in a cupboard filled with old love letters that beautiful medal presented to him by the Pope to prove that he can gain the approbation of Holy Church as well as her disapproval?

It was all in the day's work.

Meanwhile he fully intended to enjoy himself hugely and

VOLTAIRE GOES TO SCHOOL IN ENGLAND

crowd his days and weeks and months and years with a strange and colorful assortment of the most variegated experiences.

By birth Voltaire belonged to the middle class. His father was what for the lack of a better term we might call a sort of private trust company. He was the confidential handy-man of a number of rich nobles and looked after their legal and financial interests. Young Arouet (for that was the family name) was therefore accustomed to a society a little better than that of his own people, something which later in life gave him a great advantage over most of his literary rivals. His mother was a certain Mademoiselle d'Aumard. She had been a poor girl who did not bring her husband a cent of dowry. But she was possessed of that small "d'" which all Frenchmen of the middle classes (and all Europeans in general and a few Americans in particular) regard with humble awe, and her husband thought himself pretty lucky to win such a prize. As for the son, he also basked in the reflected glory of his ennobled grandparents and as soon as he began to write, he exchanged the plebeian François Marie Arouet for the more aristocratic François Marie de Voltaire, but how and where he hit upon this surname is still a good deal of a mystery. He had a brother and a sister. The sister, who took care of him after his mother's death, he loved very sincerely. The brother, on the other hand, a faithful priest of the Jansenist denomination, full of zeal and rectitude, bored him to distraction and was one of the reasons why he spent as little time as possible underneath the paternal shingles.

Father Arouet was no fool and soon discovered that his little "Zozo" promised to be a handful. Wherefore he sent him to the Jesuits that he might become versed in Latin hexameters and Spartan discipline. The good fathers did their best by him. They gave their spindly-legged pupil a sound training in the rudiments of both the dead and living tongues. But they found it impossible to eradicate a certain bump of "queerness" which from the very beginning had set this child apart from the other scholars.

At the age of seventeen they willingly let him go, and to please his father, young François then took up the study of the law. Unfortunately one could not read all day long. There were the long hours of the lazy evenings. These hours François whiled away either writing funny little pieces for the local newspapers or reading his latest literary compositions to his cronies in the nearest coffee-house. Two centuries ago such a life was generally believed to lead straight to perdition. Father Arouet fully appreciated the danger his son was running. He went to one of his many influential friends and obtained for M. François a position as secretary to the French Legation at the Hague. The Dutch capital, then as now, was exasperatingly dull. Out of sheer boredom Voltaire began a love affair with the not particularly attractive daughter of a terrible old woman who was a society reporter. The lady, who hoped to marry her darling to a more promising party, rushed to the French minister and asked him to please remove this dangerous Romeo before the whole city knew about the scandal. His Excellency had troubles enough of his own and was not eager for more. He bundled his secretary into the next stage-coach for Paris and François, without a job, once more found himself at the mercy of his father.

In this emergency Maître Arouet bethought himself of an expedient which was often used by such Frenchmen as had a friend at court. He asked and obtained a "lettre de cachet" and placed his son before the choice of enforced leisure in a jail or industrious application in a law school. The son said that he would prefer the latter and promised that he would be a model of industry and application. He was as good as his word and applied himself to the happy life of a free lance pamphleteer with such industry that the whole town talked about it. This was not according to the agreement with his papa and the latter was entirely within his rights when he decided to send his son away from the flesh-pots of the Seine and packed him off to a friend in the country, where the young man was to remain for a whole year.

There, with twenty-four hours' leisure each day of the week (Sundays included) Voltaire began the study of letters in all seriousness and composed the first of his plays. After twelve months of fresh air and a very healthy monotony, he was allowed to return to the scented atmosphere of the capital and at once made up for lost time by a series of lampoons upon the Regent, a nasty old man who deserved all that was said about him but did not like this publicity the least little bit. Hence, a second period of exile in the country, followed by more scribbling and at last a short visit to the Bastille. But prison in those days, that is to say, prison for young gentlemen of Voltaire's social prominence, was not a bad place. One was not allowed to leave the premises but otherwise did pretty much as one pleased. And it was just what Voltaire needed. A lonely cell in the heart of Paris gave him a chance to do some serious work. When he was released, he had finished several plays and these were performed with such tremendous success that one of them broke all records of the eighteenth century and ran for forty-five nights in succession.

This brought him some money (which he needed badly) but it also established his reputation as a wit, a most unfortunate thing for a young man who still has to make his career. For hereafter he was held responsible for every joke that enjoyed a few hours' popularity on the boulevards and in the coffeehouses. And incidentally it was the reason why he went to

England and took a post-graduate course in liberal statesmanship.

It happened in the year 1725. Voltaire had (or had not) been funny about the old but otherwise useless family of de Rohan. The Chevalier de Rohan felt that his honor had been assailed and that something must be done about it. Of course, it was impossible for a descendant of the ancient rulers of Brittany to fight a duel with the son of a notary public and the Chevalier delegated the work of revenge to his flunkeys.

One night Voltaire was dining with the Duc de Sully, one of his father's customers, when he was told that some one wished to speak to him outside. He went to the door, was fallen upon by the lackeys of my Lord de Rohan and was given a sound beating. The next day the story was all over the town. Voltaire, even on his best days, looked like a caricature of a very ugly little monkey. What with his eyes blackened and his head bandaged, he was a fit subject for half a dozen popular reviews. Only something very drastic could save his reputation from an untimely death at the hands of the comic papers. And as soon as raw beefsteak had done its work, M. de Voltaire sent his witnesses to M. le Chevalier de Rohan and began his preparation for mortal combat by an intensive course in fencing.

Alas! when the morning came for the great fight, Voltaire once more found himself behind the bars. De Rohan, a cad unto the last, had given the duel away to the police, and the battling scribe remained in custody until, provided with a ticket for England, he was sent traveling in a northwestern direction and was told not to return to France until requested to do so by His Majesty's gendarmes.

Four whole years Voltaire spent in and near London. The British kingdom was not exactly a Paradise, but compared to France, it was a little bit of Heaven.

A royal scaffold threw its shadow over the land. The thirtieth of January of the year 1649 was a date remembered by all those in high places. What had happened to sainted King Charles might (under slightly modified circumstances) happen to any one else who dared to set himself above the law. And as for the religion of the country, of course the official church of the state was supposed to enjoy certain lucrative and agreeable advantages, but those who preferred to worship elsewhere were left in peace and the direct influence of the clerical officials upon the affairs of state was, compared to France, almost negligible. Confessed atheists and certain bothersome non-conformists might occasionally succeed in getting themselves into jail, but to a subject of King Louis XV the general condition of life in England must have seemed wellnigh perfect.

In 1729, Voltaire returned to France, but although he was permitted to live in Paris, he rarely availed himself of that privilege. He was like a scared animal, willing to accept bits of sugar from the hands of his friends, but forever on the alert and ready to escape at the slightest sign of danger. He worked very hard. He wrote prodigiously and with a sublime disregard for dates and facts, and choosing for himself subjects which ran all the way from Lima, Peru, to Moscow, Russia, he composed a series of such learned and popular histories, tragedies and comedies that at the age of forty he was by far the most successful man of letters of his time.

Followed another episode which was to bring him into contact with a different kind of civilization.

In distant Prussia, good King Frederick, yawning audibly among the yokels of his rustic court, sadly pined for the companionship of a few amusing people. He felt a tremendous admiration for Voltaire and for years he had tried to induce him to come to Berlin. But to a Frenchman of the year 1750 such a migration seemed like moving into the wilds of Virginia and it was not until Frederick had repeatedly raised the ante that Voltaire at last condescended to accept.

He traveled to Berlin and the fight was on. Two such hopeless egotists as the Prussian king and the French playwright could not possibly hope to live under one and the same roof without coming to hate each other. After two years of sublime disagreement, a violent quarrel about nothing in particular drove Voltaire back to what he felt inclined to call "civilization."

But he had learned another useful lesson. Perhaps he was

right, and the French poetry of the Prussian king was atrocious. But His Majesty's attitude upon the subject of religious liberty left nothing to be desired and that was more than could be said of any other European monarch.

And when at the age of almost sixty Voltaire returned to his native land, he was in no mood to accept the brutal sentences by which the French courts tried to maintain order without some very scathing words of protest. All his life he had been greatly angered by man's unwillingness to use that divine spark of intelligence which the Lord on the sixth day of creation had bestowed upon the most sublime product of his handiwork. He (Voltaire) hated and loathed stupidity in every shape, form and manner. The "infamous enemy" against whom he directed most of his anger and whom, Cato-like, he was forever threatening to demolish, this "infamous enemy" was nothing more or less than the lazy stupidity of the mass of the people who refused to think for themselves as long as they had enough to eat and to drink and a place to sleep.

From the days of his earliest childhood he had felt himself pursued by a gigantic machine which seemed to move through sheer force of lethargy and combined the cruelty of Huitzilopochtli with the relentless persistency of Juggernaut. To destroy or at least upset this contraption became the obsession of his old years, and the French government, to give this particular devil his due, ably assisted him in his efforts by providing the world with a choice collection of legal scandals.

The first one occurred in the year 1761.

In the town of Toulouse in the southern part of France there lived a certain Jean Calas, a shop-keeper and a Protestant. Toulouse had always been a pious city. No Protestant was there allowed to hold office or to be a doctor or a lawyer, a bookseller or a midwife. No Catholic was permitted to keep a Protestant servant. And on August 23rd and 24th of each year the entire community celebrated the glorious anniversary of the massacre of Saint Bartholomew with a solemn feast of praise and thanksgiving.

Notwithstanding these many disadvantages, Calas had lived

all his life in complete harmony with his neighbors. One of his sons had turned Catholic, but the father had continued to be on friendly terms with the boy and had let it be known that as far as he was concerned, his children were entirely free to choose whatever religion pleased them best.

But there was a skeleton in the Calas closet. That was Marc Antony, the oldest son. Marc was an unfortunate fellow. He wanted to be a lawyer but that career was closed to Protestants. He was a devout Calvinist and refused to change his creed. The mental conflict had caused an attack of melancholia and this in time seemed to prey upon the young man's mind. He began to entertain his father and mother with long recitations of Hamlet's well-known soliloquy. He took long solitary walks. To his friends he often spoke of the superior advantages of suicide.

This went on for some time and then one night, while the family was entertaining a friend, the poor boy slipped into his father's storeroom, took a piece of packing rope and hanged himself from the doorpost.

There his father found him a few hours later, his coat and vest neatly folded upon the counter.

The family was in despair. In those days the body of a person who had committed suicide was dragged nude and face downward through the streets of the town and was hanged on a gibbet outside the gate to be eaten by the birds.

The Calas' were respectable folks and hated to think of such a disgrace. They stood around and talked of what they ought to do and what they were going to do until one of the neighbors, hearing the commotion, sent for the police, and the scandal spreading rapidly, their street was immediately filled with an angry crowd which loudly clamored for the death of old Calas "because he had murdered his son to prevent him from becoming a Catholic."

In a little town all things are possible and in a provincial nest of eighteenth century France, with boredom like a black funeral pall hanging heavily upon the entire community, the most idiotic and fantastic yarns were given credence with a sigh of profound and eager relief.

The high magistrates, fully aware of their duty under such suspicious circumstances, at once arrested the entire family, their guests and their servants and every one who had recently been seen in or near the Calas home. They dragged their prisoners to the town hall, put them in irons and threw them into the dungeons provided for the most desperate criminals. The next day they were examined. All of them told the same story. How Marc Antony had come into the house in his usual spirits, how he had left the room, how they thought that he had gone for one of his solitary walks, etc., etc.

By this time, however, the clergy of the town of Toulouse had taken a hand in the matter and with their help the dreadful news of this bloodthirsty Huguenot, who had killed one of his own children because he was about to return to the true faith, had spread far and wide throughout the land of Languedoc.

Those familiar with modern methods of detecting crime might think that the authorities would have spent that day inspecting the scene of the murder. Marc Antony enjoyed quite a reputation as an athlete. He was twenty-eight and his father was sixty-three. The chances of the father having hanged his son from his own doorpost without a struggle were small indeed. But none of the town councilors bothered about such little details. They were too busy with the body of the victim. For Marc Antony, the suicide, had by now assumed the dignity of a martyr and for three weeks his corpse was kept at the town hall and thereupon it was most solemnly buried by the White Penitents who for some mysterious reason had made the defunct Calvinist an ex-officio member of their own order and who conducted his embalmed remains to the Cathedral with the circumstance and the pomp usually reserved for an archbishop or an exceedingly rich patron of the local Basilica.

During these three weeks, from every pulpit in town, the good people of Toulouse had been urged to bring whatever testimony they could against the person of Jean Calas and his family and finally, after the case had been thoroughly thrashed out in the public press, and five months after the suicide, the trial began.

One of the judges in a moment of great lucidity suggested

that the shop of the old man be visited to see whether such a suicide as he described would have been possible, but he was over-ridden and with twelve votes against one, Calas was sentenced to be tortured and to be broken on the wheel.

He was taken to the torture-room and was hanged by his wrists until his feet were a meter from the ground. Then his body was stretched until the limbs were "drawn from their sockets." (I am copying from the official report.) As he refused to confess to a crime which he had not committed, he was then taken down and was forced to swallow such vast quantities of water that his body had soon "swollen to twice its natural size." As he persisted in his diabolical refusal to confess his guilt, he was placed on a tumbril and was dragged to the place of execution where his arms and legs were broken in two places by the executioner. During the next two hours, while he lay helpless on the block, magistrates and priests continued to bother him with their questions. With incredible courage the old man continued to proclaim his innocence. Until the chief justice, exasperated by such obstinate lying, gave him up as a hopeless case and ordered him to be strangled to death.

The fury of the populace had by this time spent itself and none of the other members of the family were killed. The widow, deprived of all her goods, was allowed to go into retirement and starve as best she could in the company of her faithful maid. As for the children, they were sent to different convents with the exception of the youngest who had been away at school at Nîmes at the time of his brother's suicide and who had wisely fled to the territory of the sovereign city of Geneva.

The case had attracted a great deal of attention. Voltaire in his castle of Ferney (conveniently built near the frontier of Switzerland so that a few minutes' walk could carry him to foreign ground) heard of it but at first refused to be interested. He was forever at loggerheads with the Calvinist ministers of Geneva who regarded his private little theater which stood within sight of their own city as a direct provocation and the work of Satan. Hence Voltaire, in one of his supercilious moods, wrote that he could not work up any enthusiasm for this so-called

Protestant martyr, for if the Catholics were bad, how much worse those terribly bigoted Huguenots, who boycotted his plays! Besides, it seemed impossible to him (as to a great many other people) that twelve supposedly respectable judges would have condemned an innocent man to such a terrible death without very good reason.

But a few days later the sage of Ferney, who kept open house to all comers and no questions asked, had a visit from an honest merchant from Marseilles who had happened to be in Toulouse at the time of the trial and who was able to give him some first-hand information. Then at last he began to understand the horror of the crime that had been committed and from that moment on he could think of nothing else.

There are many sorts of courage, but a special order of merit is reserved for those rare souls who, practically alone, dare to face the entire established order of society and who loudly cry for justice when the high courts of the land have pronounced sentence and when the community at large has accepted their verdict as equitable and just.

Voltaire well knew the storm that would break if he should dare to accuse the court of Toulouse of a judicial murder, and he prepared his case as carefully as if he had been a professional attorney. He interviewed the Calas boy who had escaped to Geneva. He wrote to every one who could possibly know something of the inside of the case. He hired counsel to examine and if possible to correct his own conclusions, lest his anger and his indignation carry him away. And when he felt sure of his ground, he opened his campaign.

First of all he induced every man of some influence whom he knew within the realm of France (and he knew most of them) to write to the Chancellor of the Kingdom and ask for a revision of the Calas case. Then he set about to find the widow and as soon as she had been located, he ordered her to be brought to Paris at his own expense and engaged one of the best known lawyers to look after her. The spirit of the woman had been completely broken. She vaguely prayed that she might get her daughters out of the convent before she died. Beyond that, her hopes did not extend.

Then he got into communication with the other son who was a Catholic, made it possible for him to escape from his school and to join him in Geneva. And finally he published all the facts in a short pamphlet entitled "Original Documents Concerning the Calas Family," which consisted of letters written by the survivors of the tragedy and contained no reference whatsoever to Voltaire himself.

Afterwards, too, during the revision of the case, he remained carefully behind the scenes, but so well did he handle his publicity campaign that soon the cause of the Calas family was the cause of all families in all countries of Europe and that thousands of people everywhere (including the King of England and the Empress of Russia) contributed to the funds that were being raised to help the defense.

Eventually Voltaire gained his victory, but not until he had fought one of the most desperate battles of his entire career.

The throne of France just then was occupied by Louis XV of unsavory memory. Fortunately his mistress hated the Jesuits and all their works (including the Church) with a most cordial hatred and was therefore on the side of Voltaire. But the King loved his ease above all other things and was greatly annoyed at all the fuss made about an obscure and dead Protestant. And of course as long as His Majesty refused to sign a warrant for a new trial, the Chancellor would not take action, and as long as the Chancellor would not take action, the tribunal of Toulouse was perfectly safe and so strong did they feel themselves that they defied public opinion in a most high-handed fashion and refused to let Voltaire or his lawyers have access to the original documents upon which they had based their conviction.

During nine terrible months, Voltaire kept up his agitation until finally in March of the year 1765 the Chancellor ordered the Tribunal of Toulouse to surrender all the records in the Calas case and moved that there be a new trial. The widow of Jean Calas and her two daughters, who had at last been returned to their mother, were present in Versailles when this decision

was made public. A year later the special court which had been
ordered to investigate the appeal reported that Jean Calas
had been done to death for a crime which he had not committed.
By Herculean efforts the King was induced to bestow a small
gift of money upon the widow and her children. Furthermore,
the magistrates who had handled the Calas case were deprived of
their office and it was politely
suggested to the people of Toulouse that such a thing must not
happen again.

CALAS

But although the French government might take a lukewarm
view of the incident, the people
of France had been stirred to
the very depths of their outraged
souls. And suddenly Voltaire
became aware that this was not
the only miscarriage of justice
on record, that there were many
others who had suffered as inno-
cently as Calas.

In the year 1760 a Protestant
country squire of the neighborhood of Toulouse had offered
the hospitality of his house to a visiting Calvinist minister. For
this hideous crime he had been deprived of his estate and had
been sent to the galleys for life. He must have been a terribly
strong man for thirteen years later he was still alive. Then
Voltaire was told of his plight. He set to work, got the unfortunate man away from the galleys, brought him to Switzerland
where his wife and children were being supported by public
charity and looked after the family until the crown was induced
to surrender a part of the confiscated property and the family
were given permission to return to their deserted homestead.

Next came the case of Chaumont, a poor devil who had been
caught at an open-air meeting of Protestants and who for that
crime had been dispatched to the galleys for an indeterminate

period, but who now, at the intercession of Voltaire, was set free.

These cases, however, were merely a sort of grewsome hors-d'œuvre to what was to follow.

Once more the scene was laid in Languedoc, that long suffering part of France which after the extermination of the Albigensian and Waldensian heretics had been left a wilderness of ignorance and bigotry.

In a village near Toulouse there lived an old Protestant by the name of Sirven, a most respectable citizen who made a living as an expert in medieval law, a lucrative position at a time when the feudal judicial system had grown so complicated that ordinary rent-sheets looked like an income tax blank.

Sirven had three daughters. The youngest was a harmless idiot, much given to brooding. In March of the year 1764 she left her home. The parents searched far and wide but found no trace of the child until a few days later when the bishop of the district informed the father that the girl had visited him, had expressed a desire to become a nun and was now in a convent.

Centuries of persecution had successfully broken the spirit of the Protestants in that part of France. Sirven humbly answered that everything undoubtedly would be for the best in this worst of all possible worlds and meekly accepted the inevitable. But in the unaccustomed atmosphere of the cloister, the poor child had soon lost the last vestiges of reason and when she began to make a nuisance of herself, she was returned to her own people. She was then in a state of terrible mental depression and in such continual horror of voices and spooks that her parents feared for her life. A short time afterwards she once more disappeared. Two weeks later her body was fished out of an old well.

At that time Jean Calas was up for trial and the people were in a mood to believe anything that was said against a Protestant. The Sirvens, remembering what had just happened to innocent Jean Calas, decided not to court a similar fate. They fled and after a terrible trip through the Alps, during which one of their grandchildren froze to death, they at last reached Switzerland. They had not left a moment too soon. A few months later, both the father and the mother were found guilty (in their absence) of the crime of having murdered their child and were ordered to be hanged. The daughters were condemned to witness the execution of their parents and thereafter to be banished for life.

A friend of Rousseau brought the case to the notice of Voltaire and as soon as the Calas affair came to an end, he turned his attention to the Sirvens. The wife meanwhile had died. Remained the duty of vindicating the husband. It took exactly seven years to do this. Once again the tribunal of Toulouse refused to give any information or to surrender any documents. Once more Voltaire had to beat the tom-tom of publicity and beg money from Frederick of Prussia and Catherine of Russia and Poniatowski of Poland before he could force the crown to take an interest. But finally, in the seventy-eighth year of his own life and in the eighth year of this interminable lawsuit, the Sirvens were exonerated and the survivors were allowed to go back to their homes.

So ended the second case.

The third one followed immediately.

In the month of August of the year 1765 in the town of Abbeville, not far from Amiens, two crucifixes that stood by the side of the road were found broken to pieces by an unknown hand. Three young boys were suspected of this sacrilege and orders were given for their arrest. One of them escaped and went to Prussia. The others were caught. Of these, the older one, a certain Chevalier de la Barre, was suspected of being an atheist. A copy of the Philosophical Dictionary, that famous work to which all the great leaders of liberal thought had contributed, was found among his books. This looked very suspicious and the judges decided to look into the young man's past. It was true they could not connect him with the Abbeville case but had he not upon a previous occasion refused to kneel down and uncover while a religious procession went by?

De la Barre said yes, but he had been in a hurry to catch a stage-coach and had meant no offense.

Thereupon he was tortured, and being young and bearing the pain less easily than old Calas, he readily confessed that he had mutilated one of the two crucifixes and was condemned to death for "impiously and deliberately walking before the Host without kneeling or uncovering, singing blasphemous songs, tendering marks of adoration to profane books," and other crimes of a similar nature which were supposed to have indicated a lack of respect for the Church.

The sentence was so barbarous (his tongue was to be torn out with hot irons, his right hand was to be cut off, and he was to be slowly burned to death, and all that only a century and a half ago!) that the public was stirred into several expressions of disapproval. Even if he were guilty of all the things enumerated in the bill of particulars, one could not butcher a boy for a drunken prank! Petitions were sent to the King, ministers were besieged with requests for a respite. But the country was full of unrest and there must be an example, and de la Barre, having undergone the same tortures as Calas, was taken to the scaffold, was decapitated (as a sign of great and particular favor) and his corpse, together with his Philosophical Dictionary and some volumes by our old friend Bayle, were publicly burned by the hangman.

It was a day of rejoicing for those who dreaded the ever-growing influence of the Sozzinis and the Spinozas and the Descartes. It showed what invariably happened to those ill-guided young men who left the narrow path between the right and the wrong and followed the leadership of a group of radical philosophers.

Voltaire heard this and accepted the challenge. He was fast approaching his eightieth birthday, but he plunged into the case with all his old zeal and with a brain that burned with a clear white flame of outraged decency.

De la Barre had been executed for "blasphemy." First of all, Voltaire tried to discover whether there existed a law by which people guilty of that supposed crime could be condemned to death. He could not find one. Then he asked his lawyer friends. They could not find one. And it gradually dawned upon the community that the judges in their unholy eagerness had "invented" this bit of legal fiction to get rid of their prisoner.

There had been ugly rumors at the time of de la Barre's execution. The storm that now arose forced the judges to be very circumspect and the trial of the third of the youthful prisoners was never finished. As for de la Barre, he was never vindicated. The review of the case dragged on for years and when Voltaire died, no decision had as yet been reached. But the blows which he had struck, if not for tolerance at least against intolerance, were beginning to tell.

The official acts of terror instigated by gossiping old women and senile courts came to an end.

Tribunals that have religious axes to grind are only successful when they can do their work in the dark and are able to surround themselves with secrecy. The method of attack followed by Voltaire was one against which such courts had no means of defense.

Voltaire turned on all the lights, hired a voluminous orchestra, invited the public to attend, and then bade his enemies do their worst.

As a result, they did nothing at all.

Chapter XXVI

THE ENCYCLOPEDIA

THERE are three different schools of statesmanship. The first one teaches a doctrine which reads somewhat as follows: "Our planet is inhabited by poor benighted creatures who are unable to think for themselves, who suffer mental agonies whenever they are obliged to make an independent decision and who therefore can be led astray by the first ward-heeler that comes along. Not only is it better for the world at large that these 'herd people' be ruled by some one who knows his own mind, but they themselves, too, are infinitely happier when they do not have to bother about parliaments and ballot-boxes and can devote all their time to their work-shops, their children, their flivvers and their vegetable gardens."

The disciples of this school become emperors, sultans, sachems, sheiks and archbishops and they rarely regard labor unions as an essential part of civilization. They work hard and build roads, barracks, cathedrals and jails.

The adherents of the second school of political thought argue as follows: "The average man is God's noblest invention. He is a sovereign in his own right, unsurpassed in wisdom, prudence and the loftiness of his motives. He is perfectly capable of looking after his own interests, but those committees through which he tries to rule the universe are proverbially slow when it comes to handling delicate affairs of state. Therefore, the masses ought to leave all executive business to a few trusted friends who are not hampered by the immediate necessity of making a living and who can devote all their time to the happiness of the people."

Needless to say the apostles of this glorious ideal are the logical candidates for the job of oligarch, dictator, first consul and lord protector.

They work hard and build roads and barracks, but the cathedrals they turn into jails.

But there is a third group of people. They contemplate man with the sober eye of science and accept him as he is. They appreciate his good qualities, they understand his limitations. They are convinced from a long observation of past events that the average citizen, when not under the influence of passion or

THE ENCYCLOPEDIST

self-interest, tries really very hard to do what is right. But they make themselves no false illusions. They know that the natural process of growth is exceedingly slow, that it would be as futile to try and hasten the tides or the seasons as the growth of human intelligence. They are rarely invited to assume the government of a state, but whenever they have a chance to put their ideas into action, they build roads, improve the jails and spend the rest of the available funds upon schools and universities. For they are such incorrigible optimists that they believe that education of the right sort will gradually rid this world of most of its ancient evils and is therefore a thing that ought to be encouraged at all costs.

And as a final step towards the fulfillment of this ideal, they usually write an encyclopedia.

Like so many other things that give evidence of great wisdom and profound patience, the encyclopedia-habit took its origin in China. The Chinese Emperor K'ang-hi tried to make his subjects happy with an encyclopedia in five thousand and twenty volumes.

Pliny, who introduced encyclopedias in the west, was contented with thirty-seven books.

The first fifteen hundred years of the Christian era produced nothing of the slightest value along this line of enlightenment. A fellow countryman of Saint Augustine, the African Felix Capella, wasted a great many years of his life composing something which he held to be a veritable treasure house of miscellaneous knowledge. In order that people might the more easily retain the many interesting facts which he presented to them, he used poetry. This terrible mass of misinformation was duly learned by heart by eighteen successive generations of medieval children and was held by them to be the last word in the fields of literature, music and science.

Two hundred years later a bishop of Sevilla by the name of Isidore wrote an entirely new encyclopedia and after that the output increased at the regular rate of two for every hundred years. What has become of them all, I do not know. The bookworm (most useful of domestic animals) has possibly acted as our deliverer. If all these volumes had been allowed to survive, there would not be room for anything else on this earth.

When at last during the first half of the eighteenth century, Europe experienced a tremendous outbreak of intellectual curiosity, the purveyors of encyclopedias entered into a veritable Paradise. Such books, then as now, were usually compiled by very poor scholars who could live on eight dollars a week and whose personal services counted for less than the money spent upon paper and ink. England especially was a great country for this sort of literature and so it was quite natural that John Mills, a Britisher who lived in Paris, should think of translating the successful "Universal Dictionary" of Ephraim Chambers into the French language that he might peddle his product among the subjects of good King Louis and grow rich. For this purpose he associated himself with a German professor and then approached Lebreton, the king's printer, to do the actual publishing. To make a long story short, Lebreton, who saw a chance to make a small fortune, deliberately swindled his partner and as soon as he had frozen Mills and the Teuton doctor out of the enterprise, continued to publish the pirated edition on his own account. He called the forthcoming work the "Encyclopédie ou Dictionnaire Universel des Arts et des Sciences" and issued a series of beautiful prospectuses with such a tremendous selling appeal that the list of subscribers was soon filled.

Then he hired himself a professor of philosophy in the Collège de France to act as his editor-in-chief, bought a lot of paper and awaited results.

Unfortunately, the work of writing an encyclopedia did not prove as simple as Lebreton had thought. The professor produced notes but no articles, the subscribers loudly clamored for Volume I and everything was in great disorder.

In this emergency Lebreton remembered that a "Universal Dictionary of Medicine" which had appeared only a few months before had been very favorably received. He sent for the editor of this medical handbook and hired him on the spot. And so it happened that a mere encyclopedia became the "Encyclopédie." For the new editor was no one less than Denis Diderot and the work which was to have been a hack job became one of the most important contributions of the eighteenth century towards the sum total of human enlightenment.

Diderot at that time was thirty-seven years old and his life had been neither easy nor happy. He had refused to do what all respectable young Frenchmen were supposed to do and go to a university. Instead, as soon as he could get away from his Jesuit teachers, he had proceeded to Paris to become a man of letters. After a short period of starvation (acting upon the principle that two can go hungry just as cheaply as one) he had married a lady who proved to be a terribly pious woman and an uncompromising shrew, a combination which is by no means as rare as some people seem to believe. But as he was obliged to support her, he had been forced to take all sorts of odd jobs and to compile all sorts of books from "Inquiries concerning Virtue and Merit" to a rather disreputable rehash of Boccaccio's "Decameron." In his heart, however, this pupil of Bayle remained faithful to his liberal ideals. Soon the government (after the fashion of governments during times of stress) discovered that this inoffensive looking young author maintained grave doubts about the story of creation as rendered in the first chapter of Genesis and otherwise was considerable of a heretic. In consequence whereof Diderot was conducted to the prison of Vincennes and there held under lock and key for almost three months.

It was after his release from jail that he entered the service of Lebreton. Diderot was one of the most eloquent men of his time. He saw the chance of a lifetime in the enterprise of which he was to be the head. A mere rehash of Chambers' old material seemed entirely beneath his dignity. It was an era of tremendous mental activity. Very well! Let the Encyclopedia of Lebreton contain the latest word upon every conceivable subject and let the articles be written by the foremost authorities in every line of human endeavor.

Diderot was so full of enthusiasm that he actually persuaded Lebreton to give him full command and unlimited time. Then he made up a tentative list of his coöperators, took a large sheet of foolscap and began, "A: the first letter of the alphabet," etc., etc.

Twenty years later he reached the Z and the job was done. Rarely, however, has a man worked under such tremendous disadvantages. Lebreton had increased his original capital when he hired Diderot, but he never paid his editor more than five hundred dollars per year. And as for the other people who were supposed to lend their assistance, well, we all know how those things are. They were either busy just then, or they would do it next month, or they had to go to the country to see their grandmother. With the result that Diderot was obliged to do most of the work himself while smarting under the abuse that was heaped upon him by the officials of both the Church and the State.

To-day copies of his Encylopedia are quite rare. Not because so many people want them but because so many people are glad to get rid of them. The book which a century and a half ago was howled down as a manifestation of a pernicious radicalism reads to-day like a dull and harmless tract on the feeding of babies. But to the more conservative element among the clergy of the eighteenth century, it sounded like a clarion call of destruction, anarchy, atheism and chaos.

Of course, the usual attempts were made to denounce the editor-in-chief as an enemy of society and religion, a loose reprobate who believed neither in God, home or the sanctity of the family ties. But the Paris of the year 1770 was still an overgrown village where every one knew every one else. And Diderot, who not only claimed that the purpose of life was "to do good and to find the truth," but who actually lived up to this motto, who kept open house for all those who were hungry, who labored twenty hours a day for the sake of humanity and asked nothing in return but a bed, a writing desk and a pad of paper, this simple-minded, hard-working fellow was so shining an example of those virtues in which the prelates and the monarchs of that day were so conspicuously lacking, that it was not easy to attack him from that particular angle. And so the authorities contented themselves with making his life just as unpleasant as they possibly could by a continual system of espionage, by everlastingly snooping around the office, by raiding Diderot's home, by confiscating his notes and occasionally by suppressing the work altogether.

These obstructive methods, however, could not dampen his enthusiasm. At last the work was finished and the "Encyclopédie" actually accomplished what Diderot had expected of it— it became the rallying point for all those who in one way or another felt the spirit of the new age and who knew that the world was desperately in need of a general overhauling.

It may seem that I have dragged the figure of the editor slightly out of the true perspective.

Who, after all, was this Denis Diderot, who wore a shabby coat, counted himself happy when his rich and brilliant friend, the Baron D'Holbach, invited him to a square meal once a week, and who was more than satisfied when four thousand copies of his book were actually sold? He lived at the same time as Rousseau and D'Alembert and Turgot and Helvétius and Volney and Condorcet and a score of others, all of whom gained a much greater personal renown than he did. But without the Encyclopédie these good people would never have been able to exercise the influence they did. It was more than a book, it was a social and economic program. It told what the leading minds of the day were actually thinking. It contained a concrete statement of those ideas that soon were to dominate the entire world. It was a decisive moment in the history of the human race.

France had reached a point where those who had eyes to see and ears to hear knew that something drastic must be done to avoid an immediate catastrophe, while those who had eyes to see and ears to hear, yet refused to use them, maintained with an equal display of stubborn energy that peace and order could only be maintained by a strict enforcement of a set of antiquated laws that belonged to the era of the Merovingians. For the moment, those two parties were so evenly balanced that everything remained as it had always been and this led to strange complications. The same France which on one side of the ocean played such a conspicuous rôle as the defender of liberty and freedom and addressed the most affectionate letters to Monsieur Georges Washington (who was a Freemason) and arranged delightful week-end parties for Monsieur le Ministre, Benjamin Franklin, who was what his neighbors used to call a "sceptic" and what we call a plain atheist, this country on the other side of the broad Atlantic stood revealed as the most vindictive enemy of all forms of spiritual progress and only showed her sense of democracy in the complete impartiality with which she condemned both philosopher and peasant to a life of drudgery and privation.

Eventually all this was changed.

But it was changed in a way which no one had been able to foresee. For the struggle that was to remove the spiritual and social handicaps of all those who were born outside the royal purple was not fought by the slaves themselves. It was the work of a small group of disinterested citizens whom the Protestants, in their heart of hearts, hated quite as bitterly as their Catholic oppressors and who could count upon no other reward than that which is said to await all honest men in Heaven.

The men who during the eighteenth century defended the cause of tolerance rarely belonged to any particular denomination. For the sake of personal convenience they sometimes went through certain outward motions of religious conformity which kept the gendarmes away from their writing desks. But as far as their inner life was concerned, they might just as well have lived in Athens in the fourth century B. C. or in China in the days of Confucius.

They were often most regrettably lacking in a certain reverence for various things which most of their contemporaries held in great respect and which they themselves regarded as harmless but childish survivals of a bygone day.

They took little stock in that ancient national history which the western world, for some curious reason, had picked out from among all Babylonian and Assyrian and Egyptian and Hittite and Chaldean records and had accepted as a guide-book of morals and customs. But true disciples of their great master, Socrates, they listened only to the inner voice of their own conscience and regardless of consequences, they lived fearlessly in a world that had long since been surrendered to the timid.

Chapter XXVII

THE INTOLERANCE OF REVOLUTION

THE ancient edifice of official glory and unofficial misery known as the Kingdom of France came crashing down on a memorable evening in the month of August of the year of grace 1789.

On that hot and sultry night, after a week of increasing emotional fury, the National Assembly worked itself into a veritable orgy of brotherly love. Until in a moment of intense excitement the privileged classes surrendered all those ancient rights and prerogatives which it had taken them three centuries to acquire and as plain citizens declared themselves in favor of those theoretical rights of man which henceforth would be the foundation-stone for all further attempts at popular self-government.

As far as France was concerned, this meant the end of the feudal system. An aristocracy, which is actually composed of the "aristoi," of the best of the most enterprising elements of society, which boldly assumes leadership and shapes the destinies of the common country, has a chance to survive. A nobility, which voluntarily retires from active service and contents itself with ornamental clerical jobs in diverse departments of government, is only fit to drink tea on Fifth Avenue or run restaurants on Second.

The old France therefore was dead.

Whether for better or for worse, I do not know.

But it was dead and with it there passed away that most outrageous form of an invisible government which the Church, ever since the days of Richelieu, had been able to impose upon the anointed descendants of Saint Louis.

Verily, now as never before, mankind was given a chance.

Of the enthusiasm which at that period filled the hearts and souls of all honest men and women, it is needless to speak.

The millennium was close at hand, yea, it had come.

And intolerance among the many other vices inherent in an

autocratic form of government was for good and all to be eradicated from this fair earth.

Allons, enfants de la patrie, the days of tyranny are gone! And more words to that effect.

Then the curtain went down, society was purged of its many iniquities, the cards were reshuffled for a new deal and when it was all over, behold our old friend Intolerance, wearing a pair of proletarian pantaloons and his hair brushed à la Robespierre, a-sitting side by side with the public prosecutor and having the time of his wicked old life.

Ten years ago he had sent people to the scaffold for claiming that authority maintaining itself solely by the grace of Heaven might sometimes be in error.

Now he hustled them to their doom for insisting that the will of the people need not always and invariably be the will of God.

A ghastly joke!

But a joke paid for (after the nature of such popular fancies) with the blood of a million innocent bystanders.

What I am about to say is unfortunately not very original. One can find the same idea couched in different if more elegant words in the works of many of the ancients.

In matters pertaining to man's inner life there are, and apparently there always have been, and most likely there always will be two entirely different varieties of human beings.

A few, by dint of endless study and contemplation and the serious searching of their immortal souls will be able to arrive

REVOLUTION

at certain temperate philosophical conclusions which will place them above and beyond the common worries of mankind.

But the vast majority of the people are not contented with a mild diet of spiritual "light wines." They want something with a kick to it, something that burns on the tongue, that hurts the gullet, that will make them sit up and take notice. What that "something" is does not matter very much, provided it comes up to the above-mentioned specifications and is served in a direct and simple fashion and in unlimited quantities.

This fact seems to have been little understood by historians and this has led to many and serious disappointments. No sooner has an outraged populace torn down the stronghold of the past (a fact duly and enthusiastically reported by the local Herodoti and Taciti), than it turns mason, carts the ruins of the former citadel to another part of the city and there remolds them into a new dungeon, every whit as vile and tyrannical as the old one and used for the same purpose of repression and terror.

The very moment a number of proud nations have at last succeeded in throwing off the yoke imposed upon them by an "infallible man" they accept the dictates of an "infallible book."

Yea, on the very day when Authority, disguised as a flunkey, is madly galloping to the frontier, Liberty enters the deserted palace, puts on the discarded royal raiment and forthwith commits herself to those selfsame blunders and cruelties which have just driven her predecessor into exile.

It is all very disheartening, but it is an honest part of our story and must be told.

No doubt the intentions of those who were directly responsible for the great French upheaval were of the best. The Declaration of the Rights of Man had laid down the principle that no citizen should ever be disturbed in the peaceful pursuit of his ways on account of his opinion, "not even his religious opinion," provided that his ideas did not disturb the public order as laid down by the various decrees and laws.

This, however, did not mean equal rights for all religious denominations. The Protestant faith henceforth was to be tolerated, Protestants were not to be annoyed because they worshiped in a different church from their Catholic neighbors, but Catholicism remained the official, the "dominant" Church of the state.

Mirabeau, with his unerring instinct for the essentials of political life, knew that this far-famed concession was only a half-way measure. But Mirabeau, who was trying to turn a great social cataclysm into a one-man revolution, died under the effort and many noblemen and bishops, repenting of their generous gesture of the night of the fourth of August, were already beginning that policy of obstructionism which was to be of such fatal consequence to their master the king. And it was not until two years later in the year 1791 (and exactly two years too late for any practical purpose) that all religious sects, including the Protestants and the Jews, were placed upon a basis of absolute equality and were declared to enjoy the same liberty before the law.

From that moment on, the rôles began to be reversed. The constitution which the representatives of the French people finally bestowed upon an expectant country insisted that all priests of whatsoever faith should swear an oath of allegiance to the new form of government and should regard themselves strictly as servants of the state, like the school-teachers and postal employees and lighthouse-keepers and customs officials who were their fellow citizens.

Pope Pius VI objected. The clerical stipulations of the new constitution were in direct violation of every solemn agreement that had been concluded between France and the Holy See since the year 1516. But the Assembly was in no mood to bother about such little trifles as precedents and treaties. The clergy must either swear allegiance to this decree or resign their positions and starve to death. A few bishops and a few priests accepted what seemed inevitable. They crossed their fingers and went through the formality of an oath. But by far the greater number, being honest men, refused to perjure themselves and, taking a leaf out of the book of those Huguenots whom they had persecuted during so many years, they began to say mass in deserted stables and to give communion in pigsties, to preach their sermons behind country hedges and to pay clandestine visits to the homes of their former parishioners in the middle of the night.

Generally speaking, they fared infinitely better than the Protestants had done under similar circumstances, for France was too hopelessly disorganized to take more than very perfunctory measures against the enemies of her constitution. And as none of them seemed to run the risk of the galleys, the excellent clerics were soon emboldened to ask that they, the non-jurors, the "refractory ones" as they were popularly called, be officially recognized as one of the "tolerated sects" and be accorded those privileges which during the previous three centuries they had so persistently refused to grant to their compatriots of the Calvinist faith.

The situation, for those of us who look back at it from the safe distance of the year 1925, was not without a certain grim humor. But no definite decision was taken, for the Assembly soon afterwards fell entirely under the domination of the extreme radicals and the treachery of the court, combined with the stupidity of His Majesty's foreign allies, caused a panic which in less than a week spread from the coast of Belgium to the shores of the Mediterranean and which was responsible for that series of wholesale assassinations which raged from the second to the seventh of September of the year 1792.

From that moment on the Revolution was bound to degenerate into a reign of terror.

The gradual and evolutionary efforts of the philosophers came to naught when a starving populace began to suspect that their own leaders were engaged in a gigantic plot to sell the country to the enemy. The explosion which then followed is common history. That the conduct of affairs in a crisis of such magnitude is likely to fall into the hands of unscrupulous and ruthless leaders is a fact with which every honest student of history is sufficiently familiar. But that the principal actor in the drama should have been a prig, a model citizen, a hundred-percenting paragon of Virtue, that indeed was something which no one had been able to foresee.

THE TOLERANCE OF REVOLUTION

When France began to understand the true nature of her new master, it was too late, as those who tried in vain to utter their belated words of warning from the top of a scaffold in the Place de la Concorde could have testified.

Thus far we have studied all revolutions from the point of view of politics and economics and social organization. But not until the historian shall turn psychologist or the psychologist shall turn historian shall we really be able to explain and understand those dark forces that shape the destinies of nations in their hour of agony and travail.

There are those who hold that the world is ruled by sweetness and light. There are those who maintain that the human race respects only one thing, brute force. Some hundred years from now, I may be able to make a choice. This much, however, seems certain to us, that the greatest of all experiments in our sociological laboratory, the French revolution, was a noisy apotheosis of violence.

Those who had tried to prepare for a more humane world by way of reason were either dead or were put to death by the very people whom they had helped to glory. And with the Voltaires and Diderots and the Turgots and the Condorcets out of the way, the untutored apostles of the New Perfection were left the undisputed masters of their country's fate. What a ghastly mess they made of their high mission!

During the first period of their rule, victory lay with the out-and-out enemies of religion, those who had some particular reason to detest the very symbols of Christianity; those who in some silent and hidden way had suffered so deeply in the old days of clerical supremacy that the mere sight of a cassock drove them into a frenzy of hate and that the smell of incense made them turn pale with long forgotten rage. Together with a few others who believed that they could disprove the existence of a personal God with the help of mathematics and chemistry, they set about to destroy the Church and all her works. A hopeless and at best an ungrateful task but it is one of the characteristics of revolutionary psychology that the normal becomes abnormal and the impossible is turned into an everyday occurrence. Hence a paper decree of the Convention abolishing the old Christian calendar; abolishing all saints' days; abolishing Christmas and Easter; abolishing weeks and months and re-dividing the year into periods of ten days each with a new pagan Sabbath on every tenth. Hence another paper pronunciamento which abolished the worship of God and left the universe without a master.

But not for long.

However eloquently explained and defended within the bare rooms of the Jacobin club, the idea of a limitless and empty void was too repellent to most citizens to be tolerated for more than a couple of weeks. The old Deity no longer satisfied the masses. Why not follow the example of Moses and Mahomet and invent a new one that should suit the demands of the times?

As a result, behold the Goddess of Reason!

Her exact status was to be defined later. In the meantime a comely actress, properly garbed in ancient Greek draperies, would fill the bill perfectly. The lady was found among the dancers of his late Majesty's corps de ballet and at the proper hour was most solemnly conducted to the high altar of Notre Dame, long since deserted by the loyal followers of an older faith.

As for the blessed Virgin who, during so many centuries, had stood a tender watch over all those who had bared the wounds of their soul before the patient eyes of perfect understanding, she too was gone, hastily hidden by loving hands before she be sent to the limekilns and be turned into mortar. Her place had been taken by a statue of Liberty, the proud product of an amateur sculptor and done rather carelessly in white plaster. But that was not all. Notre Dame had seen other innovations. In the middle of the choir, four columns and a roof indicated a "Temple of Philosophy" which upon state occasions was to serve as a throne for the new dancing divinity. When the poor girl was not holding court and receiving the worship of her trusted followers, the Temple of Philosophy harbored a "Torch of Truth" which to the end of all time was to carry high the burn-ing flame of world enlightenment.

The "end of time" came before another six months.

On the morning of the seventh of May of the year 1794 the French people were officially informed that God had been reëstablished and that the immortality of the soul was once more a recognized article of faith. On the eighth of June, the new Supreme Being (hastily constructed out of the second-hand material left behind by the late Jean Jacques Rousseau) was officially presented to his eager disciples.

Robespierre in a new blue waistcoat delivered the address of welcome. He had reached the highest point of his career. The obscure law clerk from a third-rate country town had become the high priest of the Revolution. More than that, a poor demented nun by the name of Catherine Théot, revered by thousands as the true mother of God, had just proclaimed the forthcoming return of the Messiah and she had even revealed his name. It was Maximilian Robespierre; the same Maximilian who in a fantastic uniform of his own designing was proudly dispensing reams of oratory in which he assured God that from now on all would be well with His little world.

And to make doubly sure, two days later he passed a law by which those suspected of treason and heresy (for once more they were held to be the same, as in the good old days of the Inquisition) were deprived of all means of defense, a measure so ably conceived that during the next six weeks more than fourteen

ROBESPIERRE

hundred people lost their heads beneath the slanting knife of the guillotine.

The rest of his story is only too well known.

As Robespierre was the perfect incarnation of all he himself held to be Good (with a capital G), he could, in his quality of a logical fanatic, not possibly recognize the right of other men, less perfect, to exist on the same planet with himself. As time went by, his hatred of Evil (with a capital E) took on such proportions that France was brought to the brink of depopulation.

Then at last, and driven by fear of their own lives, the enemies of Virtue struck back and in a short but desperate struggle destroyed this Terrible Apostle of Rectitude.

Soon afterwards the force of the Revolution had spent itself. The constitution which the French people then adopted recognized the existence of different denominations and gave them the same rights and privileges. Officially at least the Republic washed her hands of all religion. Those who wished to form a church, a congregation, an association, were free to do so but they were obliged to support their own ministers and priests and recognize the superior rights of the state and the complete freedom of choice of the individual.

Ever since, the Catholics and Protestants in France have lived peacefully side by side.

It is true that the Church never recognized her defeat, continues to deny the principle of a division of state and church (see the decree of Pope Pius IX of December 8th, 1864) and has repeatedly tried to come back to power by supporting those political parties who hope to upset the republican form of government and bring back the monarchy or the empire. But these battles are usually fought in the private parlors of some minister's wife, or in the rabbit-shooting-lodge of a retired general with an ambitious mother-in-law.

They have thus far provided the funny papers with some excellent material but they are proving themselves increasingly futile.

Chapter XXVIII

LESSING

On the twentieth of September of the year 1792 a battle was fought between the armies of the French Revolution and the armies of the allied monarchs who had set forth to annihilate the terrible monster of insurrection.

It was a glorious victory, but not for the allies. Their infantry could not be employed on the slippery hillsides of the village of Valmy. The battle therefore consisted of a series of solemn broadsides. The rebels fired harder and faster than the royalists. Hence the latter were the first to leave the field. In the evening the allied troops retreated northward. Among those present at the engagement was a certain Johann Wolfgang von Goethe, aide to the hereditary Prince of Weimar.

Several years afterwards this young man published his memoirs of that day. While standing ankle-deep in the sticky mud of Lorraine, he had turned prophet. And he had predicted that after this cannonade, the world would never be the same. He had been right. On that ever memorable day, Sovereignty by the grace of God was blown into limbo. The Crusaders of the Rights of Man did not run like chickens, as they had been expected to do. They stuck to their guns. And they pushed those guns forward through valleys and across mountains until they had carried their ideal of "Liberty, Equality and Fraternity" to the furthermost corners of Europe and had stabled their horses in every castle and church of the entire continent.

It is easy enough for us to write that sort of sentence. The revolutionary leaders have been dead for almost one hundred and fifty years and we can poke as much fun at them as we like. We can even be grateful for the many good things which they bestowed upon this world.

But the men and women who lived through those days, who

one morning had gayly danced around the Tree of Liberty and then during the next three months had been chased like rats through the sewers of their own city, could not possibly take such a detached view of those problems of civic upheaval. As soon as they had crept out of their cellars and garrets and had combed the cobwebs out of their perukes, they began to devise measures by which to prevent a recurrence of so terrible a calamity.

But in order to be successful reactionaries, they must first of all bury the past. Not a vague past in the broad historical sense of the word but their own individual "pasts" when they had surreptitiously read the works of Monsieur de Voltaire and had openly expressed their admiration for the Encyclopédie. Now the assembled works of Monsieur de Voltaire were stored away in the attic and those of Monsieur Diderot were sold to the junkman. Pamphlets that had been reverently read as the true revelation of reason were relegated to the coal-bin and in every possible way an effort was made to cover up the tracks that betrayed a short sojourn in the realm of liberalism.

Alas, as so often happens in a case like that when all the literary material has been carefully destroyed, the repentant brotherhood overlooked one item which was even more important as a telltale of the popular mind. That was the stage. It was a bit childish on the part of the generation that had thrown whole cartloads of bouquets at "The Marriage of Figaro" to claim that they had never for a moment believed in the possibilities of equal rights for all men, and the people who had wept over "Nathan the Wise" could never successfully prove that they had always regarded religious tolerance as a misguided expression of governmental weakness.

The play and its success were there to convict them of the opposite.

The author of this famous key play to the popular sentiment of the latter half of the eighteenth century was a German, one Gotthold Ephraim Lessing. He was the son of a Lutheran clergyman and had studied theology in the University of Leipzig. But he had felt little inclination for a religious career and had played hooky so persistently that his father heard of it, had told him to come home and had placed him before the choice of immediate resignation from the university or diligent application as a member of the medical department. Gotthold, who was no more of a doctor than a clergyman, promised everything that was asked of him, returned to Leipzig, went surety for some of his beloved actor friends and upon their subsequent disappearance from town was obliged to hasten to Wittenberg that he might escape arrest for debt.

His flight meant the beginning of a period of long walks and short meals. First of all he went to Berlin where he spent several years writing badly paid articles for a number of theatrical papers. Then he engaged himself as private secretary to a rich friend who was going to take a trip around the world. But no sooner had they started than the Seven Years' War must break out. The friend, obliged to join his regiment, had taken the first post-chaise for home and Lessing, once more without a job, found himself stranded in the city of Leipzig.

But he was of a sociable nature and soon found a new friend in the person of one Eduard Christian von Kleist, an officer by day and a poet by night, a sensitive soul who gave the hungry ex-theologian insight into the new spirit that was slowly coming over this world. But von Kleist was shot to death in the battle of Kunersdorf and Lessing was driven to such dire extremes of want that he became a columnist.

Then followed a period as private secretary to the commander of the fortress of Breslau where the boredom of garrison life was mitigated by a profound study of the works of Spinoza which then, a hundred years after the philosopher's death, were beginning to find their way to foreign countries.

All this, however, did not settle the problem of the daily Butterbrod. Lessing was now almost forty years old and wanted a home of his own. His friends suggested that he be appointed keeper of the Royal Library. But years before, something had happened that had made Lessing persona non grata at the Prussian court. During his first visit to Berlin he had made the acquaintance of Voltaire. The French philosopher was nothing if not generous and being a person without any idea of "system" he had allowed the young man to borrow the manuscript of the "Century of Louis XIV," then ready for publication. Unfortunately, Lessing, when he hastily left Berlin, had (entirely by accident) packed the manuscript among his own belongings. Voltaire, exasperated by the bad coffee and the hard beds of the penurious Prussian court, immediately cried out that he had been robbed. The young German had stolen his

LESSING

most important manuscript, the police must watch the frontier, etc., etc., etc., after the manner of an excited Frenchman in a foreign country. Within a few days the postman returned the lost document, but it was accompanied by a letter from Lessing in which the blunt young Teuton expressed his own ideas of people who would dare to suspect his honesty.

This storm in a chocolate-pot might have easily been forgotten, but the eighteenth century was a period when chocolate-pots played a great rôle in the lives of men and women and Frederick, even after a lapse of almost twenty years, still loved his pesky French friend and would not hear of having Lessing at his court.

And so farewell to Berlin and off to Hamburg, where there was rumor of a newly to be founded national theater. This enterprise came to nothing and Lessing in his despair accepted the office of librarian to the hereditary grand duke of Brunswick. The town of Wolfenbüttel which then became his home was not exactly a metropolis, but the grand-ducal library was one of the finest in all Germany. It contained more than ten thousand manuscripts and several of these were of prime importance in the history of the Reformation.

Boredom, of course, is the main incentive to scandal-mongering and gossip. In Wolfenbüttel a former art critic, columnist and dramatic essayist was by this very fact a highly suspicious person and soon Lessing was once more in trouble. Not because of anything he had done but on account of something he was vaguely supposed to have done, to wit: the publication of a series of articles attacking the orthodox opinions of the old school of Lutheran theology.

These sermons (for sermons they were) had actually been written by a former Hamburg minister, but the grand duke of Brunswick, panic-stricken at the prospect of a religious war within his domains, ordered his librarian to be discreet and keep away from all controversies. Lessing complied with the wishes of his employer. Nothing, however, had been said about treating the subject dramatically and so he set to work to revaluate his opinions in terms of the stage.

The play which was born out of this small-town rumpus was called "Nathan the Wise." The theme was very old and I have mentioned it before in this book. Lovers of literary antiquities can find it (if Mr. Sumner will allow them) in Boccaccio's "Decameron" where it is called the "Sad Story of the Three Rings" and where it is told as follows:

Once upon a time a Mahometan prince tried to extract a large sum of money from one of his Jewish subjects. But as he had no valid reason to deprive the poor man of his property, he bethought himself of a ruse. He sent for the victim and having complimented him gracefully upon his learning and wisdom, he asked him which of the three most widely spread religions, the Turkish, the Jewish and the Christian, he held to be most true. The worthy patriarch did not answer the Padishah directly but said, "Let me, oh great Sultan, tell you a little story. Once upon a time there was a very rich man who had a beautiful ring and he made a will that whichever of his sons at the time of his death should be found with that ring upon his finger should fall heir to all his estates. His son made a like will. His grandson too, and for centuries the ring changed hands and all was well. But finally it happened that the owner of the ring had three sons whom he loved equally well. He simply could not decide which of the three should own that much valued treasure. So he went to a goldsmith and ordered him to make two other rings exactly like the one he had. On his death-bed he sent for his children and gave them each his blessing and what they supposed was the one and only ring. Of course, as soon as the father had been buried, the three boys all claimed to be his heir because they had The Ring. This led to many quarrels and finally they laid the matter before the Kadi. But as the rings were absolutely alike, even the judges could not decide which was the right one and so the case had been dragged on and on and very likely will drag on until the end of the world. Amen."

Lessing used this ancient folk-tale to prove his belief that no one religion possessed a monopoly of the truth. That it was the inner spirit of man that counted rather than his outward conformity to certain prescribed rituals and dogmas and that therefore it was the duty of people to bear with each other in love and friendship and that no one had the right to set himself upon a high pedestal of self-assured perfection and say, "I am better than all others because I alone possess the Truth."

But this idea, much applauded in the year 1778, was no longer popular with the little princelings who thirty years later returned to salvage such goods and chattels as had survived the deluge of the Revolution. For the purpose of regaining their lost prestige, they abjectly surrendered their lands to the rule of the police-sergeant and expected the clerical gentlemen who depended upon them for their livelihood to act as a spiritual militia and help the regular cops to reëstablish law and order.

But whereas the purely political reaction was completely successful, the attempt to reshape men's minds after the pattern of fifty years before ended in failure. And it could not be otherwise. It was true that the vast majority of the people in all countries were sick and tired of revolution and unrest, of parliaments and futile speeches and forms of taxation that had completely ruined commerce and industry. They wanted peace. Peace at any price. They wanted to do business and sit in their own front parlors and drink coffee and not be disturbed by the soldiers billeted upon them and forced to drink an odious extract of oak-leaves. Provided they could enjoy this blessed state of well-being, they were willing to put up with certain small inconveniences such as saluting whoever wore brass buttons, bowing low before every imperial letter-box and saying "Sir" to every assistant official chimney-sweep.

But this attitude of humble obedience was the result of sheer necessity, of the need for a short breathing space after the long and tumultuous years when every new morning brought new uniforms, new political platforms, new police regulations and new rulers, both of Heaven and earth. It would be erroneous, however, to conclude from this general air of subservience, from this loud hurray-ing for the divinely appointed masters, that the people in their heart of hearts had forgotten the new doctrines which the drums of Sergeant Le Grand had so merrily beaten into their heads and hearts.

As their governments, with that moral cynicism inherent in all reactionary dictatorships, insisted chiefly upon an outward semblance of decency and order and cared not one whit for the inner spirit, the average subject enjoyed a fairly wide degree of independence. On Sunday he went to church with a large Bible under his arm. The rest of the week he thought as he pleased. Only he held his tongue and kept his private opinions to himself and aired his views when a careful inspection of the premises had first assured him that no secret agent was hidden underneath the sofa or was lurking behind the tile stove. Then, however, he discussed the events of the day with great gusto and sadly shook his head when his duly censored, fumigated and sterilized newspaper told him what new idiotic measures his masters had taken to assure the peace of the realm and bring about a return to the status quo of the year of grace 1600.

What his masters were doing was exactly what similar masters with an imperfect knowledge of the history of human nature under similar circumstances have been doing ever since the year One. They thought that they had destroyed free speech when they ordered the removal of the cracker-barrels from which the speeches that had so severely criticized their government had been made. And whenever they could, they sent the offending orators to jail with such stiff sentences (forty, fifty, a hundred years) that the poor devils gained great renown as martyrs, whereas in most instances they were scatter-brained idiots who had read a few books and pamphlets which they had failed to understand.

Warned by this example, the others kept away from the public parks and did their grumbling in obscure wine-shops or in the public lodging-houses of overcrowded cities where they were certain of a discreet audience and where their influence was infinitely more harmful than it would have been on a public platform.

There are few things more pathetic in this world than the man upon whom the Gods in their wisdom have bestowed a little bit of authority and who is in eternal fear for his official prestige. A king may lose his throne and may laugh at a misadventure which means a rather amusing interruption of a life of dull routine. And anyway he is a king, whether he wears his valet's brown derby or his grandfather's crown. But the mayor of a third-rate town, once he has been deprived of his gavel and his badge of office, is just plain Bill Smith, a ridiculous fellow who gave himself airs and who is now laughed at for his troubles. Therefore woe unto him who dares to approach such a potentate pro tem without visible manifestations of that reverence and worship due to so exalted a human being.

But those who did not stop at burgomasters, but who openly questioned the existing order of things in learned tomes and handbooks of geology and anthropology and economics, fared infinitely worse.

They were instantly and dishonorably deprived of their livelihood. Then they were exiled from the town in which they had taught their pernicious doctrines and with their wives and children were left to the charitable mercies of the neighbors.

This outbreak of the reactionary spirit caused great inconvenience to a large number of perfectly sincere people who were honestly trying to go to the root of our many social ills. Time, however, the great laundress, has long since removed whatever spots the local police magistrates were able to detect upon the professorial garments of these amiable scholars. To-day, King Frederick William of Prussia is chiefly remembered because he interfered with the teachings of Emanuel Kant, that dangerous radical who taught that the maxims of our own actions must be worthy of being turned into universal laws and whose doctrines, according to the police reports, appealed only to "beardless youths and idle babblers." The Duke of Cumberland has gained lasting notoriety because as King of Hanover he exiled a certain Jacob Grimm who had signed a protest against "His Majesty's unlawful abrogation of the country's constitution." And Metternich has retained a certain notoriety because he extended his watchful suspicion to the field of music and once censored the music of Schubert.

Poor old Austria!

Now that it is dead and gone, all the world feels kindly disposed towards the "gay empire" and forgets that once upon a time it had an active intellectual life of its own and was something more than an amusing and well-mannered county fair with excellent and cheap wine, atrocious cigars and the most enticing of waltzes, composed and conducted by no one less than Johann Strauss himself.

We may go even further and state that during the entire eighteenth century Austria played a very important rôle in the development of the idea of religious tolerance. Immediately after the Reformation the Protestants had found a fertile field for their operations in the rich province between the Danube and the Carpathian Mountains. But this had changed when Rudolf II became emperor.

This Rudolf was a German version of Spanish Philip, a ruler to whom treaties made with heretics were of no consequence whatsoever. But although educated by the Jesuits, he was incurably lazy and this saved his empire from too drastic a change of policy.

That came when Ferdinand II was chosen emperor. This monarch's chief qualification for office was the fact that he alone among all the Hapsburgs was possessed of a few sons. Early during his reign he had visited the famous House of the Annunciation, bodily moved in the year 1291 by a number of angels from Nazareth to Dalmatia and hence to central Italy, and there in an outburst of religious fervor he had sworn a dire oath to make his country one-hundred-percent Catholic.

He had been as good as his word. In the year 1629 Catholicism once more was proclaimed the official and exclusive faith of Austria and Styria and Bohemia and Silesia.

Hungary having been meanwhile married into that strange family, which acquired vast quantities of European real estate with every new wife, an effort was made to drive the Protestants from their Magyar strongholds. But backed up by the Transylvanians, who were Unitarians, and by the Turks, who were heathen, the Hungarians were able to maintain their independence until the second half of the eighteenth century. And by that time a great change had taken place in Austria itself.

The Hapsburgs were loyal sons of the Church, but at last even their sluggish brains grew tired of the constant interference with their affairs on the part of the Popes and they were willing for once to risk a policy contrary to the wishes of Rome.

In an earlier part of this book I have already told how many medieval Catholics believed that the organization of the Church was all wrong. In the days of the martyrs, these critics argued, the Church was a true democracy ruled by elders and bishops who were appointed by common consent of all the parishioners. They were willing to concede that the Bishop of Rome, because he claimed to be the direct successor of the Apostle Peter, had been entitled to a favorite position in the councils of the Church, but they insisted that this power had been purely honorary and that the Popes therefore should never have considered themselves superior to the other bishops and should not have tried to extend their influence beyond the confines of their own territory.

The Popes from their side had fought this idea with all the bulls, anathemas and excommunications at their disposal and several brave reformers had lost their lives as a result of their bold agitation for greater clerical decentralization.

The question had never been definitely settled, and then during the middle of the eighteenth century, the idea was revived by the vicar-general of the rich and powerful archbishop of Trier. His name was Johann von Hontheim, but he is better known by his Latin pseudonym of Febronius. Hontheim had enjoyed the advantages of a very liberal education. After a few years spent at the University of Louvain he had temporarily forsaken his own people and had gone to the University of Leiden. He got there at a time when that old citadel of undiluted Calvinism was beginning to be suspected of liberal tendencies. This suspicion had ripened into open conviction when Professor Gerard Noodt, a member of the legal faculty, had been allowed to enter the field of theology and had been permitted to publish a speech in which he had extolled the ideal of religious tolerance.

His line of reasoning had been ingenious, to say the least.

"God is all-powerful," so he had said. "God is able to lay down certain laws of science which hold good for all people at all times and under all conditions. It follows that it would have been very easy for him, had he desired to do so, to guide the minds of men in such a fashion that they all of them should have had the same opinions upon the subject of religion. We know that He did not do anything of the sort. Therefore, we act against the express will of God if we try to coerce others by force to believe that which we ourselves hold to be true."

Whether Hontheim was directly influenced by Noodt or not, it is hard to say. But something of that same spirit of Erasmian rationalism can be found in those works of Hontheim in which he afterwards developed his own ideas upon the subject of episcopal authority and papal decentralization.

That his books were immediately condemned by Rome (in

February of the year 1764) is of course no more than was to be expected. But it happened to suit the interests of Maria Theresa to support Hontheim, and Febronianism or Episcopalianism, as the movement which he had started was called, continued to flourish in Austria and finally took practical shape in a Patent of Tolerance which Joseph II, the son of Maria Theresa, bestowed upon his subjects on the thirteenth of October of the year 1781.

Joseph, who was a weak imitation of his mother's great enemy, Frederick of Prussia, had a wonderful gift for doing the right thing at the wrong moment. During the last two hundred years the little children of Austria had been sent to bed with the threat that the Protestants would get them if they did not go to sleep at once. To insist that those same infants henceforth regard their Protestant neighbors (who, as they all knew, had horns and a long black tail), as their dearly beloved brothers and sisters was to ask the impossible. All the same, poor, honest, hard working, blundering Joseph, forever surrounded by a horde of uncles and aunts and cousins who enjoyed fat incomes as bishops and cardinals and deaconesses, deserves great credit for this sudden outburst of courage. He was the first among the Catholic rulers who dared to advocate tolerance as a desirable and practical possibility of statecraft.

And what he did three months later was even more startling. On the second of February of the year of grace 1782 he issued his famous decree concerning the Jews and extended the liberty then only enjoyed by Protestants and Catholics to a category of people who thus far had considered themselves fortunate when they were allowed to breathe the same air as their Christian neighbors.

Right here we ought to stop and let the reader believe that the good work continued indefinitely and that Austria now became a Paradise for those who wished to follow the dictates of their own conscience.

I wish it were true. Joseph and a few of his ministers might rise to a sudden height of common sense, but the Austrian peasant, taught since time immemorial to regard the Jew as his natural enemy and the Protestant as a rebel and a renegade, could not possibly overcome that old and deep-rooted prejudice which told him to regard such people as his natural enemies.

A century and a half after the promulgation of these excellent Edicts of Tolerance, the position of those who did not belong to the Catholic Church was quite as unfavorable as it had been in the sixteenth century. Theoretically a Jew and a Protestant could hope to become prime ministers or to be appointed commander-in-chief of the army. And in practice it was impossible for them to be invited to dinner by the imperial bootblack.

So much for paper decrees.

Chapter XXIX

TOM PAINE

SOMEWHERE or other there is a poem to the effect that God moves in a mysterious way, his wonders to perform.

The truth of this statement is most apparent to those who have studied the history of the Atlantic seaboard.

During the first half of the seventeenth century the northern part of the American continent was settled by people who had gone so far in their devotion to the ideals of the Old Testament that an unsuspecting visitor might have taken them for followers of Moses, rather than disciples of the words of Christ. Cut off from the rest of Europe by a very wide and very stormy and very cold expanse of ocean, these pioneers had set up a spiritual reign of terror which had culminated in the witch-hunting orgies of the Mather family.

Now at first sight it seems not very likely that those two reverend gentlemen could in any way be held responsible for the very tolerant tendencies which we find expounded with such able vigor in the Constitution of the United States and in the many documents that were written immediately before the outbreak of hostilities between England and her former colonies. Yet such is undoubtedly the case, for the period of repression of the seventeenth century was so terrible that it was bound to create a furious reaction in favor of a more liberal point of view.

This does not mean that all the colonists suddenly sent for the collected works of Socinius and ceased to frighten little children with stories about Sodom and Gomorrah. But their leaders were almost without exception representatives of the new school of thought and with great ability and tact they infused their own conceptions of tolerance into the parchment platform upon which the edifice of their new and independent nation was to be erected.

361

They might not have been quite so successful if they had been obliged to deal with one united country. But colonization in the northern part of America had always been a complicated business. The Swedish Lutherans had explored part of the territory. The French had sent over some of their Huguenots. The Dutch Arminians had occupied a large share of the land. While almost every sort and variety of English sect had at one time or another tried to found a little Paradise of its own in the wilderness between the Hudson Bay and the Gulf of Mexico.

This had made for a variety of religious expression and so well had the different denominations been balanced that in several of the colonies a crude and rudimentary form of mutual forbearance had been forced upon a people who under ordinary circumstances would have been forever at each other's throats.

This development had been very unwelcome to the reverend gentlemen who prospered where others quarreled. For years after the advent of the new spirit of charity they had continued their struggle for the maintenance of the old ideal of rectitude. They had achieved very little but they had successfully estranged many of the younger men from a creed which seemed to have borrowed its conceptions of mercy and kindliness from some of its more ferocious Indian neighbors.

Fortunately for our country, the men who bore the brunt of battle in the long struggle for freedom belonged to this small but courageous group of dissenters.

Ideas travel lightly. Even a little two-masted schooner of eighty tons can carry enough new notions to upset an entire continent. The American colonists of the eighteenth century were obliged to do without sculpture and grand pianos, but they did not lack for books. The more intelligent among the people in the thirteen colonies began to understand that there was something astir in the big world, of which they had never heard anything in their Sunday sermons. The booksellers then became their prophets. And although they did not officially break away from the established church and changed little in their outer mode of life, they showed when the opportunity offered itself that they were faithful disciples of that old prince of Transylvania,

who had refused to persecute his Unitarian subjects on the
ground that the good Lord had expressly reserved for himself
the right to three things: "To be able to create something out
of nothing; to know the future; and to dominate man's conscience."

And when it became necessary to draw up a concrete political
and social program for the future conduct of their country, these
brave patriots incorporated their ideas into the documents in

TOM PAINE

which they placed their ideals before the high court of public
opinion.

It would undoubtedly have horrified the good citizens of Virginia had they known that some of the oratory to which they
listened with such profound respect was directly inspired by
their arch-enemies, the Libertines. But Thomas Jefferson, their
most successful politician, was himself a man of exceedingly
liberal views and when he remarked that religion could only be
regulated by reason and conviction and not by force or violence;
or again, that all men had an equal right to the free exercise
of their religion according to the dictates of their conscience,
he merely repeated what had been thought and written before by
Voltaire and Bayle and Spinoza and Erasmus.

And later when the following heresies were heard: "that no
declaration of faith should be required as a condition of obtain-

ing any public office in the United States," or "that Congress should make no law which referred to the establishment of religion or which prohibited the free exercise thereof," the American rebels acquiesced and accepted.

In this way the United States came to be the first country where religion was definitely separated from politics; the first country where no candidate for office was forced to show his Sunday school certificate before he could accept the nomination; the first country in which people could, as far as the law was concerned, worship or fail to worship as they pleased.

But here as in Austria (or anywhere else for that matter) the average man lagged far behind his leaders and was unable to follow them as soon as they deviated the least little bit from the beaten track. Not only did many of the states continue to impose certain restrictions upon those of their subjects who did not belong to the dominant religion, but the citizens in their private capacity as New Yorkers or Bostonians or Philadelphians continued to be just as intolerant of those who did not share their own views as if they had never read a single line of their own Constitution. All of which was to show itself soon afterwards in the case of Thomas Paine.

Tom Paine rendered a very great service to the cause of the Americans.

He was the publicity man of the Revolution.

By birth he was an Englishman; by profession, a sailor; by instinct and training, a rebel. He was forty years old before he visited the colonies. While on a visit to London he had met Benjamin Franklin and had received the excellent advice "to go west." In the year 1774, provided with letters of introduction from Benjamin himself, he had sailed for Philadelphia and had helped Richard Bache, the son-in-law of Franklin, to found a magazine, the "Pennsylvania Gazette."

Being an inveterate amateur politician, Tom had soon found himself in the midst of those events that were trying men's souls. And being possessed of a singularly well-ordered mind, he had taken hold of the ill-assorted collection of American grievances and had incorporated them into a pamphlet, short but sweet, which by a thorough application of "common sense" should convince the people that the American cause was a just cause and deserved the hearty coöperation of all loyal patriots.

This little book at once found its way to England and to the Continent where it informed many people for the first time in their lives that there was such a thing as "an American nation" and that it had an excellent right, yea, it was its sacred duty, to make war upon the mother country.

As soon as the revolution was over, Paine went back to Europe to show the English people the supposed absurdities of the government under which they lived. It was a time when terrible things were happening along the banks of the Seine and when respectable Britishers were beginning to look across the Channel with very serious misgivings.

A certain Edmund Burke had just published his panic-stricken "Reflections on the French Revolution." Paine answered with a furious counter-blast of his own called "The Rights of Man" and as a result the English government ordered him to be tried for high treason.

Meanwhile his French admirers had elected him to the Convention and Paine, who did not know a word of French but was an optimist, accepted the honor and went to Paris. There he lived until he fell under the suspicion of Robespierre. Knowing that at any moment he might be arrested and decapitated, he hastily finished a book that was to contain his philosophy of life. It was called "The Age of Reason." The first part was published just before he was taken to prison. The second part was written during the ten months he spent in jail.

Paine believed that true religion, what he called "the religion of humanity," had two enemies, atheism on the one hand and fanaticism on the other. But when he gave expression to this thought he was attacked by every one and when he returned to America in 1802 he was treated with such profound and relentless hatred that his reputation as a "dirty little atheist" has survived him by more than a century.

It is true that nothing happened to him. He was not hanged or burned or broken on the wheel. He was merely shunned by all his neighbors, little boys were encouraged to stick their tongues out at him when he ventured to leave his home, and at the time of his death he was an embittered and forgotten man who found relief for his anger in writing foolish political tracts against the other heroes of the Revolution.

This seems a most unfortunate sequel to a splendid beginning.

But it is typical of something that has repeatedly happened during the history of the last two thousand years.

As soon as public intolerance has spent its fury, private intolerance begins.

And lynchings start when official executions have come to an end.

Chapter XXX

THE LAST HUNDRED YEARS

TWELVE years ago it would have been quite easy to write this
book. The word "Intolerance," in the minds of most people,
was then almost exclusively identified with the idea of "religious
intolerance" and when an historian wrote that "so and so had been
a champion of tolerance" it was generally accepted that so and
so had spent his life fighting the abuses of the Church and the
tyranny of a professional priesthood.

Then came the war.

And much was changed in this world.

Instead of one system of intolerance, we got a dozen.

Instead of one form of cruelty, practiced by man upon his
fellow men, we got a hundred.

And a society which was just beginning to rid itself of the
horrors of religious bigotry was obliged to put up with the infinitely more painful manifestations of a paltry form of racial
intolerance and social intolerance and a score of petty forms of
intolerance, the existence of which had not even been suspected
a decade ago.

$$* \quad * \quad * \quad * \quad * \quad * \quad * \quad *$$

This seems very terrible to many good people who until
recently lived in the happy delusion that progress was a sort
of automatic time-piece which needed no other winding than their
occasional approbation.

They sadly shake their heads, whisper "Vanity, vanity, all is
vanity!" and mutter disagreeable things about the cussedness of
the human race which goes everlastingly to school, yet always
refuses to learn.

Until, in sheer despair, they join the rapidly increasing ranks of our spiritual defeatists, attach themselves to this or that or the other religious institution (that they may transfer their own burden to the back of some one else), and in the most doleful tones acknowledge themselves beaten and retire from all further participation in the affairs of their community.

I don't like such people.

They are not merely cowards.

They are traitors to the future of the human race.

*   *   *   *   *   *   *   *

So far so good, but what is the solution, if a solution there be?

Let us be honest with ourselves.

There is not any.

At least not in the eyes of a world which asks for quick results and expects to settle all difficulties of this earth comfortably and speedily with the help of a mathematical or medical formula or by an act of Congress. But those of us who have accustomed ourselves to consider history in the light of eternity and who know that civilization does not begin and end with the twentieth century, feel a little more hopeful.

That vicious circle of despair of which we hear so much nowadays ("man has always been that way," "man always will be that way," "the world never changes," "things are just about the same as they were four thousand years ago,") does not exist.

It is an optical illusion.

The line of progress is often interrupted but if we set aside all sentimental prejudices and render a sober judgment upon the record of the last twenty thousand years (the only period about which we possess more or less concrete information) we notice an indubitable if slow rise from a condition of almost unspeakable brutality and crudeness to a state which holds the promise of something infinitely nobler and better than what has ever gone before and even the ghastly blunder of the Great War cannot shake the firm conviction that this is true.

*   *   *   *   *   *   *   *

The human race is possessed of almost incredible vitality.

It has survived theology.

In due time it will survive industrialism.

It has lived through cholera and plague, high heels and blue laws.

It will also learn how to overcome the many spiritual ills which beset the present generation.

*   *   *   *   *   *   *   *

History, chary of revealing her secrets, has thus far taught us one great lesson.

What the hand of man has done, the hand of man can also undo.

It is a question of courage, and next to courage, of education.

*   *   *   *   *   *   *   *

That of course sounds like a platitude. For the last hundred years we have had "education" driven into our ears until we are sick and tired of the word and look longingly back to the time when people could neither read nor write but used their surplus intellectual energy for occasional moments of independent thinking.

But when I here speak of "education" I do not mean the mere accumulation of facts which is regarded as the necessary mental ballast of our modern children. Rather, I have in mind that true understanding of the present which is born out of a charitable and generous knowledge of the past.

In this book I have tried to prove that intolerance is merely a manifestation of the protective instinct of the herd.

A group of wolves is intolerant of the wolf that is different (be it through weakness or strength) from the rest of the pack and invariably tries to get rid of this offending and unwelcome companion.

A tribe of cannibals is intolerant of the individual who by his idiosyncrasies threatens to provoke the wrath of the Gods and bring disaster upon the whole village, and brutally relegates him or her to the wilderness.

The Greek commonwealth can ill afford to harbor within its sacred walls a citizen who dares to question the very fundaments upon which the success of the community has been built, and in a poor outburst of intolerance condemns the offending philosopher to the merciful death of poison.

The Roman state cannot possibly hope to survive if a small group of well-meaning zealots is allowed to play fast and loose with certain laws which have been held indispensable ever since the days of Romulus, and much against her own will she is driven into deeds of intolerance which are entirely at variance with her age-old policy of liberal aloofness.

The Church, spiritual heir to the material dominions of the ancient Empire, depends for her continued existence upon the absolute and unquestioning obedience of even the humblest of her subjects and is driven to such extremes of suppression and cruelty that many people prefer the ruthlessness of the Turk to the charity of the Christian.

The great insurgents against ecclesiastical tyranny, beset by a thousand difficulties, can only maintain their rule if they show themselves intolerant to all spiritual innovations and scientific experiments, and in the name of "Reform" they commit (or rather try to commit) the self-same mistakes which have just deprived their enemies of most of their former power and influence.

And so it goes throughout the ages until life, which might be a glorious adventure, is turned into a horrible experience and all this happens because human existence so far has been entirely dominated by fear.

*   *   *   *   *   *   *   *

For fear, I repeat it, is at the bottom of all intolerance.

No matter what form or shape a persecution may take, it is caused by fear and its very vehemence is indicative of the degree of anguish experienced by those who erect the gallows or throw fresh logs upon the funeral pyre.

*   *   *   *   *   *   *   *

Once we recognize this fact, the solution of the difficulty immediately presents itself.

Man, when not under the influence of fear, is strongly inclined to be righteous and just.

Thus far he has had very few opportunities to practice these two virtues.

But I cannot for the life of me see that this matters overmuch. It is part of the necessary development of the human race. And that race is young, hopelessly, almost ridiculously young. To ask that a certain form of mammal, which began its independent career only a few thousand years ago should already have acquired those virtues which go only with age and experience, seems both unreasonable and unfair.

And furthermore, it warps our point of view.

It causes us to be irritated when we should be patient.

It makes us say harsh things where we should only feel pity.

* * * * * * * *

In the last chapters of a book like this, there is a serious temptation to assume the rôle of the prophet of woe and indulge in a little amateur preaching.

Heaven forbid!

Life is short and sermons are apt to be long.

And what cannot be said in a hundred words had better never be said at all.

* * * * * * * *

Our historians are guilty of one great error. They speak of prehistoric times, they tell us about the Golden Age of Greece and Rome, they talk nonsense about a supposedly dark period, they compose rhapsodies upon the tenfold glories of our modern era.

If perchance these learned doctors perceive certain characteristics which do not seem to fit into the picture they have so prettily put together, they offer a few humble apologies and mumble something about certain undesirable qualities which are part of our unfortunate and barbaric heritage but which in due course of time will disappear, just as the stage-coach has given way before the railroad engine.

It is all very pretty but it is not true. It may flatter our pride to believe ourselves heir to the ages. It will be better for our spiritual health if we know ourselves for what we are—contemporaries of the folks that lived in caves, neolithic men with cigarettes and Ford cars, cliff-dwellers who reach their homes in an elevator.

For then and only then shall we be able to make a first step toward that goal that still lies hidden beyond the vast mountain ranges of the future.

*   *   *   *   *   *   *   *

To speak of Golden Ages and Modern Eras and Progress is sheer waste of time as long as this world is dominated by fear.

To ask for tolerance, as long as intolerance must of need be an integral part of our law of self-preservation, is little short of a crime.

The day will come when tolerance shall be the rule, when intolerance shall be a myth like the slaughter of innocent captives, the burning of widows, the blind worship of a printed page.

It may take ten thousand years, it may take a hundred thousand.

But it will come, and it will follow close upon the first true victory of which history shall have any record, the triumph of man over his own fear.

Westport, Connecticut
July, 19, 1925

Chapter XXXI

. . . AND AFTER TWO YEARS

In the good old days when a book was writ, 'twas writ, and no matter how much better the author wished 'twere done, there was little or no chance to add to it during his own lifetime.

For History, in the era before the machine-gun and universal suffrage, progressed with the solemn dignity of a glacier and there was no reason why one should review, reshape or retract one's opinions unless one lived to be as old as Methuselah.

But all this has been changed and to-day History borrows a few pages from the Social Register and adds a list of "Dilatory Domiciles" wherein the most recent combinations and variations upon the old and slightly shop-worn subject of the "Human Race" are neatly tabulated and the temporary whereabouts of the leading political ideas are duly chronicled for the benefit of those who are foolish enough to care for such information.

Following immediately upon our inspiring last chapter with its ringing appeal for "courage and still more courage," this new version of our "hail and farewell" might be regarded as somewhat of an anticlimax.

Why not?

Isn't the period in which we live the most grotesque anticlimax of the ages?

And why should we alone among a thousand million people set ourselves apart and try and be consistent in a world that was going to be made safe for democracy and was then left to the tender mercies of the official dictator, the private spy and their inevitable rival, the spiritual mountebank?

*   *   *   *   *   *   *   *

While I am writing this the levees that for many years past have protected the greater part of Louisana against the ever

373

threatening floods of the Mississippi River have at last given way under the pressure of this muddy current and correspondents are complaining that they do not know where to begin with their stories because the break is so enormous, the inundated region so vast, the number of homeless people so great and the general messiness of the muddle so terrible that a well-ordered survey of the extent of the disaster is entirely out of the question and that all the scribes can hope to do is to give their readers a few detached descriptions of conditions as they exist at the different points where the refugees have been temporarily gathered and where one can get some scraps of first-hand information from the survivors themselves.

Any one who undertakes to write about Tolerance in the year of Grace 1927 experiences the same feeling of dull despair—the damage done to the cause of human forbearance and decency since the ending of the war has been so enormous, the prospect for the immediate future is so absolutely dark, that only the hardiest of our professional optimists and the highest priced among the manufacturers of our Inspirational Moonshine seem able to contemplate the chaos without a feeling of absolute futility and uselessness.

We may perhaps hope that time will take care of the situation (as it usually has taken care of every other situation) and that there probably will be some sort of return to normalcy before the beginning of the next glacial period. But when hard pressed, we all must agree that the people of this generation are in for a long and severe siege of intolerance in every form and shape, and I shall try and tell you why I think that this is so and I shall do this in as few words as I can.

* * * * * * * *

Intolerance is the result of fear.

The more fear there is in this world, the more intolerance there will be, and I doubt whether at any time during the last four thousand years (the period of written history) there has been quite as much fear, as great an amount of mutual distrust, as at the present moment.

Those are the general premises of my contentions. Now, let me try and prove them.

The Great European War was in reality a world-wide revolution. It destroyed the old established and highly centralized forms of imperial and royal government which ever since the Middle Ages had administered the affairs of the greater part of the European continent. By doing so, it allowed the complete dissolution of vast groups of ill-assorted units which had never quite mixed (in the chemical sense of the word) and it removed the one element which by holding itself aloof from the common run of humanity had been able to stand forth as the generally recognized and universally accepted arbiter in all matters pertaining to politics, economics and religion.

The dynasties which had succeeded in establishing diverse groups of united states (the United States of the Hohenzollerns, the United States of the Hapsburgs, the United States of the Romanovs) were relegated to the historical dust-heap.

There were loud and prolonged rejoicings and half a hundred new national anthems arose lustily to high Heaven.

And then the misery began.

*　　*　　*　　*　　*　　*　　*　　*

Let us try and understand each other.

The old world of the absolutistic form of government was no Paradise. Far from it! But from the point of view of Tolerance, it enjoyed one great advantage. It laid down one definite standard of conduct and behavior, both political and spiritual. It said to the average citizen, "Do so and so or at least go through the gestures of making your neighbors believe that you are doing so and so and we shall bother you no further and shall not inquire too closely into the real sentiments that animate your immortal soul."

It impressed upon the mind of the masses of the people the necessity of paying a certain outward homage to certain articles of faith which had been devised fifteen hundred years before for the benefit of the people in Asia Minor and which were supposed to contain all that was necessary for ultimate salvation.

But that was all.

In Russia one could not go forth into the street and denounce the outrageous régime of the local governor. In Austria it was not safe to agitate for a decent divorce law or question the right of the Bishops of Rome to dictate to the citizens of another country their views upon the subject of matrimony and childbirth. Nor was it a good thing for the health of a humble

THE INTOLERANCE OF THE STATE

Prussian butcher or baker to inquire too closely into the original sources from which the last of the Hohenzollerns had derived their knowledge of political economy.

As a result, there were certain definite subjects which the State made clear were to be regarded as "taboo"—which must be left alone—which could not be turned into a topic for a public debate. Once, however, the average citizen had accepted these unavoidable restrictions upon his sovereign rights as a member of the human race, he enjoyed an extraordinarily large range of personal liberty in every field of science, behavior or speculation. There were whole orchards from which he could pluck every kind and variety of dangerous fruit if only he would be careful not to damage the shrubs that had been reserved for the exclusive use of the imperial uncles and aunts and nephews and nieces. As for the field of pure speculation, the sky was the limit and investigations of the Milky Way and the most remote of our solar systems were not only tolerated but were actually encouraged, provided the stellar pioneers did not interfere with that restricted part of Heaven which the faithful regarded as a necessary and integral part of the Christian cosmology.

In short, there was an officially established and officially recognized and officially accepted form of State-Intolerance.

That was a nuisance and it led to many grievous abuses. On the other hand, the system was not without a certain advantage to those whose mental activities reached beyond the sphere of cogitation of the cows and the daffodils.

Since the state undertook to be the sole purveyor of Intolerance it followed that the state would brook no rivalry. If there were any laws to be enforced, if there was any hanging or shooting to be done, if there were any books to be burned or music to be suppressed, the state would see to it and would enforce, hang, shoot, burn or suppress through the officially appointed judges, hangmen and censors and through no one else.

Mark that well: *through no one else.*

The amateur Torquemadas, the village Comstocks, the small-town Jeffries' were not only not encouraged. They were actually clapped into jail as soon as they made the slightest gesture which seemed to betray a desire to indulge in a little private heresy hunting.

It was an essentially undemocratic arrangement.

But those classes of society which are to-day most exposed to attacks upon their intellectual and spiritual liberties fared comparatively well under this system.

They were taught from childhood on to be on their guard against the servants of His Majesty, but they were safe from their neighbors, and they ceased to enjoy this immunity when the world passed through that terrible ordeal which for lack of a better word I would like to call a "vertical revolution."

* * * * * * * *

All those who have ever read a page of history are familiar with the stereotype, or what I would like to call the "horizontal type," of revolution: the struggle between two different groups of society—one side trying to hold what it has in riches and in sinecures and in privileges—the other trying to obtain its share of these much-coveted riches, sinecures and privileges, for the benefit of themselves and their supporters.

These "horizontal revolutionary outbreaks" usually consisted of a pitched battle between individuals or groups of individuals who lived more or less on the same plane of society—between a king who tried to rule with autocratic powers and his faithful knights who hoped to do likewise (as happened in England in the thirteenth and in France in the sixteenth century)—between one small body of successful merchants who had come to

THE HORIZONTAL REVOLUTION

regard the common country as their private possession and another which, although equally rich, was excluded from participation in the government (as happened in Venice, in Genoa, in Holland, in practically all of the commercial republics)—or between one set of land owners who believed that they had been divinely appointed to administer the affairs of the universe and others who asked with pertinent insistence, "What is the matter with us?" and got a haughty sneer for their impudence, as happened, soon or later, in practically every part of feudal Europe and America.

But all these insurrections and rebellions and brawls and quarrels could have been summed up in the witty French saying, "You get up from that comfortable chair and let me sit in it for a while and let me enjoy the benefits of those comfortable cushions and let me have the feeling that for the time being I too am a fine gentleman."

They were "horizontal revolutions" and represented a clash of interest between parties that lived on the same plane and that were at outs over some very tangible spoils.

      *   *   *   *   *   *   *   *

Now we come to the second variety, the "vertical revolutions," and these are comparatively new.

In the olden days of Egypt and Babylon and Greece there had been many slave uprisings but as a rule they bore a closer resemblance to the stampeding of a herd of cattle than to a deliberately organized effort of certain miserable people to improve their living conditions. And the first really serious outbreak of a "vertical revolution" took place in France only a century and a half ago.

There the inhabitants of the cellars, exasperated by the arrogance of those whose lifelong servants they were supposed to be, finally arose in righteous anger, left their dungeons, pushed in the doors of the first floor, dumped the blessed denizens of the parlors and boudoirs into the cellars or pitched them out of the windows and established themselves firmly among the silks and the brocades of the parlor, bedroom and bath to enjoy those advantages which thus far had been exclusively reserved for their "betters."

The Great War, while much less spectacular in its social consequences than the French Revolution, brought about a similar state of affairs. It suddenly shifted the economic emphasis from one class of society to another. In central and eastern Europe it definitely destroyed the power of the old landed gentry which

THE VERTICAL REVOLUTION

in those far distant countries had maintained itself uninterruptedly from the days of the great migrations to the hour of the Serajevo murder. For the war began as a mere struggle between those different combinations of dynastic and feudal interests which in the majority of Continental countries represented the idea of government and authority, but when it was all over it became clear that these old enemies had eaten each other up (after the classical example of the Kilkenny cats) and that their vacant country-houses and their vacant schools and their vacant churches and universities were now at the disposal of that vast group of "middle-class" people and proletarians who had been tolerated as convenient tax-payers and cannon-fodder but had never been given their full share of those social and educational advantages which had been reserved for those who were supposed to have been called by God himself to handle the affairs of state, the good, the wealthy and the wise.

Thereupon our misery began. For those new masters, each of them firmly convinced that he and his friends were right, were in such terrible fear of their neighbors that they were ready to fight to the bitter end to make their own ideas prevail.

"This," so all of them seemed to argue, "is our one supreme chance to establish the millennium according to our own recipe and prevent all others from establishing their erroneous Utopias. We know exactly what we hold to be true (whether it be the spontaneous generation of the human race, the existence of a deity called Jehovah, the necessity for a complete reorganization of the economic system along the principles laid down by the late Carl Marx, or the acknowledged superiority or inferiority of certain races of men according to the shape of their skulls or the color of their skins) and we insist that we must triumph here and now or forever surrender our chance of victory."

* * * * * * * *

It would be easy to continue my present argument for several hundred pages more, but what I am saying is no deep secret and it has been a commonplace topic of our editorial pages for more than seven years.

During the war, which was in reality a Vertical Revolution, the old standards (good, bad and indifferent) were all of them destroyed and it will be several decades before we can reasonably expect a new set of rules that shall once more remove the fears and suspicions which now turn the whole of society into an armed camp and make every man the enemy of his neighbor.

That does not sound very cheerful.

But what will you?

After all, this planet was not created for our fun.

We just have to make the best of things as we find them.

* * * * * * * *

The Abbé Sieyès, when asked what he had done during the great French Revolution, answered, "My friends, I survived."

It was not a very heroic attitude.

"But what," so the Abbé reasoned, "is the use of trying to argue with a volcanic eruption, a flood or a popular uprising?" And so he saved whatever he could and waited for the end of the disaster.

And that, it seems to me, is the only thing we can hope to do during the present crisis.

We can't stop the flood.

We cannot lead it back to its river-bed.

We must wait until the waters shall have receded sufficiently to allow us to communicate with those of our neighbors who share our views and who are willing to coöperate with us in the work of reconstruction.

There is of course a chance that it will be too late, that they shall have perished, that the waves shall have done their work too well and shall have killed the few men who might have shown us a way out of our difficulties.

There is that chance.

But there is no alternative.

For the moment the watchword is "Survive!"

For further instructions, please meet me at the crossroads three hundred years hence.   Au revoir!

New York, June 21, 1927.

THE END